MAR 3 0 2009

East Meadow Public Library
1886 Front Street
East Meadow, New York 11554
516-794-2570
www.eastmeadow.info

I LOVE A MAN
IN UNIFORM

I LOVE A MAN IN UNIFORM

A Memoir of Love, War, and Other Battles

LILY BURANA

WEINSTEIN
BOOKS

ISBN: 978-1-60286-083-4

First Edition
10 9 8 7 6 5 4 3 2 1

*This book is dedicated to soldiers
and those who love them,
fighting all kinds of wars in all kinds of ways.*

And, of course, to Mike.

I want to be with people who submerge in the task, who go into the fields to harvest and work in a row and pass the bags along, who stand in the line and haul in their places, who are not parlor generals and field deserters but move in a common rhythm.

—Marge Piercy

I LOVE A MAN IN UNIFORM

I Hate That Girl

I'm being followed by an invisible woman. Pesky girl, she trails me almost everywhere I go. She's not here at the moment, so I can tell you about her: she's probably baking something delicious in her spotless kitchen. Or writing a thank-you note, or packing up the tenth care package she's mailed to her deployed husband this month, or having an engaging but noncontroversial conversation with her girlfriends. She's the Perfect Army Wife, a mythical creature who seamlessly, selflessly performs every domestic task with patriotic resolve that would make Uncle Sam sit down and weep Yankee Doodle tears. She's mindful, graceful, emotionally composed, and eternally in the right. She never falters, and heavens to Betsy, she never swears. For all I know, once the sun sets, she dons a red, white, and blue cape and flies around military installations solving crimes. Because she's invisible, I can't tell you what she looks like, but I can tell you one thing: I hate that girl.

Understand that there is nothing in my suburban punk-rock past that indicated that in 2002, I would marry an Army officer, thereby becoming an Army wife myself. My one connection to the military was tenuous—my dad was drafted into the Korean War, but that was long before I was born. In my family, my father's stint in the Army was mentioned only in passing, like his former hobby of playing the saxophone or the fact that, when he packed out of sleepy little Sandusky County, Ohio, to attend Harvard on scholarship, his only suit was a helplessly out-of-date plaid. My husband was the first Army officer I had ever met. I was so military-ignorant, I didn't know how to even talk to a soldier. When he called me "ma'am," I busted his chops. "Did you call me that because you're trying to be polite, or because you think I'm old?"

Thus began the relationship between Army Guy and Anarchy Girl. Ours isn't a red state–blue state relationship—more like red state and smash the state. It baffled everyone at first, especially me.

There are more than a million military wives in the United States today, and millions more women who are married to retired veterans, so it stands to reason that there would be one or two (or one or two thousand) wild cards. To be honest, I'm hardly a Johnny Cash–caliber "I shot a man in Reno just to watch him die" badass, but I'm not exactly glowing under the radiant light of my own halo, either. I do my best to make my way within a military lifestyle that is by turns rewarding, anxiety-making, exciting, and tough as hell.

I'd never try to tell another woman how to be a military

wife. Books like that already exist, and they are helpful. When I first married Mike, I read them all. Some taught me a ton; others scared the living daylights out of me. Nancy Shea's postwar-era classic *The Army Wife* told me to expect to be closely watched—and that my behavior, comportment, and hostess skills would be judged as an extension of my husband's career. "As an officer has an efficiency report file in Washington," Shea writes, "just so has his wife an 'unwritten efficiency report,' unfiled but known, labeled, and catalogued throughout the service. The unwritten efficiency report may be the means of bringing special assignments of honor to an officer or it may deprive him of an enviable detail for which he has worked faithfully. If she is the stormy petrel type, or the too ambitious type, she may have hurt her husband's career permanently." In other words, if I messed up, my husband's professional prospects would suffer, so I'd better mind the rules. The female cognate to the soldier's imperative to "Man up" when facing a challenge was "Watch yourself, little lady." The book also told me that my "trousseau" required, among other things, girdles, hostess pajamas, and daytime dresses for cocktail parties with matching purses and hats. If this standard still held, I was in need of a massive wardrobe expansion and possibly a time machine.

I learned early on that such measures are no longer required to be an upstanding military wife. But over time, it's been made clear to me that other standards may come into play. At a West Point luncheon one day last summer, a woman who has been an Army wife for fifteen years—the length of her husband's entire career—said to me, "You know, some of the other wives might not like you because you haven't done the time." I felt as if I'd been kicked in the chest. Not *like* me? For days afterward, I felt a sore spot whenever I thought of it. But if I would be judged for not having been married long enough, then another woman would be judged for having been married too long—or too many times. Or because she's got too many tattoos, too many kids, or no kids at all. She works outside the home. Or she doesn't. She's in the military, too. Or she isn't. She's too emotional, or she comes off as cold. She seems a little wild, or she's too tame to trust. It's the classic judgment-go-round concealed in camouflage and wrapped in the flag. When faced with such scrutiny, you can raise your defenses, you can raise your middle finger, or you can raise the white flag. As for me, I surrender. I am who I am, and I present my take on life as an Army wife as mine alone.

I'll be blunt: There's a Green Curtain rule in effect when it comes to communicating about the military with people who are strangers to that world. Unless she's a soldier herself, an Army wife is a civilian; still, a militaristic sense of discretion is expected of her. But six years into a tough war, I don't see an upside to sugarcoating the occasional hard truth. We've got a strong Army made of strong soldiers, and the whole gig won't crumble from a little honesty or a dash of political incorrectness. We're a nation built on a foundation of free speech, and anyway, I doubt you'd believe me if every page of this book broadcast, "Hey, everything's 100 percent fine! 100 percent of the time!" Beware of women bearing relentlessly good tidings.

Still, I do sometimes worry that I'll say something truly over the line, and the next thing I know, Mike will be handing out basketballs at the West Point gym and I'll be the fourth Dixie Chick. And because of OPSEC (Operations Security) regulations, there is some information that I simply cannot share. But I can give you a crash course in Army Wife 101—how a soldier courts, talks, thinks. What it's like to see your man off to war, and to welcome him home again, as is. I can share the emotional duress of a months-long deployment and the majesty of 200-plus years of tradition that lives on at the United States Military Academy at West Point. The trial of moving, and the thrill of a husband's promotion. The language, the rules (both written and implied), the customs, the joy, the anguish, and the searing, pulse-quickening pride. To know, and tend, the fierce heart that beats beneath an armed forces uniform. To watch soldiers go from being background noise to rock stars in the wake of national tragedy. To be married to the military during an exceptionally challenging war. And what it's like to ponder the answers to the questions that shape every military marriage: *What if?* and *What next?*

When it comes to speaking the truth about being an Army wife, there is no "we" in this book. There is only me. I won't whitewash who I am, but I'll happily offer a trade:

If you lend me your reader's eyes for the length of my tes-
timony, I will give you undiluted dispatches from one military wife's real, imperfect life.

So here we are. You and me. And her, the see-through
specter of military spouse perfection, flying around us
both, stirring the air and making me nervous. But I'm willing to believe that what intimidates us also instructs us,
so when Mrs. ArmyPants, the World's Most Perfect Military Wife, is buzzing about, I don't just swat her away. She
shows me, in part, who I'd like to be, and who, by choice
or by nature, I have no chance of becoming.

So I may say I hate her, but for all she has to teach me,
I kind of love her, too.

I

The Mating Call of the High and Tight

Before leaving the house, I carefully dot con-
cealer on the small, pitted scar over my upper lip, where
I used to wear a stainless-steel ring, and on the spot just
slightly right of my lower lip, where I wore a small dia-
mond stud. Over the years, my hair has been dyed ultra-
violet purple, shaved into a Mohawk, shorn close to the
scalp with a fringe of dime-store-bleach bangs, and worn
down my back in long black and platinum stripes like a
gothic vampire princess. But on this day in August 2003,
it is side-parted, brushed straight, and skimming my shoulders; I'm your basic all-American salon-born blonde.

On my husband's arm—and since he's an Army officer,
I am to hold onto his arm when he's in uniform; he must
not hold my hand or wrap his arm around my waist—I'm
a weirdo passing for arrow straight. He is ushering me
across the grand Plain at the United States Military Academy at West Point to a reception for newly arrived personnel and their families. In many ways, it is our first public

appearance as a military couple. Certainly, it is our most auspicious. In a pale yellow sundress, low heels, and no makeup except for a little red lipstick, I am traveling in my own camouflage, deep under the cover of normal.

I have been married for less than a year, and I've been in the physical presence of my new husband for a total of seventy-eight days. He returned from the war barely more than a month ago, and we were married just nine weeks before he left. Women like me, who screech to the altar right before a beloved's deployment, are called "war brides," though that makes it sound as though we pledged union with the war itself, not with a man who signed up to fight it. The term is a holdover from the selective-service days of the two World Wars, Korea, and Vietnam; lately, soldiers elect to serve and it is their families, should they have them, who are drafted. And the modern Army wife? Well, she falls somewhere in between a volunteer support system and an adventuress—curious to see where she'll go in a marriage where the military calls the shots.

At the West Point Club, my husband guides me through the receiving line—as the wife, I go ahead of him and we each shake hands with the Academy top brass. I'm introduced to the superintendent, General Bill Lennox, and his wife, Anne. Afterward, we move into the dining hall and mingle with Mike's new boss and his wife. Once I'm through the buffet line, the boss's wife introduces me to a small group of other wives. I put down my plate of Swedish meatballs, eager to make new friends.

One of the women looks me over. "Is your husband an Academy graduate?"

He isn't, I explain. He received his commission through ROTC.

She nods, her lips pursed.

When she discovers that my husband is a major, she makes a point of telling me that hers is a colonel. She asks where we were stationed before, how long we have been married, and if we have any children. The expression on her face shifts with every question I answer, and I get the sense that our conversation is not so much a friendly exchange of personal history as a way of gathering information that can, and will, be used against me.

"So," she says, "where did you meet your husband?" She pauses for a chilly, bristling beat. "In a bar?"

In this moment, I'm reeling from being dropkicked into a totally foreign culture—the United States Army. I am surrounded in this crowded room by women who have already been in this life for ten, twenty, and in a few cases, thirty years. I don't get it. What did I do wrong? Is it my lipstick? It is, isn't it? The shade is too dark, more appropriate for a cocktail waitress. Right? Or maybe this verbal hazing is part of the getting-to-know-you process. I can't tell if this woman expects me to fire back; I didn't get my secret Army wife decoder ring. All I know is that she intended to make me feel bad and she succeeded. We are a nation at war, yet right now the biggest threat to this woman is the new girl with the too-red lipstick.

I cherish and rely on the kindness of other women—I am what my nearest and dearest call "a friend to girls." As far back as ancient Greece, Euripedes wrote, "Woman is woman's natural ally," and centuries later, I believe it. But I don't sense a friendly corner here. Instead, I feel like I'm standing in the cafeteria at a new school, scanning the tables full of laughing Queen Bees, and I can't find a place to sit down with my tray.

I excuse myself and walk away from the group. I look out the floor-to-ceiling windows at the sweeping Hudson River view. Wrapping around a naturally occurring S-curve that forms the narrowest and deepest point in the river, the water slowly winds its way through the steep green hills, the current's course leading sixty miles south to New York City—not just any city but my city, rich with variety and blessed with anonymity. I want the deep water to swallow me up and carry me off, back to a place I know and understand. Back to my home turf.

My husband comes up behind me. "Are you getting along okay?"

"Sure."

"Meeting any nice women?"

I fake a smile. "You bet."

He walks away and I turn back to the picture window with a sigh. Have you ever had the sinking feeling that you're just not going to fit in?

* * *

In fact, I didn't meet my husband in a bar. I met him in a graveyard, three years earlier. If I hadn't moved back to New York after living in Wyoming for two years, and if I hadn't agreed to help my friend Molly with her project for the Daughters of the American Revolution, Mike and I never would have met, no way, no how. But I did move back and I did agree to help Molly, and *whoa-ho-ho*, of all the historic graveyards in the world, he had to walk into mine.

My dear friend Molly is convinced she missed her era, that she would have been better suited to being a refined 1950s lady who lunched at the counter at Schrafft's, hosted a nightly cocktail hour, and greeted every day in the right pair of gloves. Fueled by the spirit of feminine tradition and a yen for genealogy, she helped revive the Peter Minuit Chapter of the Daughters of the American Revolution in Manhattan.

During a guided tour of Brooklyn's Green-Wood Cemetery in 1999, Molly discovered the gravestone of Joshua Sands, an unheralded commissary captain from the Revolutionary War. As part of its commitment to historic preservation, the DAR will mark the grave of any documented patriot of the Revolution, and Molly had supplied the proper paperwork for Mr. Sands.

On the day of the grave-marking ceremony, in October 2000, I tagged along with Molly in case she needed a hand. Also, I was curious about this stuffy organization she'd been trying to get me to join. Molly had pored over my genealogy records and prepared the lengthy DAR application for me, even though I felt conflicted about joining an organization—however patriotic and civic-minded—that was organized around something beyond your control: your family tree. My family's heritage is boiled-potato Ohio Valley pacifist on my father's side, and warrior hillbilly (cut with some latter-day Norwegian mariner blood) on my mom's side—both lines dating back to the Revolutionary War. Little about this impresses me, except for the family legend that my father's people were so committed to their pacifism that they locked themselves in a church during one of the battles of the Revolution and were burned to death, and that my great-great-grandfather on my mother's side was so eager to join the Confederate Army that he ran away from his family's home in Tazewell, Virginia, to sign on with the infantry at age sixteen. These two stories reveal a lot to me about my family's hereditary tendency toward stubborn adherence to belief and poor impulse control.

The weather in Brooklyn that day was crisp and clear. After a display from the local Junior ROTC color guard, an Army officer from the Department of History at West Point was scheduled to say a brief word about patriot Joshua Sands, then there would be brunch. When the major stepped out of his car, autumn sun catching the medals on his uniform, I was standing alongside Molly under the Green-Wood's elaborate Gothic stone gate. The major opened his mouth to speak, and, though I couldn't have known it at the time, my life changed with a single word: ma'am.

Dropping an Army officer in the midst of an all-female volunteer group organized around patriotism was like dropping an Alka-Seltzer into a glass of pink champagne: pure estrogen fizz. At the post-ceremony brunch, the ladies couldn't get enough of him, plying him for stories about his military career and asking him if he'd had enough to eat.

What did I think of him? I thought he was handsome in his dark green uniform, certainly, with a stern Italianate visage reminiscent of a Sopranos thug crossed with Sam the Eagle from *The Muppet Show*. But I viewed him as a bit of an oddity—a representative from the straitlaced Establishment and also, I assumed, a bloodthirsty hawk with politics so radically rigid, he'd make Strom Thurmond look like a dope-smokin' hippie.

One of the older women in the group, businesslike in her boxy suit and Pappagallo flats, tried to flirtatiously engage him with references to her genteel Southern roots. "You know," she said, practically batting her eyes behind her croissant, "the Civil War wasn't really about slavery. It was about states' rights."

The major's response to her was an elegant, learned takedown. He didn't want to be right; he wanted *her* to be right. I couldn't help but be impressed. And chastened. He was a deep thinker, and no raving ideologue. I asked what it was like to be a historian at heart but a soldier by profession. His reply was to offer our DAR chapter a tour of West Point the following month. During this outing at the military academy, we called him Major, then Major Mike. Then, finally and in perpetuity, just Mike.

He seemed like an okay guy, but really, what did I care? He wasn't available, as evinced by his yellow-gold wedding band, and I was preoccupied with my long-distance relationship with my fiancé, which, I could no longer deny, was slowly creaking apart.

A year later, in June of 2001, Mike and I were both living in sad-sack breakup shacks, a couple of miles apart in the Hudson Valley. I e-mailed to ask if he could help me find a West Point press contact for a friend who was researching an article on women at the service academies. He e-mailed back, and after a few more cheerful volleys during which we both revealed that we were on our own, he asked me for coffee. We met at a café in the charming village of Cold Spring, for one of those cautious coffee dates that seem to the battle-scarred like a safe way back into the fray. Nothing committal, nothing that requires a man to wear a tie or a woman to shave her legs.

I never thought I would say yes to a date with an Army man; it was an utter impossibility. I came of age in the punk scene of the East Village, writing for indie fanzines, piercing my ears with sewing needles, and trying not to get my toes broken by the roil of moshers at the CBGB's hardcore matinees. I had stomach-churning encounters with

The Man, including getting caught up in the Tompkins Square riots, where the police brutality was so violent, a man was dragged by his arms down the street between two officers galloping on horseback. In my eyes, if you wore a uniform, you were a puppet of the system and not to be trusted.

My disdain for authority went way back to my childhood, when I was a troublemaker with skinned knees and pink dresses, prone to weeping and truancy. My passion for alternative culture started in sixth grade when my friend Rachel's dad let us watch *Rock 'n' Roll High School* on cable. By fourteen, I was obsessed with hardcore punk and goth music and my wardrobe shifted to gloomster black. I moved to New York City when I was eighteen, and within months, started working in a sleazy Times Square peep show—a choice motivated by a little defiance and a lot of financial desperation. I took a break from the grungy sex business when my yoga teacher, David, offered me a job managing the restaurant he co-owned with Cathy, his former wife—Life Café, on Tenth Street and Avenue B, later made famous in the musical *Rent*. I'd sit at the bar reading *The Autobiography of Malcolm X* and roust junkies from the bathroom who had passed out on the toilet after shooting up. One poor obese guy had a heart attack and died in the back bathroom, which was so small, the EMTs had to crawl through the tiny window, climb over his body, and remove the door from its hinges to get him out. At twenty-one, I moved to San Francisco and ran with a crew of brainy bad girls who were determined to expand the limits of gender and feminism, and extend the worldwide base of girl power. This was the height of the ACT UP era of grassroots activism, and we were emboldened by the mouthiness of the movement. Some of us transitioned out of unsatisfying jobs or relationships; some of us, through gender reassignment surgery, transitioned from women to men. Throughout my early twenties, I bounced in and out of the sex industry as a peep-show girl and stripper, and then finally, at twenty-seven, bounced out of the business for good and moved back to New York to become a full-time freelance writer. Then, in 1998, I moved west to Wyoming for two years, lured by the promise of love and low overhead. Despite both of us having moved a lot, I couldn't imagine that this career Army officer and I would have much in common beyond mutual curiosity.

But what did I have to lose? Maybe he would surprise me. As much as I had been invested in seeing uniformed people as stereotypes, I knew a bit about being stereotyped, myself. I was a former stripper who could use her words—compound words, even!—and a good share of getting to know someone involved proving that I wasn't necessarily who they thought. The least I could do was show up and see who he was apart from the camouflage cover.

I arrived at the café in jeans and a T-shirt, and was surprised to see *him* in jeans and a T-shirt. He looked so normal, but I had my reservations nonetheless. I worried that he would be a follower, and I worried that underneath the surface friendliness, he would be cruel. And what if he was some humorless taskmaster, like every drill sergeant in every cartoon and military movie ever made? I wasn't interested in being barked at by Sarge from *Beetle Bailey*.

We ordered our drinks at the counter and sat down at a quiet table near the window. It didn't appear at first that we had many similarities. I was the youngest of five kids; he had one sister who was two years his junior, and a half-sister and half-brother a full generation younger. His parents were divorced; mine had been married for over forty years. He had attended Manhattan's prestigious Stuyvesant High School and held a master's degree in history from Penn State, while I was never more than a ball of unfulfilled academic potential and squeaked out of an adult high school at seventeen with a diploma that was mailed to me in a tube. But Mike was decisive in his speech, which I loved. He told great stories, he laughed easily, and his eyes were wide, long-lashed, gaze-to-the-core-of-your-being brown. And did I tell you about the eyebrows? Impeccable Dr. Zhivago hotness. But more than good looks, dry wit is my Achilles' heel, and I knew I was in trouble when he looked down at his second cappuccino and droned robotically, "I love you, my dark master."

There's a popular saying in the alternative scene: "Military intelligence is an oxymoron." In my punker days, I wore the slogan proudly on my black leather biker jacket, along with a Dead Kennedys button and a thrift-store sterling silver crucifix. So the irony was not at all lost on me when Mike told me his operational specialty: military intelligence. He couldn't be infantry or aviation or field artillery. Oh, no. He had to be the one branch that by its very name showed up my self-righteous political pieties and brought me to my know-it-all knees. I was bent into an infatuation headlock, and Cupid gave me a noogie.

Of course, I was only a fraction of the rebel I used to be, having come to favor country music just as much as *Rock 'n' Roll High School*. Sometime in my early twenties, I had realized that punk rock might not be able to deliver on its messianic zeal. Even my idol, Dead Kennedys singer Jello Biafra, had started sounding less like a mordant political wit than a cranky old man shouting, "Hey you kids, get off my lawn!" In one of his later songs, he asked a question that echoed my own doubt: "Anarchy sounds great, but who would fix the sewers?"

I mourned my loss of outlier faith as much as I welcomed the drift inward from the margins. The punk scene wasn't hallowed ground or some infallible brain trust, it was just a bunch of strivers flailing around in search of answers, no better (though surely no worse) than anyone else. The far-flung dream of anarchy wore itself thin. Ideologically, I was fair game.

Mike and I met a few more times for coffee, then, on a warm and muggy night in mid-June, we took our first road trip together. Mike drove me around "deepest darkest

Queens" to show me where he had grown up. Woodhaven Boulevard. Forest Park. Jamaica Avenue, where you'd stop your conversation on the street and do the "El-train pause" whenever the elevated train roared overhead. We stopped for cheeseburgers at the Georgia Diner on Queens Boulevard. His childhood neighborhood contrasted starkly with mine, a welter of 1970s split-levels parked on cul-de-sacs carved into rural stretches of New Jersey dairy land. Queens and Morris County, New Jersey, are only fifty miles apart, yet they are totally different worlds. As we cruised around, we shared our passion for country music, George Strait singing "Amarillo by Morning." We drove the busy streets singing along, mutual fondness unfolding to a two-step beat.

A military man's courtship rites may not be poetic, but then, they're not cryptic, either. Even if he's bashful, when he fancies you, you know it, because you can't hide a lover's blush under the Army's signature high-and-tight haircut. When Mike reddened with excitement, it traveled from the shorn nape of his neck all the way up to the tips of his exposed ears. He may have acted cool, but the glowing, red beet ears gave him away.

Though my assumptions about Mike's politics gave me pause initially, I enjoyed getting to know him, because if nothing else, he marched in, unambiguous in his interest. The Army teaches a man many things—chief among them is the creed of Mission First, a sense of duty and priority that leaps nimbly from the battlefield to matters of the heart.

* * *

During my first few dates with Mike, I was still reeling from the pain and confusion of a broken engagement. The final months with my fiancé had been an erratic back-and-forth of traveling between New York and Wyoming, the two of us clinging to each other in desperate need, then watching the fire go out, then around we go again. The guy whom I had bet on being my happily-ever-after turned out to be a disaster narrowly averted.

Day-to-day, we got along well. He was affectionate and attentive—which you maybe don't expect from a Wyoming cowboy. He wasn't a bad person by any means. He just wasn't in love with who I am; he was in love with who I used to be. I couldn't forget the time he referred to me as his "sexy *Playboy* model." It was 2001. I had modeled for *Playboy* in 1996. I was in *Playboy in the previous century.* If he'd built his esteem for me on something I couldn't possibly sustain, then where could we go from there? There's no such thing as an eternal vixen, even the dorky, alterna-girl variety. You get bored. You burn out. You turn thirty. The job description includes built-in obsolescence. I didn't want to be some post-stripper ghost-bride—forever toting the shadow of my old self with me through my married life, stunted and soured by my own over-reliance on my past. It would mean living as a twisted Dickens heroine, wedded but locked in to the persona I had already outgrown, becoming more snarled and diminished by the day. Miss Havisham of the pole.

Heartbroken and homesick for New York, I left that relationship, and Wyoming, for good, with my notion of "the perfect man" blown to bits. But that shattered illusion turned out to be my saving grace; if I hadn't ditched my western romance novel idea of Prince Charming, I never would have entertained the idea of getting to know a guy who, I could only assume, was entirely wrong for me. No longer held in the thrall of some tumbleweed Mister Right fantasy, I was willing to try anything. I couldn't have known it then, but because of a chance meeting one fall afternoon in a windy graveyard in Brooklyn, I went from groping numbly out of the wreckage of dashed hope to a life hijacked by possibility.

2

Simple as Alpha Bravo Charlie

There was only one problem with Mike: Half the time I didn't understand what he was talking about.

"Greenspeak" is the mysterious tongue unique to the military, a strange mix of slang and acronyms. Is it any wonder that I was confused when confronted with a statement like, "I met with my assignments officer at 1300. It turns out that my TDY at Fort Meade is going to be a PCS. Which is okay. At least I'm not being sent OCONUS like I'd originally thought. After that, I'm pretty sure I'll be able to rotate back to West Point. My assignments officer is pretty STRAC, but the one I had before her was a pogue"? (Translation: "I met with the Army human resource officer who directs the course of my career at 1 p.m. It turns out that my temporary duty at Fort Meade is going to be a permanent change of station—i.e., a move—which is okay. At least I'm not being sent overseas like I'd originally thought. After that, I think I'll be going back to West Point.

My assignments officer is competent, but the guy I had before her was an idiot.")

He patiently translated for me, and soon I found my own speech peppered with green. I'd say "roger that," instead of "okay," and if Mike asked me for a favor, I'd say "WILCO" ("will comply"). After a lavish dinner out, I'd look at the table crowded with empty plates and say, "Maybe we should ask the waitress to 'police up' all these dishes to make room for the dessert." I could even spell my name with the military alphabet: "Lima-India-Lima-Yankee." With Mike having been assigned as a battalion executive officer at Fort Meade, an Army post in Maryland, only five hours from where I lived in New York, I let my heart unfurl a little bit more.

I appreciated the officer-and-a-gentleman polish he exhibited on our first dates—the formality was perfectly appropriate. I was delighted to have doors held open for me, and to have help putting on my coat. But I knew there was no way that Mike could've made it through years of rigorous training and all that time downrange talking about European travel and *Harper's*. The lofty, big-brain part of him was delectable, but I wanted to know the muddy side of the man, too.

I persuaded him to share with me the raunchy Jody calls used to set the marching rhythm of all-male units, like the one he was in during Desert Storm. One of my favorites:

> *I wish all the ladies*
> *Were pies on a shelf.*
> *And I was the baker,*
> *I'd eat 'em all myself.*

Knowing I was a bat-and-spiderweb-loving goth as a teen, he thought that I'd appreciate this next stanza:

> *I wish all the ladies*
> *Were bats in the steeple.*
> *And I was the King Bat,*
> *There'd be more bats than people.*

The adage is that an Army marches on its stomach. But if the scores of filthy Jody calls tell the true tale, then the organ that the Army actually marches on is located farther down the torso.

I wasn't disturbed by the fact that when something went wrong, he said it had gone "Tango Uniform" ("Tits Up"), or that, when he was tired, he'd say, "My bags are smoked." But I reached my saturation point when I heard the expression "grinds my sack." As in, "I'm telling you, the lack of organization in this unit really grinds my sack."

I'd worried that Mike might be too uptight for me, too duty bound and formal. But how uptight can a guy be when he cheerfully admits he likes sleeping in a "fart sack" (i.e., sleeping bag)? In the grossness lay the promise.

* * *

In a best-case scenario, your new heartthrob has much to teach you. I was constantly learning new things from Mike—about the Army, about history, about the bridge that might be built between our two very different worlds. But perhaps the most hard-earned lesson I learned from Mike is this: Never trust a walrus.

Trust was not my strong suit, I admit. Not when it came to romantic relationships, anyway, where you are expected to merge hearts and souls and checking accounts. I've paid a lot of lip service to commitment over the years—as evidenced by my prior engagement—but the truth was, in any relationship, I had always had a suitcase packed and parked by the door. I was self-conscious about this. Weren't women supposed to be the joiners and the yielders and the "Can we go to Pottery Barn and pick out a new comforter set—something we both like?" beseechers? But the reasoning behind my restraint was this: If you build a world around a guy, and he leaves, then what happens to that world? It's blown to bits—a scorched-earth strike right in the heart. I had done the cohabitation, the comforter shopping. But in the midst of all the optimism and future planning and eating dessert off each other's plates was a small voice saying, "Yeah. For now. For however long it lasts. The other shoe will drop eventually." I believed that I was some kind of mutant strain of girl because I so deeply doubted the fairy tale of Forever.

But Mike made an effort to show me that even though he was moving to Fort Meade in July, and we would be living three states apart, his interest in me was sincere. On our first date as a potential long-distance couple, we went to the Coney Island Mermaid Parade. The date would, ever after, be referred to as the New York Aquarium Incident.

Mike picked me up in his dark green Mitsubishi Montero. He was dressed in an old St. Johns University hat, cargo shorts, running shoes, and a Yankees T-shirt. He held open the passenger-side door for me and helped me up into the seat. I held the hem of my sundress with one hand as I climbed up into the SUV. I was wearing flip-flops that I could easily slip off to dig my toes in the sand, and a huge black picture hat that I'd bought for nine bucks at Wal-Mart. On the drive down the Brooklyn-Queens Expressway, Mike told me about his last visit to the aquarium, when he was a teenager. "I was looking at this female walrus lying in the sun. She noticed I was watching her, and she flashed me."

"What do you mean she 'flashed' you?"

"I mean, she saw that I was watching her, she looked me straight in the eye, and showed me her, ah, um . . . lady parts."

I felt my face bunch up into a skeptical sneer. "Man, you are more full of crap than a city dump."

"I'm serious!"

People lie all the time to keep the story spicy and the

conversation rolling: The fish that got away was *this* big. Angus Young really did throw his guitar pick right to me— and only me—at that AC/DC show. Stuff like that. I had to admit, a flashing lady walrus was a pretty funny lie—it was an obvious whopper, but it did make me laugh. And that he wanted to make me laugh meant a lot.

I love Coney Island. Love it. The walloping smell of sea salt mixed with city bus exhaust as you walk down Surf Avenue, the clattering conversations of the old Russians blending with hip-hop beats that pulse out of the car windows. Run-down and funky, but full of hidden treasure like the burned-out pot of gold at the end of the subway line rainbow, Coney Island had been one of my favorite destinations since I used to make the hour-long train ride from the East Village to visit my friend Boogie. Boogie lived on Surf Avenue in a dilapidated seafoam green row house with a red lobster perched on top, claws raised in salute to the sun. We liked to shop together at the twenty-four-hour Stillwell Avenue Pathmark in the middle of the night. Since Boogie was a health nut and a vegetarian, he got by on the white-label generic jars of peanut butter, beans, and vegetable ramen. When he was really short on money, he'd go to the store with his baggy black bondage pants tucked into his boots. We'd find an empty aisle, where he'd open a jar of vitamins, pull out his waistband, and pour them down his pant leg.

It was a great day for Coney Island. Whenever Mike and

I got hungry, we hit an ice cream stall for a pistachio soft-serve cone, or ordered cheese fries from Nathan's Famous, which we ate with a two-pronged red plastic fork. We watched the Mermaid Parade, the revelers melting under their bright purple and turquoise wigs in the ninety-degree heat. Several times the ocean breeze grabbed my hat and sent it sailing down the boardwalk, and Mike would run after it and return it to me. We strolled the boardwalk behind a man sporting a full-back tattoo of an underwater scene—an old-fashioned deep-sea diver, a squid, a great white shark, a hammerhead, a treasure chest brimming with gold and jewels, a submarine, a guy in a wet suit, even a family of sea horses. Man, did he love that tattoo—enough to risk burning the skin on his back as he strolled the sunny promenade with his T-shirt slung over his shoulder.

"Look at that," I whispered.

"It's like kitchen-sink-of-the-sea," Mike whispered back.

After watching the parade, we decided to escape the heat by visiting the New York Aquarium on 8th Street. We moved with the crowd through the dimly lit underwater viewing area and stepped up to the glass to watch the walruses swim. Despite their heft, they moved with grace, turning slowly and easily in the murky water. The males, having had their tusks removed so they couldn't fight, were at first hard to distinguish from the females, except for their impressive size. After a few minutes, I noticed that the largest male walrus had an enormous erection, a great wavering sea monster phallus, dark seaweed brown and the size of Rambo's arm. I leaned into Mike's side. "Hey, check that out!"

The walrus swam up to the glass right in front of me, erection bobbing before him. I have no idea why he singled me out among an entire crowd of people, but he was staring right into my eyes, with a look that said, "Hey, baby. I know what you want. I got what you need." That walrus knew exactly what he was doing. Then, to my shock, he curled his head down and started fellating himself, skillfully and with great vigor.

There are a few things I want out of any good date: I want the guy to think I'm fun. I would love for him to think I'm cute. And, more than anything, I want him to see me as sensible and together. Like I can handle the basics of life. It is really hard to look sensible, or cute, or even remotely together when you're slapping your picture hat against a window to shield a child's eyes from the sight of a self-fellating walrus. But I had to do something before one of the kids surrounding us asked the inevitable "Mommy, what's that?" As I held my hat in place, Mike and I laughed hysterically. Most of the parents around us looked grateful, though they, too, were overcome with laughter.

The walrus swam away, and Mike and I made our wobbly way to the next exhibit, still laughing so hard our knees buckled. "That was some good thinking with that hat there," Mike said. "*Now* do you believe me about that lady walrus?"

"I will never doubt you again."

In a way, the exhibitionist walrus was a test. Like, if Mike didn't find that terribly funny, there wasn't much hope for us in the long term. More importantly, I knew that his tale of being flashed by the lady walrus was likely to be true. He had more than a sense of humor; he had credibility. This was very promising. I mentally crossed my fingers. *Please, please turn out to be as awesome as I think you are.*

The greenspeak term that would best apply to the aquarium incident was "Whiskey Tango Foxtrot." As in, "What the Fuck?" Is there any other response to a walrus giving himself an underwater hummer? As the sun dipped over Brooklyn, we headed to the car. We drove up Surf Avenue toward the Brooklyn-Queens Expressway with the air-conditioner blasting, sunburned but happy, full of french fries and burgeoning trust, holding hands and chuckling over the mysteries of the deep.

In July, Mike packed up his history textbooks, closed out his three-year faculty position at the military academy, and moved down to Maryland to start his job as the XO (executive officer) of an intelligence battalion. A military intelligence unit is tasked with collecting, analyzing, processing, and disseminating intelligence gathered about enemy operations in order to help friendly forces stay one step ahead, and as the XO, Mike would be responsible for helping the commanding officer set the unit's agenda—sort of the equivalent of a corporate chief operating officer. Thinking he was only going to be there for two years before returning to a West Point staff job, he rented a two-bedroom apartment in a bland commuter complex in Odenton, about fifteen minutes from Fort Meade. The apartment had beige carpet and a push-button gas fireplace. His neighbors, it appeared, were all civilians, up early, travel mugs in hand, to cruise the highways to Baltimore or Washington, D.C., both a half-hour's drive away.

Whenever I drove down for a visit, my indoctrination into greenspeak continued. Perhaps the most important word in the greenspeak glossary is *hooah*—the Army's *cri de coeur*. For the uninitiated:

Dictionary definition of *hooah*

hooah (hoo ah) adj., adv., n., v., conj., interj., excla. (Orig. unknown) Slang. **1:** Referring to or meaning anything and everything except "no" **2:** What to say when at a loss for words **3a:** Good copy **b:** Roger **c:** Solid copy **d:** Good **e:** Great **f:** Message received **g:** Understood **h:** Acknowledged **4a:** Glad to meet you **b:** Welcome **5:** All right! **6a:** I don't know the answer, but I'll check on it **b:** I haven't the foggiest idea **7:** I am not listening **8:** That is enough of your drivel; sit down! **9:** Yes **10:** You've got to be kidding me! **11:** Thank you **12:** Go to the next slide **13:** You've taken the correct action **14:** I don't know what that means, but I'm too embarrassed to ask for clarification **15:** Squared away (He's pretty *hooah*) **16:** Amen!

It is not enough to *say* hooah, I learned. One must *be* hooah, to embody this essence of warrior spirit. By Labor Day weekend of 2001, I decided I was going to have to *be* hooah because it was time to have The Conversation. It's the part of stripping that never dies, the social tariff of being a woman with a past. Bottom line: I have to ask someone if he (a) disapproves of me and (b) would consider me an embarrassment moving forward. I knew that to an Army officer, reputation was important, so it meant something to me when I asked him if he thought that dating a former stripper—a somewhat public former stripper—might affect his career negatively. He said, "Do you know what my response would be if someone got on my case about you?" He raised his hand and flipped a big ol' bird, and a frozen, doubtful spot inside of me started melting.

Would he tolerate me stripping now? No. That was a part of me that he was not willing to share, he said. "I care for you and I don't want Joe Shit the Ragbag to be able to touch you, or God forbid say something to you that would make you upset."

Previously, if a man had said that to me, my response would have been indignant—how dare you tell me what to do with my body? But I'd mellowed enough to see it as a statement of concern, and an indicator of the reasonable possessiveness that any person who cares for you might have. Is it really that out of line for a guy to not want his girlfriend to be naked and vulnerable in front of a bunch of strange men who may or may not know how to behave themselves? Is it so bad for him to think she deserves better? His response might have been a problem if it had come from a controlling or judgmental place. But it didn't—it was chivalry in brass knuckles.

For a guy with top-secret security clearance, Mike proved surprisingly easy to get to know. He had a comedic deadpan that any stand-up yukster would envy. He used episodes of *The Simpsons* as teaching material when he taught history to West Point cadets. We could split an entire large pizza between us in one sitting. And I loved that as a teenager in Queens, he took banjo lessons. I pictured him strutting down Jamaica Avenue, with his poufy '80s Guido hair and gold Christ head pendant dangling from a rope chain around his neck, swinging a banjo case the way Tony Manero swung his paint can as he cruised down a similar street in *Saturday Night Fever*.

Mike was unashamed of his geekiness, and I liked that about him. It meant that he valued his intellect more than his image. During one of our bowling dates at the lanes at Fort Meade, he told me, "I admit it. I became a historian because they get all the chicks."

"Right. Like Martha Washington. Betsy Ross . . ."

"Susan B. Anthony . . . Margaret Thatcher. She *still* calls me."

If we flipped past CSPAN while watching TV, he'd see Doris Kearns Goodwin and yell out, "Doris!"

Had Mike been dreadfully wedded to his machismo, it

wouldn't have worked out. Men like that can't ever really relax. They're always on alert against people, situations, conversations, things that make them look—heaven forbid—"soft." There's just no future with a guy whose life mission is to relentlessly defend his bullshit fortress of Dude.

Basically, if someone wanted to cook up controversy from Mike's relationship with me, a single Google search of my name would provide enough intel to do the job. But stripping was just the most recent scandal. Somewhere out there, not online but in the bowels of the New York Police Department, I had a mug shot and, possibly, a moldering juvie FBI file.

I was an accidental teenage communist. As a yearning, politically aware peace punk, I had all the idealistic energy required to change the world, and none of the common sense. My junior year in high school, I had joined an activist group opposing the arms race, government censorship, and pretty much anything Washington, D.C., had to offer. The whole time I sat in on meetings at the NYU student union and flyered city high schools and helped plan protests, I was unaware that the organization was an offshoot of the Revolutionary Communist Party. I knew there were RCP members in the group—they were easy to spot in their old Army jackets, berets, jump boots, and keffiyeh. They all looked like Che Guevara but with less fashion sense. I assumed they were part of a larger, big-tent anarchist/activist/whatever-ist youth collective, and I was too naïve to make any real inquiry as to the group's origin. I thought if we were on the same page and wanted a better world that was all that mattered.

My friend Jeanette and I were psyched the day of our first protest. We dressed like postapocalyptic ghouls, drawing on fake radiation burns with lipstick and eyeliner. We made signs and shook rattles and marched with our noisy righteous throng all the way from Herald Square to the Village.

When the group took a right turn off of Sixth Avenue onto Eighth Street, the police were there, setting up a blockade. We stopped in front of a small jewelry store and started chanting. The store owner came out and told us to move. When Jeanette refused, saying she had a First Amendment right to be there, one of the police officers stepped forward and snapped a pair of handcuffs on her. Patrice and Lulu, two of the RCP true believers, followed soon after.

I panicked. I didn't know what to do—if I let Jeanette get arrested alone, her mother and father would kill me. So I did the only thing I could do: I stepped forward into the shopkeeper's doorway so that the police had to arrest me, too.

The paddy wagon was hot and stuffy. Through the wire window guards, I could see Lower Manhattan rolling by: Broadway, Canal Street, Chinatown. Butcher-shop windows filled with greasy ducks hanging by their crooked necks, stalls selling knockoff purses and cheap paper parasols and fans. The paddy wagon finally stopped in an underground garage and the four of us were led through a heavy steel door and marched down a series of window-less concrete hallways. No one told us where we were, but Lulu, who had been in the group for years and arrested at half a dozen protests, whispered, "Central Booking."

Female officers led us through another series of narrow hallways brightly lit with yellowy-green fluorescent light. Because we were underage, Jeanette and I were locked in our own cell. In the adjoining adult cell, Patrice and Lulu began singing Clash songs—"Career Opportunities," "Radio Clash." They'd been arrested several times already, and they sounded like they were having a grand old time. I don't think they were even remotely scared. The police never offered us a phone call. But we did get mug shots taken, and then we were fingerprinted and strip-searched.

Jeanette and I sat on the hard bench in the cell, con-fused and terrified. At one point, they let an underage pros-titute into our cell. She was stick thin and wearing a red sequined minidress. She sat on the floor and ignored us, looking bored. The guards brought us dinner—a bologna sandwich on a paper plate and pea soup in a Styrofoam cup. I had no idea what time it was—they'd taken our watches. I didn't trust the bologna, so I just had a couple of small bites of the bread. I dumped the soup down the toilet. After dinner, they opened our cell once again and let in a plump middle-aged woman with long, blond hair. You could tell by the streaks on her swollen face that she'd been crying. She'd been caught shoplifting accessories at Bloom-ingdale's and she had been so unnerved by the tough women in the adult pen that they had moved her into our cell so she could calm down. She sat cross-legged on the floor of the cell, rocking back and forth, weeping and play-ing with her hair.

We were led into a courtroom in the morning. Jeanette's mom, Cathy, sat in the front row. I had no idea how she got there. Who had called her? How did she know where we were? She looked odd, and I didn't know why at first. But then I figured it out. Her expression. It was the first time I'd ever seen her angry.

The judge gave us a date for our sentencing and we were dismissed. Cathy took us to the Second Avenue Deli for something to eat. She poured cream from a small metal pitcher into her cup of coffee. "If your uncle Gary wasn't a New York City police officer, I'd have no idea where you are right now." She didn't seem mad anymore, just scared and exhausted. "I waited for you in that courtroom since seven last night. When I didn't hear from you by dinner, I called Gary and asked him to look into the system to see if you two were in there somewhere. That's how I found out they'd taken you to Central Booking."

Cathy looked at me. "Your mother was really worried about you, by the way. When I called to let her know I was coming to get you out of jail, I told her the last thing Jeanette's dad said to you at the train station was, 'Don't get arrested.'"

Weeks later, when Jeanette and I showed up at City Hall for sentencing, the civil rights attorney William Kunstler stood on behalf of our group and told the judge we'd been denied our phone call and Miranda rights. The judge dismissed the charges against all of us immediately and we were free to go.

After that, my teenage revolutionary ardor cooled considerably. I knew then that whatever change I might hope to effect in this world, I'd have to do it by working within the system. I couldn't hack it as a radical.

When talking it over, Mike and I realized that I'd been taking the train into the city to leaflet Stuyvesant High School just a few years after he'd graduated. (By the time I got there, he was in officer training.) As far as any personal ramifications, my flirtation with being a teen radical was of no concern to him. Whenever I brought up some adolescent memory, he'd say, "Oh? When was that? Back when you were a communist?" Really, he just saw it as an excellent opportunity to make fun of me.

Things became decidedly less humorous on September 11. Mike was down at Fort Meade, and I was in New York, having woken up to a warm day with an unusually vivid blue sky. When I turned on the television and saw the smoke pouring out of the Twin Towers, I panicked. Then came the news of the plane hitting the Pentagon and my immediate thought was: Mike. Was Fort Meade or any of the other military posts in the D.C. area next on the list?

Thank goodness, I still had phone service—I wouldn't by the end of the day—and I was able to get through to him. He couldn't talk long, his entire office was in an uproar, but he assured me that he was okay. "I'm telling you right now," he said, "if terrorists are behind these attacks, every single thing about life in this country is going to change. Especially for the military." Through the numbness of shock, a dark, slow chill went down my spine.

The terror attacks of 9/11 kicked off the military's own Extreme Makeover. Before that tragic event, the image of the military was lackluster, particularly in my little sheltered corner of the world—servicepeople were seen as a bunch of green collar grunts, prone to drinking, domestic violence, and primitive, chest-thumping jingoism. Then the Twin Towers fell, Flight 93 crashed, and one side of the Pentagon was reduced to a smoking crater. People immediately understood that we need the military, and anyone close to a service member noticed a sudden upgrade in popular reception.

In fifty years, when little children ask their grandparents what it was like to live in the United States in the days after 9/11, they'll be told that it was a time when the country exploded into a yellow ribbon wonderland overnight. American flags everywhere, every day the Fourth of July. There was an immediate, desperate need to reconnect to a sense of national identity. My friend Meryl, who owned a tattoo studio in Jersey, said her shop was flooded with guys who wanted screaming eagles and fighter jets—

any kind of aggressive, rockets-red-glare Americana they could get inked on a bicep, on a shoulder, over an angry, patriotism-swelled heart.

The first time I visited Mike at Fort Meade after September 11, he came to pick me up at the train station still wearing his BDUs (battle dress uniform, a.k.a. camouflage), pant legs *whoosh whoosh*ing with every heavily starched step. The crowd parted around him like the Red Sea at Moses' command. A woman approached him, her eyes shining with tears. "I feel so much safer knowing you're here!" People smiled, waved, and stood a little straighter when he walked by. When the two of us ran errands at Target, a toddler stood transfixed by Mike's side.

"Andrew," the boy's father said, "do you want to salute the soldier?"

Andrew shyly raised his little arm in salute, John-John-style. That young boy summed up a burgeoning sentiment of admiration mixed with starstruck awe. Soldiers have always fascinated children, but now adults were spellbound, too. Earlier that summer, when I'd tell people I was dating a soldier, they'd be all, *Whatever*. Then, after 9/11, when they found out I was involved with a soldier, they'd say, *Wow, really?* From whatever to wow. It was as if I'd been dating a guy in a struggling no-name garage band that had suddenly rocketed to the top of the charts. Like his awesomeness was believable now. Tragedy begat credibility.

While the average American was now high on the military, within my own social circle, the news that I was considering throwing my lot in with a soldier was met with mixed reception. A lot of my friends were surprised that he was educated. Others were more skeptical. "I could never get involved with someone who would willingly sign up to kill people," said my colleague Janet.

Janet's abruptness took me aback, but I couldn't fault her. Dating a soldier is not just a choice of the heart. It's a choice of conscience, too. Ultimately, it's a matter of trust—that the man I cared for would have this authority and this power, and not abuse it.

Not everyone was so resistant. I got some grudging approval from my friend John, a former marine. "So sorry you hit bottom and had to settle for an Army guy," he chided in an e-mail. I shot back: "Tell me, friend, is it hard to type without opposable thumbs?" *Oorah* is the Marines' cognate to *hooah*, and John was *oorah* enough to reply, "Me no type. Just bash out words with forehead."

Most of my friends, family, and fellow writers were generally supportive, more curious than anything. They would quiz me: Has Mike ever been in combat? (Yes.) Does he have an arsenal of weapons in his house? (No. Not one. On principle. His only firearm is his Army-assigned pistol, which is locked in his unit's arms room, and which he has to show his weapons card—with the gun's serial number on it—to sign out). Has he ever killed anybody? I'd posed that question myself. We'd been dating for three months and I thought we were close enough for me to ask. As soon as the words left my lips, his usual thoughtful demeanor turned stormy, ominous black clouds and lightning flashes all around. I knew I'd crossed a line.

I watched the ground while we walked. "Am I not supposed to ask?"

"Let me tell you something," he said. "I have friends in the Army I've known for fifteen years, and we don't even ask each other that question."

It was then that I felt the full gravity of his profession. This was a real warrior, with real principles. Not a bang-bang Hollywood type, not a bendable dress-up doll in a hot uniform. A soldier, a soul. Life and death decisions were not an academic exercise for him, and he was not playing at this.

Dating Mike highlighted my ignorance about the military. For instance, I had no idea that a commissioned Army officer's First Amendment rights are curtailed. Per Article 88 of the Uniform Code of Military Justice: "Any commissioned officer who uses contemptuous words against the President, the Vice President, Congress, the Secretary of Defense, the Secretary of a military department, the Secretary of Transportation, or the Governor or legislature of any State, Territory, Commonwealth, or possession in which he is on duty or present shall be punished as a court-martial may direct."

Mike said, "I serve in the army of a democracy, but the Army is not a democracy."

Knowing I would have to let the magnitude of that sink

in, I asked Mike some other questions I had. "So, once a military intelligence officer is granted top-secret clearance, do you get a shoe phone like Maxwell Smart?"

"No."

"Have you had any secret meetings with spacemen or hostile alien life forms?"

"No."

"Would you be allowed to tell me even if you did?"

"No."

The first time Mike fired a weapon he was fourteen—a .22 rifle, during Boy Scout camp at Camp Ranachqua, Delaware. He practiced shooting paper targets hung from little wooden frames in a field. The next time, he was twenty, at an ROTC field-training exercise at Fort Dix. The weapon was an M-16. For him, it was a very grown-up moment. "It made me realize the seriousness of what I was undertaking," he said. "That being a soldier was more than ending up as an equestrian statue poised on the edge of a parade field."

Of course, this story prompted the big question: why he joined the Army to begin with. "First of all," Mike said, "it's not a bad way for a butcher's kid from Queens to move solidly into the middle class and get a master's degree." He paused, with a wry smile. "Thanks, Uncle Sugar."

"I know it sounds predictable," he continued. "But I joined the Army because I wanted to be part of something larger than myself. You're working in close quarters and for long hours as part of an organization that has an identity—it's a team. In the Army, you connect with other human beings in a way that you don't anywhere else—you may one day have to give your life for another soldier, or vice versa. There's an implicit contract that you'd do that for one another. You see the best and worst of people in a way that you don't in any other walk of life."

Within the greenspeak lexicon is the phrase "I've got your six." It's an aviation term used by a pilot who's another's flight buddy, with a literal meaning of "I'm flying right behind you at the six o'clock position." Figuratively, it means, "I'm here." I've got your back. You can count on me. When I heard the meaning behind "I've got your six," my eyes started to tear up, because it represented a spot of tenderness under all that masculine armor. Also, it emphasized the tremendous loyalty among troops, which, I was coming to realize, had a depth beyond my comprehension.

The stripping. The arrest. None of it fazed Mike. In fact, he had reservations about whether he was good for *me*. He worried that I'd see him as helplessly boring and square, illustrating his point by making an "L7" with his hands. But if I needed something, he was there, and by the end of September, I found myself wanting to see him more and more. It became impossible to get him off my mind.

When Mike came up to visit me in New York in October,

he walked around my little cottage in the woods, checking out the furniture and the books. "Wow, you're pretty squared away." At the time, I didn't fully realize what a compliment that was. "Squared away" is high praise from a soldier. From there, it's a short trip to "I love you." Squared away means *You have your shit together; I think I can rely on you*—and to a soldier, that is everything. At first, I had my doubts that we'd make it past the superficial stunt-dating stage, but by now, I was feeling quite different.

I left Mike at my house during a quick trip to Chicago for a writing assignment, and when I came home, I found him outside in the sunshine, carefully cleaning out brushes and rollers. While I was gone, he'd painted my chipped and peeling front porch. My heart soared. I love the traditional niceties of romance—dinners, cards, a pretty bouquet—but nothing compares to the gift of sweat equity, which I view as the he-man's true statement of intent. Far better than spending money on me, he'd spent some of his precious free time. Bring me flowers and I'm charmed; swing a hammer and I'm yours.

Within the jumble of acronyms, strange euphemisms, crude gestures, and *Simpsons* quotes was an emerging bond—Mike wanted to show me who he was and where he came from, and I wanted to know. We shared a desire to understand each other, and the more we saw, the better things got. And if there was one place where we met, heart, mind, and soul, it was in our ideals. Between his

Armyism and my activism, we both hoped that we could improve the world somehow. Granted, he might know more about M-16s and I might know more about the Sex Pistols, but we were learning that we spoke the same language after all.

3

Embedded

From the beginning, Mike liked to refer to himself as a "planner by nature and profession," which worked out beautifully for me, since I'm a worrier by nature and profession. I mull things over, churn, process, and either fashion a comment out of the chaos, or struggle to figure out a way around the mess. Being with someone who valued order and organization made me feel more relaxed. Not genuinely relaxed—I didn't think that was possible for me—but definitely less stressed than usual.

On our way out for a Sunday afternoon walk before I made the drive back up to New York, Mike said, picking up his things from the kitchen counter, "I always like to carry my wallet and my cell phone in case I come across a lemonade stand or a man down," which encapsulated what I loved most about him.

We wound around the secluded nature trail that bordered the apartment complex, the pathway shaded with oak, white poplar, and loblolly pine. He reached for my hand. "Do you think you could live here?"

Could I? For him, absolutely. I liked Maryland—being so close to D.C., and Baltimore, where my mother grew up. I liked the hazy sunsets, the slower pace, and the fact that Maryland was Southern enough for the supermarket to stock five kinds of Glory brand canned greens—collard, kale, mustard, mixed, and turnip. I even liked Fort Meade, with its run-down cinder-block official buildings, enormous state-of-the-art commissary, and the bowling alley, which served the best bowling alley nachos I'd ever had.

In July of 2002, we sat down to merge his gift for planning with my obsession over detail. Within three days, we'd crafted the strategy for moving in together. We made lists and bought boxes and rented a U-haul van, and just *did it*. After packing up everything in my little cottage, we convoyed down I-95 from New York to Maryland, he in the van and I in my truck, communicating by walkie-talkie. "Hey, you thirsty?"

"Roger that."

"Then meet me at the next rest stop. We'll get a soda."

"WILCO."

Fort Meade was short on living quarters, so Mike was able to live off post thanks to the generous BAH (basic allowance for housing). He purchased a new two-bedroom condo in the same complex as the apartment he'd rented. He told me he'd bought it because of the small sunny parlor with French doors off the living room; he pictured me using it as an office. I was touched. He understood that I would not—could not—stop working, no matter where our relationship went. Fortunately, I had a perfectly portable career. If not, how could we have gotten to this point?

Setting up house together was interesting because Mike is far neater than I. "I admit it," he said, folding his undershirts as if they were to be on shelf display. "I'm kind of anal."

Was it the Army or his core nature that made him so fastidious? Certainly, the Army helped. I watched in wonder as he dressed in his uniform. When he had to wear his camo for work, he'd puff the pant legs out over the tops of his boots with special bands called blousing rubbers. The boot polishing was a ritual unto itself—spit and classic black Parade Gloss Kiwi polish, applied layer upon layer with a soft cloth and buffed to a soft, perfectly even glow. He "shined" the plastic faux patent dress shoes with paper towels and a few generous shots of Windex or WD-40. And the beret—dear Lord, the beret. When it was new, it had to be shaved with a razor to remove any wool fuzz, then came the endless soaking and scrunching and flattening and shaping until the cover molded neatly to the shape of his head, with a firm peak over his left eye.

When he was being particularly strict about domestic order, I needled him with the nickname Anal Boy, which he'd sing back to me with bravado, like a two-note trumpet blast or superhero fanfare. "Anal *Boy!*" Had I really worried when we met that this man was a follower? Just folding a contour sheet with the guy held all the tension of a hostage negotiation. "No," he'd correct me. "Fold it to the left."

"What does it matter as long as it gets folded?"

He'd start pulling. "Now stretch it taut."

"I *am* stretching it taut."

"No, I know. But tauter."

"*Tauter* isn't a word."

These chores usually ended with me muttering under my breath. But I had to admit it was nice to have a neat man about the house. I never wanted to get stuck cleaning up after a guy, and now, I most assuredly wouldn't.

We shopped together for things we needed to make our household complete—some throw pillows, a printer stand for my office, framed Li-Leger prints for the walls. I drove to Fort Meade to meet him after work so we could go to the PX—the Army's general goods store. Military police with rifles stood guard at the installation gate—we were in the post-9/11 Army now. The guards asked what my business was at Fort Meade, checked my driver's license, searched my trunk, and waved me through the barricade.

At the PX, Mike disappeared into the uniform section to find a pair of trousers for his Class B uniform. I stood staring at the wall full of rank insignia, medals, ribbons, and patches—hundreds of emblems of affiliation and achieve-

ment. The medals and ribbons that Mike wore racked on
his dress uniform jackets made a colorful, well-ordered
grouping that he called his "fruit salad." He'd patiently explained to me what each medal was for, but as I looked at
the vast array of merchandise on display, I wondered how
I'd ever sort it all out. So many stripes and shapes in black-
ened bronze and gold and silver, the enormity of the Army
symbolically laid out before me.

When Mike and I left the PX and headed toward the
parking lot, we approached a trio of young soldiers, also in
uniform. As we walked past, they saluted Mike, each man
snapping his right hand up toward his brow, *thwip, thwip,
thwip.* "Evening, sir."

He saluted back, "Good evening."

I can't lie—I viewed him as a regular guy under that uniform, but there's an irrevocable shift in perception that occurs once you've seen the man you regularly fight for the
remote control being addressed as "sir."

A couple of months after moving in together, we started
talking about marriage. I had fantasized about a traditional
military wedding—my beloved in his finest uniform festooned with rows of miniature medals; a white dress for
me, and things old, new, borrowed, and blue. We'd leave
the chapel by walking under an arch of sabers held high
by fellow soldiers, and as I passed the last one, he would
tap my rear with his sword, per custom, saying, "Welcome
to the Army, ma'am."

But our betrothal landed far afield of tradition, his proposal predicated not so much on *"Will you?"* but *"What if?"* The jungle drums of war were beating and he sensed a deployment was imminent. We had to act fast.

We discussed the situation. "You know that if there's a war in Iraq, I'm going, right?" he asked me.

I nodded.

"And," his tone turned solemn, "you know what might happen when I go?"

So we made an appointment to go to Baltimore City Hall and say *I do*, just in case.

I didn't have time to stage an emergence as Mrs. Army Fashionista, so on November 18, the big day, I pieced together an ensemble befitting a clothes-conscious postpunk war bride—head-to-toe black: knit pullover, pencil skirt, wide-mesh fishnets, and round-toed slingbacks buffed to military-grade polish. I grabbed my vintage leopard-print trench coat to cover up in the November chill, and we were off to City Hall. I didn't pass under an arch of sabers like a traditional military bride, but I did have to go through a metal detector.

The security guard exhibited the heart of a true romantic. Upon hearing that we were there to get married, he stage-whispered to Mike, "The emergency exit is thataway."

My friend Deb came down from New York to be our witness. Deb had been my dearest friend since we shared an illegal sublet on East Eleventh Street in the East Village.

The Greek-Sicilian Jeff to my Waspy Mutt, she barely squeaks in over five feet tall, but she plays a Fender Strat like a guitar giant. We'd been through almost everything together, from rat infestations in our crappy tenement apartment to stupid relationships to a riotous joint birthday party in 1989 that featured a watercooler full of punch so polluted that half of our guests couldn't even walk home, and where Richie Stotts from the Plasmatics, who was almost seven feet tall, hit his head on my loft bed. There was no other choice for my "babe of honor." Our only other wedding attendants were eight men in orange prison jumpsuits being led down the corridor with their ankles and wrists chained together. Mike and I had met in a graveyard and now here we were getting hitched in immediate proximity to prisoners in handcuffs. Someone at the Department of Obvious Symbolism was working overtime on our behalf.

On the way up to the chapel in the elevator, I realized that I wasn't a war bride; I was a War on Terror bride. I appreciated the image it suggested, like I was a gore- and blood-drizzling matrimonial zombie freak. If it came down to a B-movie catfight, *War on Terror Bride vs. Bridezilla*, I would win—I wasn't weighed down by ten pounds of lace-trimmed fluff, and with Uncle Sugar breathing down my neck, I was in a hurry. I was motivated.

We found the little chapel on the fourth floor. Mike put his hand on the doorknob. "Ready?"

I held up our marriage license. "Ready."

He opened the door, and we looked around the vacant room. It was so, so sorry. Worse than anything you'd see on a Vegas bender. Even the cheesiest Elvis impersonator would have taken one look at the Home Depot PVC lattice arch over the altar and said, *No, thanks. I can't bring you kids into this mess.* I was glad our parents weren't there to see it—my mom would've wept at the urns of faux fruit on pedestals, all white plaster gilded with a misting of gold spray paint. The swags of tulle that marked off the "aisle"— which dead-ended at a foldable partition wall behind four rows of chairs—were graying under a thick coat of dust. It was what it was—a fluorescent-lit conference room modified by the lowest bidder. We crossed the threshold. Our heels sank into the maroon carpet.

Mike and I sat on the white folding chairs and held hands while we waited for the officiant to show up. My palms started to sweat. I knew that marrying a soldier meant marrying the military as well—I'd have the government as a sort of hectoring, ever-present mother-in-law. And if a conflict in Iraq did happen, the sphere of influence within our marriage would broaden further still—if the Army was to be an intractable third party in our union, the war would be a fourth. It started to feel awfully crowded in that empty chapel.

I had the nervousness of a new bride, excited butterflies but with an added overlay of fear: What would the future be like for us when this war really got here? Could I give him what he needed? Did we know each other well enough to make this work? I had almost gotten this far with someone else and backed out. Was I Army spouse material? Statistically speaking, yes—the average Army spouse is under thirty-five, 95 percent of spouses are female, and the majority of wives work—but was I really up to the task? The justice of the peace came into the room and we stood. I swallowed my fear and we stepped up to the cheapo garden-store wedding arch.

We exchanged our vows under the banks of buzzing fluorescent lights. We signed our marriage certificate and added our names to the city registry, and with a kiss, it was official: In sickness and in health, in war and in peace, we were wed.

We took Deb out to lunch at the Pizzeria Uno in Harbor Place, then, after dropping her off at the train station, we returned to our condo and, since we didn't have a wedding cake, split a pack of Hostess chocolate cupcakes. In a quick, nondescript ceremony, my life began a radical shift—not just from singleton to wife, but from free-flying civilian chick to "trailing spouse"—the household member who packs up house and goes along wherever the Army sends the soldier.

The day I really became an Army wife carried the mark of bureaucratic flourish—when I received my military ID, otherwise known as my DEERS (Defense Enrollment Eligibility Reporting System) card. With our marriage certificate in hand, Mike and I went to the issuing office at Fort Meade, where the clerk greeted us warmly.

"She's here for her dependent ID," Mike said.

The clerk shook her head and mouthed, "Noooooo."

"I'm sorry," I said to her. "What?"

"We don't call spouses 'dependents' anymore." Susie Campfollower stereotype be damned, military spouses had sufficiently cast off their "dependent" label. I passed her the necessary paperwork—my Social Security card, my passport, Mike's military ID, and our marriage certificate. From there, my information would be processed and re- duced to a digitized code on the back of the card that could only be read by a scanner, a detail that felt at once impressively advanced and vaguely Orwellian. Yes, dear. Yes, DEERS.

In no time at all, the clerk had entered my vital data and the card was almost ready to print. She pointed a small webcam my way. "Okay, straight into the camera and on the count of three, smile!"

While we waited for the card to print, she said, "Don't lose this. You'll need it for everything—to get on post, to shop at the commissary, the PX, and the Class Six (i.e., liquor store), and to get your medical." I may not be depend- ent on my husband, but apparently, I was very much de- pendent on this card.

My card started chugging out of the printer. This was go- ing a hundred times faster than any trip I'd ever taken to the Department of Motor Vehicles. Random as it seemed,

I was suddenly reminded of the time I posed for *Playboy*. When I'd recalled the experience for Mike, he was shocked at how time- and labor-intensive creating a pinup could be. Who knew that getting into the Army system and getting into *Playboy* had anything in common? But both involved lots of sitting and waiting while the experts bustled around me, trying to fit me within an existing template.

In 1995, *Playboy* issued a casting call for a layout called "Women of the Internet," because at that time, the Internet still was a novelty. *Playboy* loves the novelty shoot— Women of MENSA, Women of Hooters, Women of Enron, Women of Olive Garden. I hosted a couple of private on-line conferences in a nerdy Bay Area Internet community, which seemed like good enough qualifications, so I sent in my photo and didn't hold out much hope, but a couple of months later, I got a call from an assistant photo editor named Stephanie Barnett. She said, "We'd like to shoot you," and offered to fly me out to Los Angeles later that month.

The Good Citizens of Bunnyland do not mess around— they sent someone to Los Angeles International Airport to take me to a hotel by the beach and give me a list of preparations for the shoot: show up shaved, moisturized, with your manicure and pedicure done, your hair clean, and your face free of makeup.

The following morning, a car picked me up at nine o'clock and took me to Playboy Studio West, where I was shown the set they'd built for me: a makeshift stage with a tinsel curtain, a stripper pole, and a bank of video monitors. They had a contract and photo release ready to sign. I changed into a white terry-cloth robe and slippers and was shown into the makeup room. I emerged two hours later, with huge teased and lacquered hair and a Pamela Anderson makeup job—two rows of false eyelashes, smoky eyeliner, brows tweezed and penciled to a high arch, and a thick coat of oil-slick gloss over MAC Spice liner and Faux lipstick. I couldn't believe the transformation. I felt like I was wearing a clay mask and looked like a cross between a drag queen and a Fembot factory second.

I belted my robe and wandered around the wardrobe area while the stylists decided what to dress me in. The clothes were stocked in a two-story storeroom with lingerie eight racks high—every possible configuration of fluff, lace, feathers, leather, satin, velvet, and animal print. It was like peeking inside Barbie's Dream Closet. The stylists considered my build and my coloring and, using their own professional metric, chose to outfit me in nothing but piles of rhinestone necklaces and belly chains, black patent platform sandals, and a rhinestone-drizzled black mesh shrug.

The photographer was Stephen Wayda, who is a *Playboy* legend, which was both a blessing and a curse. I knew I could count on him to take wonderful pictures—he spent five hours shooting, just for one image. But he was clearly used to much more experienced models, and his frustration with me became obvious. Madonna's "Erotica" played on repeat as Wayda did his best to coach me: "Lengthen your waist. Chin up. Raise your arms over your head and grab the pole behind you." *Erotic. Erotic.* Shut up, Madonna, I'm stretching so far upward I'm about to break in half. He kept encouraging me to turn this way and that, but I was so anxious, I clung to the pole like the shyest girl on Amateur Night. The most humiliating thing was how he kept asking me to pose with my arms over my head—I knew this trick. It lifts your breasts. Sorry about the gravitational pull, dude. They're real.

When we took a break for lunch, one of the photographer's sympathetic assistants said, "We've got a bag of mini Reese's Peanut Butter Cups, if you want some."

I'm a nervous eater, so I couldn't keep away from those Reese's Cups. I ate a good two-dozen or so during the shoot, and to this day, whenever I hear Madonna's "Erotica," I crave peanut butter.

Hours later, we finally wrapped. I was exhausted, feeling like I'd completed a systemic circuit—this once-in-a-lifetime event was just business as usual for everyone else there. Another day at the cheesecake factory.

I awaited the issue's release, honored that I was part of a very particular feminine tradition. Finally, in April of 1996, the spread was slated to run. There was only one thing off about the photo. It didn't look like me. At all.

When the issue hit the stands, my dear friend Deb called

me. "I had to flip through the magazine four times to find you," she said. "You look like some Texas oilman's wife named Babs."

The clerk handed me my new military ID, still warm from the laminating machine. "Here you go, ma'am."

Whoa. I had officially become a "ma'am." I was part of the big green Army machine.

I looked down at the photo, a black-and-white shot floating on a light brown background. Yep, just as I suspected. Didn't look a thing like me.

I put the card in my wallet. As a rite of passage, the process of integrating into the Army system felt oddly powerful—like I was gaining not just the support of my husband, but the fortification of legitimacy and institutional might. The sense of a foundation beneath my feet offset the nervousness I felt about sacrifices I would be asked to make in aid to Mike's career. I was now a member of a team that was more than a million strong. And to me, as with legions of other women married to military men, the lover's breathless pledge of "I'll follow you anywhere" was no longer some abstract romantic notion. It was now a way of life.

4

Deployment

DEPARTMENT OF THE ARMY
PERMANENT ORDER 084-002

THE FOLLOWING ORGANIZATION OR UNIT ACTION IS
DIRECTED:

ACTION: OCONUS DEPLOYMENT IN SUPPORT OF OPERA-
TION IRAQI FREEDOM AND RETURN.
ASSIGNED TO: UNITED STATES CENTRAL COMMAND, AREA
OF RESPONSIBILITY

NUMBER OF DAYS: 365 DAYS UNLESS EXTENDED BY COM-
MANDER, U.S. TOTAL ARMY PERSONNEL COMMAND UPON
DIRECTION OF HQDA G3.

On the January day in 2003 when Mike received his deployment orders, he was eerily calm. We'd already had the *What if* of war looming over us for months. Had I expected him to be more emotional as deployment drew closer? I don't know.

He lost his cool only twice. The night he got his orders, I shuffled around the kitchen in an insomniac haze baking chocolate-chip cookies until 2 a.m. I sealed the cookies in a plastic zip bag and doodled hearts and love notes on it with a permanent marker. When he found them on the counter in the morning, he came into the bedroom in his uniform with tears in his eys.

Days later, I found him sitting on the side of the bed, shoulders slumped. "I don't want to see any more dead people," he moaned.

He had told me only once about the hundreds of burned and mangled corpses he'd seen as a platoon leader in the First Infantry Division during the Gulf War. At the end of the exhausting hundred-hour ground war, Mike's unit was making its final drive northeast to Safwan when it ran directly across the "Highway of Death." The Iraqis, fleeing Kuwait City, had jammed Highway 80 as they tried to get back to safety. Mike and his soldiers arrived upon the scene just four hours after the road was attacked by sorties of coalition aircraft. Vehicles were still smoking, some still being licked by orange flame. The air stank of burning fuel and flesh.

Mike described the gruesome sight. Amid the twisted body parts and metal were prayer rugs, televisions, candelabras, silverware, women's dresses—war booty that had been abandoned in panic. In the backseat of a old green Peugeot, Mike discovered the body of a dead Kuwaiti hostage, bugs already settling into his bloody wounds, with his hands bound behind his back. He'd been shot through the temple, and the bullet blew out the back of his head like a trapdoor, blood and chunks of brain splattering the car upholstery. His face had a peaceful expression; by his side was a photograph of lovely woman bending over a birthday cake with a toddler. Mike wasn't sure if the man had used the photo in a failed attempt to elicit mercy while he pleaded for his life, or if he had simply begged to see it before he was shot.

I never asked Mike about anything he'd seen in combat before that, or after. I didn't feel it was within my rights to press him for details, and womanly intuition guided me to soothe rather than pry. His reluctance to talk about such personal things didn't seem uniquely male, but rather, entirely human. I accepted that my husband, like many people, preferred to process misery in private. "You'll feel better if you talk about it," is the hoary inducement to divulge. Whenever I hear that, I think, instinctively, *No*. He will tell me what he wants to tell me, when he wants to. *If* he wants to. But I wouldn't ask, even though I was curious to see over the wall between us, the one that separated my experience from his. He was part of a world that I could not—and likely would not—ever know.

He would be entering that world again very soon, and I'd be shut out. I would know little more about it than the space it would span on our calendar: 365 days. Fifty-two weeks. Twelve months. A year.

A *year*.

The big green canvas kit bag lay on the bedroom floor, zipper undone and opened wide. Mike tried to convince me that this deployment wasn't a big deal—after a few weeks of predeployment training at Fort Dix in New Jersey, the battalion would start out doing a brief stint at Camp Udairi in Kuwait, then convoy north and spend the rest of the deployment providing intelligence support in Baghdad. As the battalion executive officer, his job was to support the battalion commander in matters of logistics, intelligence, and personnel—to be his right arm. While Mike assured me over and over that he wouldn't be in danger, I wasn't convinced. Though I was more frightened by him going to Baghdad, Camp Udairi was just across the Iraq border (as if bombs recognized borders anyway). Who really knew how far this conflict would spread?

The Army issued both a stop-loss and a stop-rotation, meaning that soldiers could neither leave the Army nor report to their next duty station until further notice, regardless of what their orders were prior to the start of the war. Mike's July 1 report date at the military academy was indefinitely postponed, and our return to West Point was off the table for the foreseeable future.

"I wish I could fit you in here," Mike said as he folded his undershirts into the kit bag.

"Well, technically you could fit me in there. But when you let me out, I'd be so pissed I'd attack you like a rabid chimp." I was joking out of fear. Fear ballooned out in front of me so big and ominous that humor was the only way I could see around it. I was afraid of so many things—being alone, not knowing what to do in his absence, not knowing if he'd be safe. Just not knowing.

I gave him my small battery-operated digital alarm clock to keep by his bedside every night. "Think of me when you're tucked in, okay? It's got a thermometer, too."

He tested the buttons, turning the aqua blue glowing nightlight on and off. "That could be interesting. The temperature can get over 120 degrees over there."

"You're kidding, right?"

"No."

While he continued packing, I held a set of his dog tags, turning them over and over in my palm. Stamped into the tags was information that reduced my husband to statistical basics: name, Social Security number, blood type, religion. I'm enchanted with dog tags, a timeless military symbol, until I remember that they're designed to function as a toe tag should he be killed in combat.

Two days before Mike deployed, the battalion's families were summoned on post for the predeployment Family Readiness Group meeting. Here we were briefed on every aspect of life during separation, from facing logistical challenges to dealing with emotional fallout. Though this was my first time interacting with other military wives, it was easy for me to tell the newer wives from the old. New ones like me sat alert, taking notes, our eyes round like a bunch of owls, while the more seasoned among us sat back, looking as if they'd heard the spiel before.

The unit FRG meeting was run by volunteers from Fort Meade Army Community Services. During the briefing, a stern older woman urged us to be fiscally sensible (*Do not, I repeat, do not rush out and buy a new couch or big-screen TV!*), while her earnest younger counterpart told us that it was our job as women to make sure our returning serviceman didn't feel threatened by our wartime autonomy. She said she'd shored up her man's confidence by screwing burned-out lightbulbs into the household fixtures so he'd have something to repair when he got back. I smirked. I would keep our house together and my man together—it would be a piece of cake. No assistance from GE needed.

The FRG leaders also told us that, as wives, we may be overwhelmed and agitated by news reports about the war, so we shouldn't feel bad for wanting to avoid newspapers, radio, and television. If being in the information loop frightened you or made your family anxious, a self-imposed news embargo was perfectly okay. We shouldn't feel guilty for protecting ourselves emotionally.

Mike joined me just in time for the "marital relations" portion of the presentation. Sex and intimacy can be strained when a soldier returns home, we were told. The elder woman urged us, in a thick Massachusetts accent, to "let nature take its course." A few rows in front of us, a warrant officer's wife quieted her restless three-year-old.

Back at our apartment, Mike took down our fireproof lockbox. "Here's our marriage certificate," he said, taking it from the box. I smiled; I'd brandished the certificate in front of my delighted parents at Thanksgiving dinner, announcing our marriage to their applause. We'd then moved on to New York, stopping by his mother's house in Dutchess County, then his father's place in Queens, spreading the big news. Mike dug farther into the lockbox. "Here's your power of attorney." He held out a business-size envelope. "You'll need this, too."

"What is it?"

"It's my will."

He held it out to me, but I didn't want to touch it. I refused. He lay it on the bed.

I don't know if my refusal was superstition or denial, but it is a stark fact of military marriage that we were forced to prepare for the end of our life together before it had even begun.

When Mike finished packing his gear later that night, he sat me down in his office and handed me a blue three-ring binder. "Everything you need as far as banking and credit card stuff is in here," he said, with the new husband's pride of provision. "I know you can handle this," he told me. I wasn't sure I agreed, but I looked forward to noodling around the USAA Web site paying bills and checking the Defense Finance and Accounting Service site to make sure the princely combat stipend (i.e., "hostile-fire pay") of $225 a month was added to his paycheck.

I dropped off Mike at Fort Meade the following morning, confident that I could keep the household running smoothly while his battalion went through predeployment training at Fort Dix. But I shouldn't have been so smug. I was not to be spared the Deployment Juju that I later learned visits every military household the moment the soldier leaves the house. It's uncanny. Is it some metaphysical energetic shift or a strange cheeky demon meant to test your mettle? I don't know, but *something* puts Murphy's Law of Deployment into play: If anything can go wrong in your house, your yard, or your garage while your husband is away, it will.

The first day my husband was gone, the smoke alarm started acting up, beeping every few minutes, even after I pulled out the battery. I finally boosted myself up on a kitchen chair and attacked the alarm with a hammer and a fork, yanking the wires from the ceiling. I'm still a capable woman, I soothed myself as I climbed down from the chair, I'm just not compatible with any appliance that beeps. I eyed the microwave warily. Disabling things wasn't really fixing them, but that was a lesson I had yet to learn.

At the computer in Mike's office, I would work on the monthly bills. If I couldn't figure something out, like how to change the dates on the automatic payments, keening terror gripped me, as if my competence were directly linked to my husband's safety, and by screwing things up, I had put him at risk. Routine is the balm of the fearful, I realized, and once one little blip occurs in the program, all the pent-up anxiety bursts out, full force.

Our neighbors in the condo complex knew that Mike was gone. All civilians with corporate jobs, they'd stop me in the hallway to ask how I was doing. They'd tell me, "I can't imagine what you're going through." It was so new and surreal that neither could I. I veered between feeling bored, restive, sad, and supremely annoyed. I struggled to articulate my emotions with accuracy and tact. I heard a radio show where listeners were urged to call in with their feelings about the war. People were weepy, swooning with patriotism, adamant that anyone opposed to any aspect of the war effort should "move to Iraq!" Then, a military wife called in and said exactly what I'd been feeling, what had evaded expression: "I wish they'd just get it over with!"

War is hell and waiting is hell and war is waiting. While my husband was at Fort Dix for what I called Operation

Enduring Limbo, I visited when I could. I knew I was lucky to have the opportunity to see him during his run-up to deployment. I'd hug him and he'd smell like Army, like dried sweat and sour old canvas. He looked Schwartzkopfian (but slimmer and cuter) in his new desert camo. He was ready to go, I could see it in the set of his mouth—an authoritative bracing that turns his upper lip to a tense bow.

He toured me around post during his few off moments. On warm afternoons, we'd see young female soldiers returning from physical training in their athletic uniforms of black nylon track pants and gray pullovers, their hair pulled back in hasty ponytails. Each with an M-16 rifle slung casually over her shoulder, they sauntered along like Bryn Mawr girls coming in from the lacrosse field. I sat watching them with a combination of wonder and respect. They were bound for something I knew I didn't have the guts or physical strength to take on myself.

At night, we settled down together in the generic Fort Dix lodging, an old barracks turned hotel called, startlingly, Fort Dix Lodging. The walls were cinder block, so thin we could hear the television in the next room. Whoever the occupant was, he was watching *The Nanny*, Fran Drescher's nasal honk making him bray with laughter.

I stripped Mike out of his uniform and we snickered about "letting nature take its course," then called for delivery from the local Italian place that knew every building on Fort Dix and adjoining McGuire Air Force Base.

Afterward, we settled in front of the TV. We needed the normalizing effect of *Seinfeld* and pizza. At least an hour of news was a must. All the Hollywood movies that depict a military intelligence cadre as one big nerve center located in a top-secret icy blue underground chamber have created the illusion that everyone in the Armed Forces intel community knows exactly what's going on at all times. Ha. As often as not, my husband got his news briefings from CNN.

When we were together, I'd steer the conversation, and my thoughts, toward the light side. I didn't ponder questions like, What if he's killed? What if he has to kill someone? My concerns narrowed to the tiny lens of his comfort: What could I do to make this easier on him? It wouldn't be long before he was in the desert, subsisting on MREs (Meals Ready to Eat, or as Mike called them "Meals Ready to Excrete"), food rations so bland and uninspiring that the little bottles of Tabasco packaged with them were used as currency. He might be sleeping folded up inside a Humvee, confined by stifling layers of body armor. Surely, he'd be getting sand in places you didn't know sand could find. Since he couldn't leave the post at Dix, I'd take down lists of things he needed from the outside—a camp shower, a Tupperware tub with a lid for washing laundry, baby wipes, clothesline. A king's ransom of foot powder. Whenever I kissed him goodbye before heading home, I wondered, "Is this the last time I see him before he goes?"

Finally, in late March, just days before my birthday, he got the word. His unit was leaving the States for the Middle East in twelve hours, the flight scheduled to go wheels-up at 0035, a half tick past the witching hour. He called my cell phone while I was in Hoboken, New Jersey, visiting Deb. I had one last chance to see him before he left. My brain was whirring at a mile a minute. I left Deb's apartment and hurried the four blocks to my car.

When I got to my parking spot, I let out a stream of expletives. I had parked on the wrong side of the street and the parking police had nabbed me. My car had a boot on the front tire.

I called Deb and asked her what I should do.

"I hate to tell you this, but you have to go down to Hoboken City Hall, give them your license plate number, and pay the fine so they'll give you the combination to remove the boot. Tell you what," she said, "walk back up here, I'll meet you at the corner. We'll go over there together and maybe I can get you off the hook."

Fortunately, Hoboken is "the mile-square city" so we weren't that far from City Hall. Deb pleaded my case to the woman behind the Plexiglas window in the parking department. "You don't understand. Her husband is deploying. Tomorrow. If she doesn't get the boot off now, she won't see him before he goes." My friend, God bless her, was trying to hustle them along, and to get them to waive the $150 fee to get the combination to the lock that removed the boot. I didn't care about the money.

I scribbled out a check and slid it under the Plexiglas partition.

Deb and I took a cab back to my car, punched in the combination code on the lock, and Deb took the boot so she could return it to the city for me. I slid behind the wheel and raced along the Jersey Turnpike to Fort Dix.

When I arrived, the post had an entirely different energy. Everyone in the headquarters building seemed electrified; people bustled from office to office, holding meetings and taking phone calls. Like most Army leaders, Mike focused on his soldiers' needs to the exclusion of his own. Because of this, he still needed to do several personal errands before he left, so he finally pulled himself away and climbed in the car with me. Each errand had its own emotional gravity—last haircut, last run to the PX. Then, much too soon, last hug and last kiss. Last look in the rearview mirror. And then he disappeared from sight.

My baby was off to war.

I slowly drove off post, past the Vietnam Era tank and helicopter at the center of the traffic roundabout. It's hard to say which was more difficult—the drive down to see him for the last time before he left, or the drive back to Maryland alone, knowing it would be a year before I saw him again. Like new parents being sent home from the hospital, startled that the doctors and staff actually let you leave with the baby, I felt shockingly ill-equipped. Don't I need more preparation? Am I even remotely ready? My God, how will I do this?

But I didn't cry, and I was proud of the fact. The point was not to be strong for myself, but for Mike. I would prove to him that he could count on me. When we hugged for the final time before I left, I leaned into his neck, my parting words to him a whisper.

"I've got your six."

5

Way Gone

Dear Lily—

Day three, no ice here at Camp Udairi. 109 degrees. That means drinking water that is—you guessed it—109 degrees. Sweat pouring down the front of my calves into my boots. BDU top off, stripped down to T-shirt (I do this whenever it crests 105 degrees).

Last night: Unseasonable dust storm rattled the tent from 2 a.m.–4 a.m. On a night that never got any cooler than 88 degrees, a dust storm from the south is bad—southern winds are warm. We then buttoned up the tent to keep the dust out and the temperature soared to 95 degrees. So, you just lay there, soaking in your own sweat, while all the particulate matter blows in under the tent floor and swirls around you, clinging to your skin.

It's just too hot, too much, to work out as I need to. When you do, you put your health/hygiene at risk,

*because you can't shower every day, but every fourth
day. Really classy, huh?*

I love you. I just want this to be over.

xoxo

M

On March 19, I woke to the sight of bombs falling on
Baghdad. The Shock and Awe campaign had officially
kicked off the war. There was something spooky about
watching a war unfold in real time. History was being
made, and for the first time, I had a personal attachment
to the events. I wondered if I was already failing as a military wife because I had an uneasy feeling about the
whole thing. Wasn't I supposed to be waving the Stars and
Stripes and cheering at this show of American military
majesty?

In my solitary state, I didn't bother much with grocery
shopping, preferring instead to scrape together microwave-
able meals from the gas station mini-mart up the street.
But by the first official day of the ground war in Iraq, the
pantry was stripped down to cans of pinto beans, Cup-a-
Soup, Mike's coffee, and half a crusted-over jar of Tang, I
made my way to the Fort Meade Commissary. The Iraq
war had started; the cupboards were bare.

I showed my DEERS card to the checker at the door and
pushed my cart inside. Luckily, this wasn't one of the
cramped commissaries with arrows on the aisle floors to direct the flow of traffic in a strict military march. No, this was

freedom to roam, freedom to consume. At first, I loaded my cart with lonely bachelor fare: microwave entrees, cereal, milk, just-add-hot-water box meals. What was the point of anything more elaborate?

Then I couldn't face going home alone, so I spent an hour looping around the aisles, tossing into the cart sliced turkey breast, low-fat cookies, fresh fruit, chocolate skim milk—comfort food for the vain. I found solace in the customers who, by their mere presence, were proof that soldiers' lives go on after war: old guys in satin Korean Theater jackets with elaborate dragons embroidered on the back; Vietnam vets with khaki vests covered in patches and silvered biker braids trailing down to their belt loops. And kids and kids and kids.

I stood in a checkout line that was twenty people long until a cashier waved me over to the empty fifteen-items-or-less lane. As I unloaded my little cart of sorrow, a woman in a loose-fitting lavender sweat suit and Keds came up behind me. I recognized her from the FRG meeting in January.

She smiled at me. "How you holdin' up?"

"Okay, I guess. A little worried. You?"

"I'm doing all right." She cocked her head toward her daughter, in a pink sweat suit, sneakers with lights in the soles, and a head full of braids with barrettes on the ends. "She's the one I worry about," she said, lowering her voice. "She keeps asking if her daddy's going to be safe."

"Have you heard from him at all?" I didn't know if other

soldiers in the unit had e-mail, so I didn't say anything about how often I heard from Mike.

"Yeah, a couple times."

"But it's not enough, right?" I moved to the end of the checkout queue and started loading up my bags.

"Right."

"It's good that she can tell you she's worried about her dad, though." I didn't know if this was actually true. I hoped it was.

"I know. I know." She started unloading groceries from her cart onto the moving register belt. "Well, I guess we just gotta suck it up and drive on."

On March 20, six Iraqi missiles were fired into Kuwait. On March 23, Sergeant Hasan Akbar of the 101st Airborne Division's 326th Engineer Battalion killed two soldiers and wounded fourteen others at Camp Pennsylvania in Kuwait when he threw grenades into the command center tents and then fired on soldiers with a rifle. One of the men killed, Major Gregory Stone, was pierced with eighty-three pieces of shrapnel. Shortly thereafter, an Iraqi missile landed near a popular shopping mall in Kuwait City. After hearing this news, I immediately let go of the fantasy of Mike's safety.

How to describe the dimensional warp of deployment? After a couple of months alone, my emotions had divided along two axes: a tenderheart track of lonely/achy/weepy, and a battle-ax complement of brittle, aggressive, and testy. Every day was a roller coaster of emotion, like PMS raised to an epic level. Of course it was more than some cyclical march of hormones; it was a state of shock, basically. As a stress response, I'd split myself into someone steely, and possibly a bit cracked.

Without immediate family to worry about and care for, without that primal drive to pull myself out of self-isolation and into the game of daily life, the deployment became like the movie *Groundhog Day*, each day suspiciously similar, with little room to improve the script.

If two words could describe my state during his deployment, they would be *under control*. I was a working woman, so I did what working women do: I worked, obsessively, medicating anxiety with output. All I wanted to do was hunker at my laptop and write until I felt entirely removed from reality. I was working on a novel, my war baby, my first. Usually crippled by headache-inducing writer's block, I found the words flowed out of me with ease. I convinced myself that what I needed was not the outside world but to stay inside laying down riffs about love and longing and blood. I needed productive days as ballast for the hollow-vessel nights.

My performance was convincing, but all the while, I was aware of a shadow self, constantly on alert and roaming the halls in worry. I put myself on a bizarre diet consisting almost entirely of low-fat microwave entrees, diet soda, and ice water flavored with lemon, taking in, at most, a thousand calories a day. On Sundays, I'd treat myself to the same cheat meal: pepperoni pizza, ranch-flavor tortilla chips, and two full-size vanilla Charleston Chew bars, all from the gas station mini-mart. I began to understand eating disorders a little better—the small bliss of privation, the titillation that comes from plotting and scheduling when to eat something "bad." The psychology behind my obsession wasn't hard to figure. Could I control the outcome of the war? My husband's safety? The date of his return? No. But I could fit into my clothes. All of them, even things remanded to a high shelf years ago. I could choose my battles, and this was mine: Woman vs. Scale, and I was winning.

In our own way, Mike and I were making history because this was the first-ever war in which spouses could stay in touch via e-mail. Whenever possible, Mike bummed some computer time from another MI unit that was already set up at Camp Udairi. I got a kick out of receiving e-mails with subject lines that said, "Hi! (UNCLASSIFIED)" and "I Love You! (UNCLASSIFIED)"

Due to operations security, Mike couldn't tell me anything about his unit's preparedness, so I wouldn't find out until he got home that they had arrived ahead of their equipment. For weeks, they were lacking trucks, trailers, Humvees, antenna systems, tents, tools, maintenance supplies, and communications support. All the vehicles, plus 350 tons of additional equipment, were still at sea.

They also didn't have air-conditioning, proper lodging, or enough water for showers. Mike had to rely on baby wipes to keep clean. The only things each soldier had, in addition to a uniform and the accoutrement to wear on and over it, were a rucksack, a rifle, and a duffel bag. They were, in every sense, non-mission-capable.

Mike probably wasn't risking security by telling me about Camp Udairi's nasty overflowing latrines. The porta-johns were so full—like, mounded up over the seat-rim full—they were completely unusable until the SST (Shit-Sucking Truck) came around to empty them. I had never before considered that among the sacrifices our troops make is the challenge of obtaining proper facilities in which to "execute a Class One download." (Class One supplies are food. Figure it out.) He tried not to be an Eeyore about it. He'd share with me the more amusing latrine graffiti: The classic "FTA" (Fuck the Army), "Jesus is coming. Look busy!" and, written in huge block letters on one door, "Iraqi Space Shuttle."

On March 29, Mike sent me an e-mail titled "Happy Birthday! (UNCLASSIFIED)." I was touched but confused—my birthday was the following day. Then I checked the time zone clock I'd set up on my computer and realized it *was* my birthday. In the Middle East.

I woke on the morning of my birthday—in Maryland—with an unshakable feeling of dread. I tried to brush it off—I'm just lonely; birthdays alone are tough—but I couldn't. There were no e-mails from Mike. I would find out later—four years later, to be exact—that on that day, an Egyptian man working at Camp Udairi drove a truck into a group of soldiers, injuring fifteen. Witnesses said that after he ran the vehicle into the crowd, he flipped the truck into reverse and was headed for them again. Mike's S2, the unit security officer, fired at the man, critically wounding him. It wasn't hard for me to imagine a different ending to the scene—the man, bearing a vest full of explosives, blowing himself up, taking dozens of soldiers with him, my husband among them. Or the driver roaring back in the truck, over and over, mowing down the entire crowd.

The reason I didn't know about it when it happened is because shortly after the Shock and Awe campaign, I'd started avoiding television and newspapers. From the mouths of the volunteers who ran the FRG meeting, I'd received *express permission* to avoid television and newspapers. I couldn't distance myself from the events. The constant, minute-by-minute exposure was wearing me out. And I hated the spin. I knew that, collectively, we needed to get our fear and sadness out there so we could breathe again, but I grew tired of news shows and music videos full of deployment porn—endless footage of clutching military families sobbing on the airstrip. It was hard for me to own up to this. I felt like the women on *Oprah* who fearfully admit that motherhood isn't as fulfilling as they expected, like I was breaking a cardinal rule of womanliness by feeling irritated instead of moony and sentimental. I was supposed to be the suffering Saint Wifey, crying while I adjusted the yellow ribbons on the tree, and instead I was rolling my eyes all the time. Even the Army Family Readiness literature says that anger is an expected emotional consequence of deployment, but still, I was ashamed.

While I abhorred the notion of working my solo state for pity points, I wasn't entirely innocent of playing on people's sympathies. I did periodically tell telemarketers, No, the man of the house can't come to the phone, *he's gone to war.*

I was sitting at my computer eating my allotted 250-calorie turkey, broccoli, and cheese Lean Pocket when the phone rang. The caller ID said Unknown Caller, so I picked up, prepared to encounter yet another telemarketer.

"Hey! It's me!" Mike! Sounding like he was calling from a galaxy far, far away!

I grasped the cordless handset. "Oh my God! What are you doing? Where are you?"

"I bought a cell phone! A Saudi guy came into the camp today and set up a table. He was selling them, so I bought one. Don't freak out when you see the charge for three hundred bucks on the credit card from Saudi Arabia."

"That's so cool," I said around a steaming bite of Lean Pocket.

"Hey, in the last war, I was lucky if I could call home every two weeks. We had to go off to these huge remote banks of satellite phones."

"Wow, that sucks."

"Yeah. Old school. And we had to bang rocks together to make fire!"

"And you also had to walk forty miles through a sandstorm to get to the mess hall, right?"

"Yep, uphill both ways."

God, it was so good to hear him, joking and sounding normal. I wanted to know everything. "So how are you?"

"Sweaty and sandy," he said. "I think it's going to be that way for a while. Listen, I can't talk long. I just want you to know I love you and miss you all there is."

"Me, too!"

From then on, my cell phone became my surrogate husband, my pet, my constant companion, and, sad to say, my only friend in Maryland.

Because I hadn't lived in Maryland for very long and I didn't know any other Army wives, my days were mostly spent alone. Mike is a career active-duty officer, but his battalion was a reserve unit. As a result, the soldiers' families weren't geographically clustered near each other, and family support was not as organized as it would have been in an active-duty unit, where everyone was nearby. There was no FRG volunteer calling to check on me. The battalion's commanding officer was a bachelor, so the traditional job of information broker and morale booster, usually fulfilled by the CO's wife, was vacant. If I weren't a newbie, as the executive officer's wife the duty would have fallen to me.

I wondered how the other wives were faring, but I had no means of reaching out, and no tutelage in knowing what to say to them even if I could.

The most disturbing thing about being by myself for so long was the plague of morbid thoughts: I'd be on the couch eating salted pretzel nuggets and then suddenly imagine Mike shot in the desert, lying alone on the ground, sand sticking to his wounds like granules of rock salt. Or I'd find myself envisioning his funeral—me sitting cross-legged on our bedroom floor, polishing the shoes he would wear for his burial. Picking out his casket—would he prefer burnished brass fittings or brushed steel? Who would come? Who would he want for pallbearers? What would I wear? Then I'd start playing a sick game of Which Would Be Worse? Which would be worse—if he were killed or maimed? Which would be worse—if he were severely burned or if he lost a limb? If he lost a limb, I thought, I'm sure we could deal with that by getting a prosthesis and physical therapy, but if he were severely burned, maybe he'd think he was better off dead. But what percentage of his body being burned could he tolerate? Thirty percent? Forty? Fifty? The elaborate fantasies and mind games seemed to take shape of their own accord, perfectly ghoulish in the depth of their detail. What did it say about me that I couldn't watch the evening news, but I could spend the better part of an hour deliberating over whether my husband would rather be burned over eighty percent of his body or killed by an insurgent's bullet? Did other wives do this? Could anticipatory grief be this gruesome, or was I becoming warped in my solitude?

While in the midst of one of these morbid reveries, there was a knock at my door. I almost shot clean out of my skin. That's how they tell you: It starts with the knock. Then you open up to find the two officers standing there in their Class A uniforms, informing you that your husband is dead and life as you knew it is over. By the time I got to the door, I felt faint.

I put my eye up to the peephole to see my neighbor, Keith, a young attorney who lived in the apartment next door with his wife, Florence. When I peeked out, he said, "Hey, Florence just ordered pizza. Do you want to come over?"

I'd approached this deployment with an open mind, but right then, I established one hard-and-fast rule: If you're planning to drop by, don't show up unannounced with a knock. Call first.

I began having erratic bouts of exaggerated sympathy— one moment, I'd be so tuned in to Mike, I'd swear I could feel him sweating in the 110-degree Sandbox heat. Then the grid would crash and when some well-meaning civilian, a neighbor or someone at the gym, would say, "I know how you feel," I'd be so pissed, I was sure my brain would melt and pour out of my eyes. *No, you most certainly damn don't know how I feel!*

After the second month of Mike being overseas, I

could have said, *If you really knew how I feel, then you'd know that I don't feel.* I was suspended in the ether, having intuited that if I stayed in touch with every single emotional turn on the deployment roller coaster, I'd fry my synapses. I'd dissociated into a sort of emotional brownout, wary of anything that might disturb my precarious inner balance.

I rarely left the house, but with the deployment diet under way, I decided to advance the self-improvement campaign. I found a dermatologist in Laurel who could get rid of the spider veins on my legs.

The nurse-receptionist was about forty-five, though from a distance she looked closer to thirty. She slid a clipboard my way. "Can you fill out these forms?"

Whoever said "The legs are the last to go" never met the women in my family. By twenty-five, we've all got more road maps than a GPS. The treatment, sclerotherapy, isn't a lot of fun: Each individual spider vein gets injected with saltwater in order to dissolve the ugly little suckers.

In shorts and a T-shirt, I lay in the treatment room watching a TV someone had tuned to CNN when the doctor came in and introduced himself. He had a full head of dyed brown hair swept back like George Hamilton's. He drew saline solution into a syringe and I rolled onto my side so he could attack the cluster of veins on my upper thigh. "So where do you live?"

"Just over in Odenton. My husband is assigned to Fort Meade. He's an Army officer."

This bit of small talk opened the doctor's floodgates, and the rest of the treatment was administered with an accompanying screed about the evils of immigration, Bill Clinton, and the liberal media and its crimes—particularly CNN. I didn't bother pointing out that the television was already tuned to CNN before I came in. He was, after all, standing over me holding a syringe.

When he was finished with my treatment, I sat up and thanked him for helping me get rid of a condition that had been bothering me for a long time.

"My pleasure," he said, dropping the used needle into the red plastic container of medical waste. "My wife always says, 'Men mature, women expire.'" Turns out this guy was in the hard news business himself. At this point, I was ready to offer him a deal: I'd shoot myself in the face when I turned forty if he promised never to run for public office.

I went back out to the reception area and paid the office manager. "Oh, Army!" she said when she saw my checks, which bore the Army seal. I'd ordered them just after my wedding in a patriotic show of bridal bliss. "My ex-husband was a Marine," she said, turning away with a sour look. It was becoming clear to me that, in a way, my identity was no longer my own—people would make a host of assumptions about me that might or might not reflect who I really was, for no reason other than that I was married to a soldier.

From then on, when I went out, I was cautious. Much in the way that a pregnant woman is a totem of life, I was a totem of war. If I revealed that I was a military wife with a deployed husband, suddenly I became public property. The clerks at the local library got all excited. "Hang in there, hon!" "You take it easy now!" I know they meant well, that they wanted to offer me their support and respect, but I became allergic to anything falsely gooey and nurturing. Maybe it was the artificial intimacy that turned me off; maybe it was the presumed weakness. I wanted to yell at them, "I married a soldier! Don't you think I'm a fighter, too?" War is horrible, but heeding the call is part of the soldier's duties, and accordingly, staying strong while your man's away is the Army wife's job. Evil Army Wife says, *Don't coddle me! Man up!*

There was also an assumption that because I was married to a soldier, I supported the war. I didn't, entirely. I thought Hussein was a monster who should be removed from power, but I worried about casualties on both sides. I worried about how American tactics would affect world opinion, and I wasn't so far from my antiauthoritarian roots that concepts like "preemption" and "containment" squared easily. I married into the military-industrial complex, yes, yet I reserved the right to judge. Love is tolerant; it is not at all blind.

"You're too thin." That was the first thing my mother-in-law, Mary, said to me when I walked into her kitchen in Rhinebeck. I'd been alone for three months when Easter rolled around, and independent of each other, both Mary and my friend Molly, who had set the stage for my meeting Mike that day in the Brooklyn graveyard, invited me to New York for Easter dinner. I packed an overnight bag and drove myself to the train station for the ride up.

Mary and I are both what her Italian relatives call *chiacchieronas*—talkers. If she called me down in Maryland, I could count on at least an hour's worth of phone chat to pull me from my loneliness. "Ever since he was little, from the time he could talk, Michael asked *so* many questions: "Ma, how does this work?" "Ma, why is this the way it is? . . . Oh my God, from morning to night, he drove me crazy!"

I chuckled. "Does it surprise you to hear he hasn't changed much?"

She put a hot cup of tea in front of me and narrowed her eyes. "You've lost too much weight . . . your face," she gestured to her cheeks. She and her boyfriend, Bob, took me to a steakhouse on one of the quaint, winding country highways, and we talked about cheerful, easy things. I collapsed into her guest bed without even getting under the quilt, relaxed enough to sleep well for the first time since Mike left for training at Fort Dix in January.

On Easter morning, Mary dropped me off at the train station in Rhinecliff with a tote that held a gallon-size Ziploc bag full of sausages, beef ribs, and meatballs steeping in her signature gravy. After hopping the subway at Grand Central, I emerged at the Court Street stop in Brooklyn, turned off the sunny sidewalk into a flower shop, and bought an extravagant bouquet of fragrant Easter lilies for Molly's table.

Molly had recently married a guy named Matt, a record company executive who was about eight feet tall and wore leather pants. His legs were so long, I pictured the pants being tailored from the hide of a black cow that was shaped like a dachshund. The three of us bustled around in their tiny galley kitchen, preparing for the rest of the guests. The apartment smelled wonderfully of roasting lamb and herbs. For the second day in a row, I let myself eat—really eat. As we cooked, I crunched down handfuls of speckled chocolate malt Easter eggs, ready to follow it with Molly's lamb stuffed with garlic and fresh rosemary, new potatoes, and string beans with almonds.

Soon, there was a full house: Marjorie, Jonathan, their baby Josie, Gavin and his wife, Jen, Molly, Matt, Rob, and me. It was so wonderful to be in a crowded, friendly space after months alone. We sat in Matt and Molly's living room, clustered on the floor around their low coffee table—NPR-listening, *New Yorker*–reading, messenger-bag toting junior members of the alleged East Coast liberal media elite. Molly had recently started working for the Children's Book Council, and Jonathan was working as a software consultant from the East Village loft apartment where he and Marjorie lived. The Hell's Angels headquarters was right across the street. Jen was busy sending out applications to schools across the country to get her Ph.D. in art history. Gavin, Marjorie, Rob, and I were writers. We weren't partisan wonks. We were more the type who wrote culture pieces mourning the fact that while Oreos were now kosher, they were also less tasty for lack of lard, or who wondered whether or not hipsters adopting Pabst Blue Ribbon as their beer of choice represented the co-optation of the working class, or crafted three-thousand-word essays on why Stone Temple Pilots totally suck—which is a sort of partisanship, I suppose.

Since I'd pretty much dropped out of sight after I moved to Maryland when Mike and I got serious, they had plenty of questions for me. Together, they sounded like the introduction to the Shangri-Las' "The Leader of the Pack":

> *So, Lily's really married to an Army officer?*
> *Well, here she is. Let's ask her!*
> *Lily, is that a wedding ring you're wearing?*
> *Mmm hmm.*
> *Gee, it must be weird being around all those Army*
>   *people. Is he coming to dinner today?*
> *Uh-uh . . . he's deployed.*
> *By the way . . . where'd you meet him?*

I could tell they had a million nosy things they wanted to ask—these were mostly writers, after all, and their interviewing impulse ran deep, but they restrained themselves. Sitting among the couples made me feel spun-out and extra lonely, and maybe it showed. And maybe Molly had warned them to be especially nice to me because of the stress I was under. (We all listen to Molly. Her nickname is "The Marshal.")

As we ate the delicious meal, we toasted the chefs and talked about how sad we were that such gatherings were rare. Marjorie and Jonathan's daughter Josie circled the table, offering us plastic colored Easter eggs from a basket, and we laughed at the realization that we were now overscheduled adults. In typical Gen X city-dweller fashion, we had suspended adolescence as long as possible, but here we were, finally, with mortgages and careers and credit cards. "I mean, look at this," I said, turning over one of Matt and Molly's bread plates. "This is *Wedgwood*." We all laughed because most of us had purchased the tableware from their wedding registry when they'd married the year before. Jen picked up her saucer and looked underneath. "Yep, this one's got my name on it." Matt and Jonathan admitted that their bacchanalian impulses were confined to their annual weeklong trip to Burning Man, while their wives rolled their eyes. We sipped our white wine. The conversation had the bittersweet tenderness of a bunch of aging garage rockers finally resigning themselves to the fact that the band's just not ever gonna get back together.

The next morning, I took the Amtrak down to Maryland, feeling sated on many levels.

By May, Mike had been gone for five months, twice the length of time we'd spent together since marrying. The solitary life wasn't all bad. I made the best of it, sleeping late and spreading out across the bed like a giant squid. I let books pile up in every corner of the condo, and felt perfectly okay about picking clean clothes straight out of the dryer, never bothering with folding or hanging things up.

I tried not to overthink the downside, focusing instead on things that inspired me—like dung beetles. Mike had told me about them during one of our early dates. He said that while trekking across the desert during the Gulf War, he had noticed that whenever a creature—four-legged or two—relieved itself, a dung beetle would swoop in out of nowhere and gather up the droppings. "It looks like this little man just pushing this big ball of crap with all his might," he said. "You can even flick the beetle off with a stick or something and it'll scuttle right back up to the ball and start pushing away again." In my view, Sisyphus *in excrementum* is as apt as any metaphor for war, and war spousedom. Whether in combat or at home, on any given day, you've just got to keep the crap moving along, no matter what.

I'd lovingly put together care packages for Mike, doing what I could to send him some substitute for the comforts of home—shaving cream, baby wipes, detergent, letters and photos, interesting snacks. I made sure to follow the rules—no porn, no pork, no perishables. I even called up Katz's Deli on Houston Street in New York's Lower East Side and asked them to "send a salami to my boy in the Army"—a tradition from World War II that I thought a his-

torian would appreciate. (Kosher, so no pork!) I made sure
to keep the food separate from the hygiene and laundry
supplies—putting aftershave and soap in the same box as
candy caused scent perversion, meaning my lonely, over-
worked husband would be on his cot, tearing into a bag-
ful of Springtime Fresh Twizzlers. There was so much he
was deprived of that I wanted him to have. A steak dinner.
A massage. A cooler stocked with ice-cold water and
soda. And a hot shower. My God, a hot shower would be
better than a steak dinner, a massage, a hot fudge sundae,
and guitar lessons from Keith Richards all rolled into one.
I imbued each package with love, hugging the bound-and-
labeled cardboard box before I took the bundle into the
post office to ship overseas. I knew it was silly, that these
boxes were no substitute, but they were the best I could do.

When I spoke to Mike on the phone, the tone and con-
tent of his conversation varied: *I need you bad. Everything's
fine. Not a good day today. Worst one yet. Better now.* He was
fiendish about adhering to operations security measures, so
I never knew exactly where he was or what he was doing;
I only knew how he was doing. My outlook rose and fell in
concert with his moods.

During one call, I recited a litany of the day's complaints—your basic wifely whining—and when it was
Mike's turn to talk, his voice broke. The frustration he felt
knowing that I was upset and that he couldn't help me
overtook him. I *got* it, a swift realization like a kick in the
ribs. The complaining was additional stress that he didn't

need. His job was to lead his men and women, to support his boss, and to get them all home alive. He couldn't afford the added weight of hauling my worries around the Sandbox on top of all that.

On my nightstand, I kept a set of Mike's dog tags, his rosary, and the Playboy Bunny pendant he gave me when we were dating—the sacred and profane of him. I thought that if I had these three talismans, I held him in his entirety. And I was okay. Until I wasn't.

Weekends were the worst. During the week, I would work or run errands, and not necessarily be reminded of the glaring loneliness of my life. Weekends are family time, couple time, and you see happy arrangements of people out enjoying their togetherness. I didn't begrudge them their joy, I merely watched them with a hollowness in my heart, wishing I had some of that easy closeness for myself. Even bickering couples made me a little heartsick, because even though they weren't getting along at that moment, they were together. They could turn to each other in forgiveness later.

I avoided shopping for the house because it was something Mike and I always did together, but one day in May, I decided I needed a new shower curtain. I drove out to the Target on Route 1. In the bedding section, I heard "When I'm Gone" by 3 Doors Down come over the store's sound system. The song cut through my callused, comfortably numb hide.

I really tried not to cry when I was at home. Crying in the house meant emotionally cursing our shared space—desecrating the temple of Us. I had to keep it together, for Mike's sake. I felt like I owed it to him somehow. So I'd confine my crying to the car. But not that day, not while the singer asked the woman he loved for four simple things: To hold him when he's here, to right him when he's wrong, to hold him when he's scared, and to love him when he's gone.

I turned down an empty aisle, wiping my eyes on my sleeve. Soon I was weeping—for the reservists who put their entire lives on hold when called to duty, for the military mothers who had to keep their families together all alone, for the parents, spouses, sons, and daughters who were beset with worry, for Mike, and for the soldiers who would never come home. I only meant to buy a shower curtain, and now, quite unexpectedly, right when I least wanted it, months of pent-up loneliness, fear, and frustration were pouring out in an endless churn of hot, silent tears.

I'd suffered from insomnia my whole life, but by month five of the deployment, the real sleeplessness started. Each night, I'd end up kicking off the blankets and watching country music videos, then when CMT went off the air, I'd put on VH-1 until the sky turned pink. I'd figure out what time it was in Southwest Asia and wonder what Mike was doing at that very moment. I liked knowing that we were awake at the same time.

It wasn't the suspense that kept me turning in bed at night; it was the knowledge that he was beyond my reach. When he felt restless, I couldn't distract him. When he felt hopeless, I couldn't console him. Worst of all, when he was lonely, I couldn't hold him, or even offer a loving glance. He was the man for whom I would do anything, and I could do nothing.

There were 6,500 miles of ocean and earth between us. The only place I could hold him was in my prayers, and I knew I wouldn't be fully comfortable until he was home, safe from harm's reach, safe in my arms.

6

I Love a Man in Uniform

THE BITTEREST CREATURE UNDER HEAVEN IS THE WIFE
WHO DISCOVERS THAT HER HUSBAND'S BRAVERY IS ONLY
BRAVADO, THAT HIS STRENGTH IS ONLY A UNIFORM, THAT
HIS POWER IS BUT A GUN IN THE HANDS OF A FOOL.
—*Pearl S. Buck*

The Family Readiness Group prepares a wife for loneliness, anxiety, and the urge to impulse buy while her spouse is away, but they don't say squat about the torture of the War Hornies. One of nature's cruel tricks was that when I had sunk to my very lost and loneliest, my libido started its stalking patrol. Absence makes the heart grow fonder; what it does to the rest of you makes you want to avert your gaze whenever you pass a church.

In the countless lonely hours while Mike was away, I spent an inordinately large amount of time staring at his official Army photo, admiring the racked ribbons and medals that marked his accomplishments, crushed out like a high school girl with a belly full of butterflies. I looked at him in his Class A uniform and imagined how it would be to once again straighten his tie, and tried to remember how his hands felt on my body. I mentally indexed the individual pieces of his "fruit salad," trying to see how many I could remember. My husband's medals had meaning to me because his heart beat beneath them. In my sentimental state, I'd become his little fruit salad stalker. Forlorn, isolated, and wracked with the worst possible case of skin hunger, I was beside myself with longing. I didn't know what else to do.

Thinking and yearning, this was the sum of my lonely nights. I found one of Mike's Army undershirts at the bottom of the laundry basket and started slavering like Pavlov's dog. Next thing I knew, I was sleeping in the shirt, hugging the shirt, smelling it as if I could breathe in more than the scent of faded sweat, shampoo, and the clothes the shirt was buried beneath.

Eager for any connection to Mike, I developed an unholy attachment to my laptop and my cell phone. I slept with them both in the bed. I brought the phone into the bathroom with me when I showered and checked e-mail roughly ten times an hour. Even the briefest message from Mike could illuminate my entire day. I resolved to make my months alone a bit less weird by staying active. I signed up for a weeklong workshop in June at the ranch of a noted western writer whose work I'd admired since she first started publishing. In the ancient link between eros and art, it's been postulated that a bout of deprivation stokes the creative drive. Some artists pledged a vow of celibacy to support a period of accelerated output. I figured I'd tear a page from that playbook. What else was I going to do? Pace the bedroom in a Saran Wrap bikini?

And I wasn't the only lonely heart with too much time on her hands. In those first months of the war, the online military spouse community flourished. Some Web sites offered a generous collection of resources and opportunities for networking. Others offered homecoming tips and links to Frederick's of Hollywood and Victoria's Secret for picking out lingerie for the big reunion night. Other sites featured ads selling decals and T-shirts declaring "I (heart) My Soldier" and "Proud Marine Wife." The marketing of military spousedom was impressively wide-ranging: stickers, teddy bears, ball caps, jewelry, key chains. A bumper sticker stating, "Half my heart is in Iraq" was hotly debated in the online forums as a show of loving tribute or a way to turn your car into stalker bait.

And, as ever, the march of the yellow ribbon campaign continued. The yellow ribbon has a centuries-old significance. In a popular nineteenth-century marching song, a lovelorn soldier's girl wore a yellow ribbon around her neck for her man "far, far away." (Confession: I, like many other Americans, had thought the yellow ribbon trend started with Tony Orlando's "Tie a Yellow Ribbon [Round the Old Oak Tree]," which is about an inmate coming home from prison!) But now? A girl could do so much more. As the war rolled along, the inventory increased. I stared at my laptop screen, stupefied: pillowcases, tote bags, even thongs and shot glasses. I laughed when I came across a coffee mug that said, "Sexually Deprived for Your Freedom." I appreciated the stark irreverence. In a time of war, people become achingly earnest and puffed with sentiment. Sarcasm is in short supply, and when a little sass blows through, it's like a cool breeze clearing out a smoke-filled room.

There's strong, and then there's Army strong. Correspondingly, there's hot, and then there's Army hot. I loved that Mike was part of the ground forces—rich with history and earthy appeal. He would not be an airman or a sailor. He would not choose a specialty based on skimming the air, bulling his way through the seas, or jumping from planes. He felt no shame about his rudimentary parachutist training; after completing the required five parachute jumps, he bore the mantle "five jump chump," and his airborne wings were pounded into his chest at Fort Benning. "Want your blood wings, soldier?" the training company commander asked. Mike shouted, "Hooah, sir!" and the instructor smashed the heel of his palm into the wings so that they pierced the skin just above Mike's heart.

You know what's hot about soldiers? They know things, important things about protection and survival. The great outdoors is the great unknown to me, and to revere my man as a sage of this realm had real meaning. He taught me about chewing match heads so mosquitoes don't bite you—they are repelled by the sulfur in your bloodstream, and how to scare away coyotes nosing around your tent by making a coyote shaker out of a handful of pennies in an empty soda can sealed up with duct tape.

You know what else is hot about soldiers? They've done things. When we met, Mike's accomplishments were a big attraction, and that only ramped up when we knew he was leaving for the war, which would not be called The Iraq War by the military conversant, but rather, it would be folded into the larger, ongoing Global War on Terrorism, a.k.a. GWOT, sounding in its pronunciation—"G-WOT!"—like a sound effect from Japanese anime. He was about to accomplish yet another significant feat.

Within the soldier's outsize capability and experience is the humble element of purpose. There's something deeply stirring about a man responding to the call of duty, and in hearing war stories delivered with a strong dose of modesty. At the core, being a soldier means possessing an unselfconscious capability. Selfless service is one of the Army values. It's also a powerful aphrodisiac. A firm body catches your eye, but firm beliefs capture your heart.

While "no one hates war more than a soldier," as Mike frequently reminded me before he left, and I knew he didn't want to go, it would have been infinitely worse if he hadn't. He didn't become an Army officer because he wanted to slack. He wanted to serve, and to be deprived of that opportunity, by fate or circumstance, would be a gut-shot to his well-being, to his identity as a soldier. "Devotion is not a uniform to be worn on certain days and then to be put aside," the spiritual leader Sri Sathya Sai Baba once said. Anybody can mosey down to the Army/Navy surplus and pick up some camouflage or a dress blue to wear, but it wouldn't have the same effect as the real deal. The uniform itself is not what attracts us, it's the character of the man who wears it.

As sex appeal goes, not all uniforms are created equal. The Class B—green polyester trousers with a lighter green short-sleeve button-down, is a total dud. In colder months, the Class B can be worn with a black cardigan sweater, which only dulls it down further. Whatever, Mr. Rogers. And for me, the mess dress blue, the Army equivalent of the tuxedo, is also a nonstarter: The short jacket and high-waisted trousers make a man look like a very well-appointed waiter. Even with its finely turned braid and buttons, the mess dress blue would never move me to say, "Take me, I'm yours." I want to say, "I'll have the veal." To me, the showstopper is the classic dress blue— a dark navy jacket and blue trousers, topped with the officer's service cap, which is masculine sobriety at its finest. Then there is the breathtaking utility of camouflage, which soldiers wear to engage most intently in the act of soldiering. Nothing competes with the command of camouflage. Resistance is futile.

General Dwight D. Eisenhower asserted that "when you put on a uniform, there are certain inhibitions that you accept." From the female point of view, I'd say that a uniform makes certain inhibitions fall by the wayside. When you're married to a soldier, you have to be on the lookout for damsels who are undone by the mere sight of a man in the noble profession of arms. They're called tag chasers, barracks bunnies, or barracks whores. (There is no name for men who chase female soldiers, though I guess it's all man-skank at the end of the day. Now, is that sexism or merely verbal economy?) Women have long been vulnerable to the he-man gloss—the tag chaser of today is the direct descendant of the World War II "Victory Girl." I can't blame a gal for getting her head turned by a guy in uniform—Lord knows I've got no room to judge on that front. What's more thrilling than seeing a man in uniform? Peeling him out of it. There's pleasure in skinning a guy out of his camouflage—those boots at the bedside and the clinkity-clink of dog tags hitting your chest. It's a sensual siren set off by the powerful, instinctive force of cave-woman logic: Real Man Alert! But a girl is wise to be warned, once that uniform comes off—not for a passionate embrace, but so he can change into shorts and a sweatshirt to tune in the ball game—the fantasy evaporates and you're left with just a regular guy. What will you get once you tear through all that camouflage? Mileage varies.

As Operation Iraqi Freedom ramped up, the patriotic razzle-dazzle infected even the allegedly unbiased media. Swarms of embedded reporters went squealing off into the sand and heat, cameras and digital recorders in hand. Wrapped in body armor and wide-eyed at the spectacle of military might, some of these journalists were so caught up in the rush, they seemed to be panting to get their war on. Their dispatches described equipment and maneuvers with adrenalized Hemingway swagger. I smiled as I watched a news report in which one oh-so-proper British journalist reverently described the "butt-kicking bra-*VAH*-do" of the Marine unit he was with, his khaki Kevlar vest making him look like an Etonian turtle. I was forced to ask—is this guy on a reportorial mission or the quest for a contact high? Even levelheaded media types were in thrall to G.I. Joe.

Within all that military hotness, there are laws regarding the ways in which a soldier may (ahem) deploy it. Article 125 in the Uniform Code of Military Justice bans consensual sodomy—not just anal sex, which is considered beyond the pale by most people, even in these porn-saturated times. The ban also extends to standard-issue oral, both giving and receiving (all you ladies in the back row, *stop snickering!*). Herewith, the relevant excerpt of Article 125:

Text.

(a) Any person subject to this chapter who engages in unnatural carnal copulation with another person of the same or opposite sex . . . is guilty of sodomy. Penetration, however slight, is sufficient to complete the offense.

(b) Any person found guilty of sodomy shall be punished as a court-martial may direct.

Explanation.

It is unnatural carnal copulation for a person to take into that person's mouth or anus the sexual organ of another person . . . ; or to place that person's sexual organ in the mouth or anus of another person . . . ; or to have carnal copulation in any opening of the body, except the sexual parts, with another person. . . .

I have it on good authority from a JAG attorney that consensual sodomy between a man and a woman is rarely prosecuted. But regardless of the laxity in its application, the rule stands. What does it say, I wonder, that in the list of prohibited acts in the UCMJ, sodomy is wedged between maiming and arson?

Of course, none of this punishable behavior was relevant to me, for my soldier was 6,500 miles away. All that time alone led me online to discuss the hushed topic of how to obtain relief. I'm certain that most military wives want to be true, even as we long for an oasis in the sensual desert. When the yearning gets too strong, the sensible option, other wives informed me, is to strike up a discreet relationship with BOB—the battery-operated boyfriend. While he's a pale substitute for a real partner, BOB has some advantages—he doesn't steal the covers or snore, and in his inanimate presence, you can feel okay about letting that bikini line go.

Ask any soldier and he'll tell you that BOB is a far better substitute for his affections than Jody. The mythical Jody, the opportunistic civilian on the hunt for a girl whose soldier is away, has been a staple of military lore since World War II. The fear of being cheated on lurks in the already taxed heart of the military man—so much so that Jody, that fox in the henhouse, has several marching cadences dedicated to his wily ways. In fact, they named the genre after him—"Jody calls."

> *Ain't no use in going back*
> *Jody's got your Cadillac*
> *Ain't no use in calling home*
> *Jody's got your girl and gone*
> *Ain't no use in feeling blue*
> *Jody's got your sister, too . . .*

When I visited Mike during the unit training at Fort Dix, we'd burn up—last chance, fire-sale, forget about it. But it was nothing like the heat I felt for him while he was gone. My longing for my husband exploded in his absence; it was as though I had jet fuel coursing through my veins and someone had tossed a lit match into my mouth. While I was frustrated that there was no way he could quiet that urge, I was grateful that in my overall numb state, at least that part of my emotional being was alive and burning bright—a rebellious, life-affirming flame.

Reporters seeking the human-interest angle on the war always ask the wives left behind what they miss most about their husband, but I fear the truth is too raw to tell: loving touch. She won't say that when she receives a letter or an e-mail containing a photo of her love decked out in full battle rattle (camo, body armor, helmet, boots, weapon), she feels her stomach flip and her heart race as she's reminded why she fell in love with him in the first place.

I'm not one to advocate a retro gender politics—I want to see women as surgeons and soldiers, politicians and mothers and more. But after two centuries of feminism, I still prefer a man to open the car doors and the pickle jars. There are politics and then there are preferences, and all desire for equality aside, I'd be bereft without the masculine touch. It's that cavewoman thing, a crazy howl from the primal depths. In the wild jungle of the female heart, it's two steps forward, one step back in this ancient mating dance—I like a strong lead, as both a standard to meet and a guiding light to follow. Parity between the sexes is one thing, respect for essential difference is quite another.

The two exist, like man and woman, in ways that flatter and complement each other. I'm woman enough to boldly state my appreciation for male strength as embodied by the American soldier. For those of us who love a man in uniform, might makes Mr. Right.

7

Is That You, Baby?

From Mike, toward the end of his deployment:

Ms. Lily,

Another 120+ degree day. Another dust storm from 1130–0130 last night. It's like being in the belly of a beast. In fact, I dreamt last night that you met me in the airport and I responded that way when you asked me how it'd been.

I have a dehydration stomachache and headache. I sit here drinking water so hot it's actually uncomfortable in your throat, despite keeping it in the shade. The camp only gets 35,000 pounds of ice per day (less than 4 lbs per soldier), much of which goes to the mess hall and hospital. As for us . . . we get precious little, if any. They're hoping to raise the amount to 50,000 lbs soon. In temps like this 10 lbs per soldier per day is the minimum needed. The worst hours are from 1330–1530, when you are basically wet across every surface of your body from head to toe.

I'm in single digits now . . . I fly home in eight days, arriving in nine. In seven days I'll go down to Camp Doha to spend the day prepping to fly home— washing laundry, washing myself, trying to grab a souvenir or two if possible, maybe get some pictures developed, and try to get a good night's sleep in air-conditioning.

Still no itinerary yet . . . I'll get that in Doha tomorrow. I'm suffering from a severe cleavage deficit right now . . . just thought you should know. I miss you and love you. You are the best.

xoxoMM

Some people are born lucky. The rest of us, well, we pick up a little luck here and there—fortune cookies bearing good news, ladybugs landing on your shirt, and the toast landing butter-side up. Mike and I got lucky during this deployment. According to President Bush, who, on May 1, 2003, stood on the deck of an aircraft carrier, in front of a banner that read "Mission Accomplished," the major combat operations in Iraq were officially over. (Translation: The major combat operations in Iraq were officially "over.") This proclamation was a forcing function for the Army—they were told to lift the stop-loss and stop-rotation and let the previously stymied soldiers go, either out of the Army as they'd planned, or on to their next assignment pursuant to prior orders. The stop-rotation was lifted for an all-too-brief sixty-day window—which included the time when Mike had his report date for West Point. All hail Uncle Sugar, he was going to be able to come home early.

With Mike due to return by June, I withdrew from the workshop with the Noted Western Writer because the dates no longer lined up with my schedule. I explained to her the circumstances of Mike's return. She e-mailed back, her once-friendly tone now businesslike and curt: "Sorry you can't make it. I doubt I'll be able to fill your spot at such a late date, so I can't refund your deposit. I'm praying for peace." I read and reread the e-mail, try-ing to decode her meaning. I hadn't mentioned in our prior exchanges that my husband was in the military. Within the spare sentences, I detected the faint aura of a diss.

The reunion preparations began. I wanted everything to be perfect. My early-deployment rigidity had loosened, so my to-do list was rather long. First up, I had to whip the condo back into shape—with the crusty dishes in the sink piled up like Pompeiian ruins, grunge-ringed bathtub, and heaps of laundry everywhere, it looked like a frat house. The only things missing were an empty keg in the corner, a Bob Marley poster, and a bra swinging from a blade on the ceiling fan. Then, I had to get myself squared away—hair cut and colored, teeth brightened with White Strips, the perfect outfit chosen. I hadn't fussed so much over my appearance since the prom.

* * *

I drove to Baltimore-Washington International Airport, trying not to speed as I took the curves on the local highway. My heart beat frantically, and I took deep, slow breaths, trying to steady myself. In the quiet terminal, I paced, my high heels clicking on the tile floor. I pulled a compact from my purse, checking and rechecking my makeup. I smoothed down the legs of my new low-rise jeans and tugged at the tight, pucker-stitched bodice of my flowered, off-the-shoulder blouse. Finally, there he was. I could see Mike in the crowd, walking toward me, wearing jeans and a maroon polo shirt I didn't recognize. For security reasons, he couldn't travel in uniform, so he blended in with the mass of disembarking passengers. His neck was tanned brown as a walnut; his face was dark, too, except for two thin white stripes across his temples from the arms of his sunglasses. My pulse surged. I waved to get his attention. When he caught my eye, he waved back and gave me a fatigued smile.

I walked toward him, and then, for the first time in months, his arms were around me. Any woman who welcomes her husband safely back from war is a lucky woman indeed—after all, many military wives were not so blessed. By this time, there were 750 wounded American troops and two hundred killed in action. I knew my good fortune, but still, it was strange. He'd been gone for so long. His body felt instantly familiar yet foreign.

We retrieved one of Mike's duffel bags from baggage claim—the second was stuck in a transit container some-

where in the Middle East, having never made it to Camp
Udairi. He had none of his civilian clothes and no sneakers; he had had to buy the jeans and polo shirt he wore
home during his departure workup at Camp Doha. Exhausted from two days of traveling, he asked me to drive
home. When we got back to our building, I unlocked the
door and he stepped into our apartment, where everything
looked exactly as it had the morning he left. I instantly felt
like hell. For the life of me, I don't know why I didn't do
something special to welcome him home. I had no excuse.
The apartment looked damningly plain.

Till the day I die, I will always regret that I didn't herald his homecoming in a bigger, better way. I didn't have
a baby to bundle into his arms, or kids to send cheering
across the airport carpet, but there were ways I could've
made a fuss on my own. He had just come back from a war
and there was no banner. No flag. No fanfare. Couldn't I
at least have baked the guy a goddamn cake?

He dropped off his bags and we went out to dinner at our
favorite restaurant, where he would sit down for the first
meal in months that he didn't have to eat with his 9mm holstered on his chest, with his left hand free to draw it. He
marveled at the touches of civilization he'd missed: ice water, a cloth napkin. The plate of steak cooked medium-well,
potatoes, and a glass of soda that was magically refilled. He
couldn't drink alcohol while he was deployed, but he had no
desire to indulge now that it was allowed. He only wanted
a quiet, unhurried dinner of food that he could savor.

When we got home, he unpacked a few things. We hadn't lived in our apartment for even four months before he deployed, and in his absence, it sort of became "my" space. I'd moved things to my liking. Here was this person who, presumably, I knew better than anyone, groping around the place, opening multiple drawers to locate a bath towel or a roll of paper towels, like he was negotiating a stranger's house. Fatigued after his lengthy flight, he wanted to turn in even earlier than usual.

And so, to bed. In my lack of experience, I had expected some sort of explosive howlin' coyote second-honeymoon reunion. Of course, I hadn't had a honeymoon, but I had an idea of the thermonuclear heat they were supposed to generate. I was stoked on the promise of suggestion: all those ads for kinky lingerie on the spouse Web sites! At the very least, I thought we'd be on fire to reconnect. The Army Family Readiness volunteers advise you to "let nature take its course." But they don't tell you that the first time you lie with your soldier after his return, you will feel on his skin every mile that had come between you. Mike was distant, even to the touch. In his embrace, I found myself thinking, *You've changed.*

In the days immediately after his return, the strangest change was the silence. We'd always been the talkiest of couples. A teacher and a writer! Geek and geekette! Even when we were pissed at each other and "not talking," we talked. The silence became this *thing*, a containment vessel for everything that he'd seen and gone through—things

that I would never know. The silence enclosed that separate, impenetrable world, and as much as I understood it,
I resented it.

It was oddly stressful to return to the ordinary. Every in-
teraction begged the question: *Are we back to normal yet?*
All the suspense had been lifted, the drama was over. Now
it was just "Hello, familiar stranger." Did he want to see
friends and family? Did he want to be alone? Was he truly
okay, or was he just keeping up appearances to spare me
any worry? I didn't want to hector or pry, even though I
knew that there were blank pages in our love-and-war story
that would never be filled. In that space of not knowing,
I became attached to things from the Sandbox, as if they'd
tell me what he wouldn't—or couldn't: I kept the portable
silver alarm clock, with his name written in black Sharpie
on the back (I knew that its digital thermometer had read
120 degrees just days before); the white container of
Johnson's sandalwood-scented baby powder he bought at
Camp Udairi to keep down the prickly heat, the label written in both English and Arabic; even his underwear with
his name printed in block letters on the waistband, like a
kid at summer camp. When he got his film developed, I
laughed. Of the very few images of him on the roll, one
was of him sweating away in his desert camo, sitting at a
computer. I wanted a copy of the photo of him all tricked
out in his load-bearing vest and Kevlar helmet and, over
his body armor, the holstered pistol with the left-hand
draw, but he didn't see why I'd even care.

I was relieved when he finally dropped the G word. So much became clear when he admitted that he felt guilty for leaving his soldiers behind, even though he'd returned to go to West Point pursuant to military orders. He'd received a combat patch for this deployment, but he refused to wear it. "This time doesn't count," he shrugged. "I was just a REMF." A Rear Echelon Mother Fucker—a minor support player watching the pieces get pushed around the chessboard. I stood helpless as he beat himself up. He saw his role in the war as marginal—which made him feel ineffective; it made him feel old. I struggled to come around to his point of view, but I wasn't going to argue with the guy. He'd already made up his mind: The real estate on his right sleeve still belonged to the First Infantry Division— the Big Red One.

Usually a deep and easy sleeper, during those first weeks home Mike had trouble falling asleep—he'd drift off, then suddenly jerk as if awakened by a loud noise. Sometimes he'd wake with a start in the dead of night. I'd feel him patting around the sheets, reaching for me. "Are you there?" he'd say. Or "Is that you, baby?"

For me, relationship tension always shows up in the bedroom. Not over sex, but sleep. As a lifelong insomniac, my preferred bedtime is between 1 and 5 a.m. But Mike wanted me to be close while he slept. While he was away, I'd developed my own night-owl routine, and now that he'd returned, I wasn't in a hurry to change it. At first, I was overly attentive: What do you want? What do you need? Can I get you anything? Then, I just wanted to get back to normal—my normal. I'd lie by his side, sleep still hours away, and seethe quietly: I held down the fort while you were gone, and never complained once. I had a system in place, and it worked for me. Why can't it work for you, too? We did things your way because the Army said so, but now you're back. While you were gone, I worried and didn't complain. I kept the house in order and didn't mess up once. I rearranged my life to accommodate this deployment without a second thought. The lifestyle of sacrifice is over and now it's *my* turn. I'd flip over onto my stomach and pull the pillow over my head, feeling like a grade-A schmuck.

One night, thinking Mike might at last be asleep, I softly folded back the quilt and got out of the bed.

His voice rose out of the dark. "Where are you going?"

"Just to my office. I want to look something up."

"Okay," he mumbled. "See you later, night owl."

"I won't be up long." *I won't be up long.* Always on my top ten list of white lies.

I lingered at my desk, thinking. I had my husband back, so what was I bellyaching about? But these weren't complaints, exactly. I'd entered new territory—a spectrum of feeling I wasn't yet used to. This military-wife life meant painting with a new emotional palette. And then I realized what it was: guilt. I actually felt guilty myself that Mike had come home early. During Desert Storm, he was on the

pointy end of the spear, seeing intense combat. By comparison, Operation Iraqi Freedom was like being a camp
counselor—for a shortened season, at that. He felt like he
hadn't given enough, and strangely, so did I. I should be
sitting through several more months alone. I didn't deserve
to have him home early, when there were so many families still splintered by this war. And he said he was never
really in harm's way, while thousands of men and women
pulled dangerous duty outside the wire. Of course, I was
relieved—I'd only prayed for his safe return, but that relief had a bittersweet bite. Who knew good luck could feel
so bad?

A few weeks after Mike's return, his next duty station was
up ahead, blinking in marquee lights: Back to historic
West Point! The United States Military Academy! The
fancy Army!

My strange deployment rituals ceased to feel necessary—I'd stopped weighing myself compulsively and started
eating, but while planning the move to West Point so Mike
could start his new position on the superintendent's staff,
my nerves returned. I felt like I was about to be thrust onstage in a role for which I wasn't prepared.

I knew it was time to study up on what, exactly, was expected of me as a new wife in the military world. I'd heard
the catchphrases: Military Spouse—The Toughest Job in
the Military. The Army Comes First. Orders Aren't Op-

tional. Soon the delivery from Amazon arrived and I had a stack of books at my side: *Married to the Military, Service Etiquette, The Army Wife Handbook,* and, just for fun, a vintage copy of the old guard Army wife guide, *The Army Wife.* The inside front cover was sweetly inscribed, "To Joan, with all my love, Buddy." The first order of business upon cracking the books: Slash through the sloganeering and get to what's real.

I was concerned about how to address people, so I picked up Oretha Swartz's *Service Etiquette,* a book that is 540 pages long, single-spaced—and covers just manners, not rules. I learned that spouses don't call their husband's superiors "sir" or "ma'am." Though Mike was required to call a colonel "sir," I should call him by his name, Colonel Fluffbottom, unless he told me to call him "Jim." But if I saw Jim in public in a group of people, then it was Colonel Fluffbottom again. Okay, got it. The thought of such formality left me feeling a little like that oily Eddy Haskell from *Leave It to Beaver*—"It's a pleasure to *see* you this fine afternoon, Colonel Fluffbottom!"—but I could handle it.

What I was most curious about was where my role as a wife intersected with Mike's job as a soldier. The military has a longstanding tradition of spousal volunteerism and community support that stretches all the way back to Martha Washington, who set the standard during the Revolutionary War by joining General Washington at the winter encampment at Valley Forge, where she assumed her husband's domestic duties, as well as the tasks of feeding, clothing, entertaining, nursing, and doing laundry and mending for his soldiers. I knew my loyalties were shifting when I started to weep while reading about how Mrs. Washington's carriages, loaded down with as many supplies as would fit, got stalled in snow at Brandywine Creek en route to Valley Forge, so she swiftly regrouped and arrived in camp by sleigh.

Flash forward 170 years and not much had changed. In the postwar era, it was widely assumed that an officer's wife would dedicate her life to supporting her husband's career through household engineering, entertaining, hostessing, and volunteer work. A wife's comportment and contribution to the military community would be weighed as factors in her husband's promotion—though not necessarily officially.

Next I read *The Army Wife* by Nancy Shea, a whiz-bang hoot of a book, first published in the 1940s, which supplies the postwar bride with instructions on everything from how, when stationed in Germany, to tell your housekeeper to bake the potatoes (*"Backen sie die Kartoffel*, Gretchen") to making clothing choices—"Army Men like feminine frippery such as froufrou lacy jabots, furs, snow-white gloves, and high-heeled slippers" (But what should *I* wear, Nancy?). Writes Shea, "An Army wife is just as much in the service of the government as her husband, because she plays an integral part in representing the Army for good or ill . . . The government really gets the full-time service of two people for the pay of one. The wife is definitely expected to pull her weight in the boat and in every way to uphold the fine traditions of the Army."

As social mores shifted later in twentieth century, so, too, did the expectations surrounding an Army spouse's contribution. In response to the changing times, the Department of Defense drafted the Working Military Spouse Policy, which states that "no commander or supervisor, nor any other Department of Defense official will, directly or indirectly, interfere with the right of every military spouse to decide whether to pursue or hold a job, attend school, or to serve on a voluntary basis." This was written not in the Women's Libber 1960s or even the Superwoman 1970s, but in 1987—the same year President Ronald Reagan stood at the Brandenburg Gate and entreated Soviet leader Mikhael Gorbachev to tear down the Berlin Wall. The Cold War era was ending in the military kitchen.

Now, with more and more women working outside the home, the role of wife as social coordinator and adjunct unit morale booster has decreased further still, to the point where a wife needn't really worry about harming her husband's professional standing by pursuing her own interests. Like any modern woman, an Army wife may not be able to have it all, but she can have as much as she can make fit around having to PCS (Permanent Change of Station, i.e., move) every two or three years, childrearing, separations caused by deployments and TDYs (Temporary Duty), and her husband's myriad professional obligations.

So the option to opt out was fully mine. But just because opting out was an option didn't mean it was well-advised. And not getting involved at all seemed to me like going to Disney World and not riding Space Mountain—something critical to the authentic experience would be missing, as would some of the thrills and chills. If there was a way I could be of assistance, I wanted to do it. The problem was, I couldn't tell what exactly I should—or shouldn't—do. Soldiers get their orders, responsibilities, and protocols presented to them in minute detail. Wives, on the other hand, pretty much get bupkis. I wanted to succeed, of course, but what did that mean? Meredity Leyva's *Married to the Military* asserted that success as a military spouse entailed "setting the standard of perfection." (Okay, so no pressure, then . . .)

Today's Military Wife, by Lydia Sloan Cline, delivered what the Army calls the BLUF (Bottom Line Up Front): "Your direct influence on your spouse's career may not be great, but your influence on his morale is." That helped, but I still didn't know how much *indirect* influence I might have on Mike's career. As I kept reading, however, I suspected that there was much more to being a military wife than courtesies and customs and regulations—things I couldn't learn by simply putting my nose in a book.

* * *

During our trip to West Point for the housing draw, Mike assured me I'd do just fine, but I wasn't sure I'd ever feel comfortable there, where two hundred years of American Army history lay nestled in the gentle Hudson Valley hills. The Academy has a roster of famous graduates, including Robert E. Lee, Ulysses S. Grant, Dwight D. Eisenhower, and Buzz Aldrin, as well as a few notable dropouts, like Edgar Allan Poe and James McNeill Whistler, of *Whistler's Mother* fame. As we walked around, I chanted the nicknames of each of the four West Point cadet years into memory: Plebe, Yuk, Cow, Firstie. Plebe, Yuk, Cow, Firstie.

Mike led me on a tour of the Academy grounds—Trophy Point, with its enormous sweeping vista of the Hudson, mounted guns and cannons seized by American troops as far back as the Revolutionary War; the battle monument, a tall, polished-granite column with a gold statue of winged Fate balanced on top; the grand Cadet Chapel; and the charming, winding path of Flirtation Walk, the only place on post where cadets couldn't get reprimanded for pubic displays of affection, and the site of countless senior-year marriage proposals (cadets are not allowed to marry until they graduate). The soul of the place was palpable. We held hands as we walked past Trophy Point and across the street to the statue of General John Sedgwick at the edge of the parade field. West Point lore has it that if a cadet is worried about failing, he or she can come out at midnight in parade uniform and spin the rowels on Sedgwick's spurs for luck. As I recited my misgivings to Mike—that I might not meet the standards for a successful officer's wife; that I might not fit in with the other women; that I might morph into some tedious spouse-bot—I spun the spurs myself.

"If I wanted a Stepford wife," Mike said, "I'd have married one."

I couldn't believe that this prestigious post was to be my home. Compared with the bland solitude of our suburban condo complex near Fort Meade, West Point seemed downright bucolic. The flag rippled lazily in the warm spring breeze. We passed neatly groomed, flower-filled yards decorated with seasonal banners, and young moms jogged along the wide sidewalks while pushing athletic strollers. People waved from cars as they drove by. It looked for all the world like a military Mayberry.

They're privatizing Army housing now, but at that time, family quarters at West Point were delegated through the post housing draw, a tense annual ritual. New personnel—or their representatives—were herded into the main auditorium of Thayer Hall to jockey for the choicest quarters. Soldiers would pore over a list of soon-to-be-vacated quarters in the various neighborhoods of West Point—Lusk Reservoir, New Brick, Gray Ghost, Lee, Old Brick, Central Post, and Stony Lonesome I and II.

Lusk was off-limits to anyone below full colonel, but if you were a major, you might get lucky and snag something among the lieutenant colonels in Lee, a beautiful neighborhood full of Gothic-looking red brick duplexes and triplexes set back among majestic old-growth oaks. Some Lee quarters had views of the river, and all of them had nice-size yards.

Each soldier was called, in order of rank and chronological order from earliest date of commission to most recent, to announce his or her choice from a podium at the front of the auditorium. Husbands and wives sat in nervous anticipation as the first soldier stepped to the microphone. The soldiers dressed for the event in their Class Bs, and the auditorium was teeming with a list-crumpling, green polyester Mr. Rogers mob. Husbands all but ran to the mike to state their selection when their name was called, goosed forward with the four-word edict from their wives: Try to get Lee.

Mike wasn't senior enough to place high in the batting order, so we had to settle for a three-bedroom, two-and-a-half bath duplex in New Brick, a modest but appealing area just a couple of blocks away from the central post, earmarked for captains and majors. The only snag was that every building in New Brick was being renovated, so we could only "tour" them by looking through the Cyclone fencing around the construction site. Didn't matter to me—it seemed very deluxe. In my entire adult life, I'd never lived in a place with so many bathrooms and central air-conditioning. As a longtime starving artist, to me New Brick was the big time.

We got back to Odenton in time to get into bed for the late news. Mike started to drift off. He didn't startle as he fell asleep, and he slid his foot over to find mine, just as he used to. He was back, finally, fully back. The sensation of his warm foot sliding against mine loosened the knot of guilt inside of me. He'd done good; we'd done enough.

I was happy to have Mike around again, but within that happiness was lingering disappointment at how he'd come home—flying back to the U.S. dressed in civilian clothes, to Baltimore-Washington International Airport on a commercial jet, like any other guy. But he wasn't any other guy. He was a soldier returning from a war, and my husband. I wanted a cattle-call return like you see on the news: an auditorium filled with anxious Army families waiting for the unit to disembark from a convoy of buses, personalized Welcome Home banners stretched between the steel rafters. "We love you! Thank you for your service!" Streaking tears. Fireworks and a brass band. Though I know it was foolish to feel slighted, I nursed a small resentment that it hadn't been that way—I didn't want the fanfare for me. I wanted it for Mike, a welcome home that was as loud and rowdy and emotional as he deserved. But then when he was in our bed at last, tucked into cool sheets and sleeping peacefully through the night, I thought, *Maybe this is how his homecoming was supposed to be.* Private. Quiet. Just me, the stillness of a near-empty airport, and my husband delivered to me whole.

8

Household Six

How to Preserve a Husband

First, take care in selecting one who is not too young,
but tender. Make your selection carefully and let it be
final. Otherwise, they will not keep.

Like wine they improve with age. Do not pickle or
keep them in hot water. This makes them sour.

Prepare as follows: Sweeten with smiles, according to
variety. The sour bitter kind is improved by a pinch of
salt of common sense. Spice with patience. Wrap well
in a mantle of charity. Preserve over a good fire of steady
devotion. Serve with peaches and cream.

The poorest varieties may be improved by this process
and kept for many years in any climate.

　　　　　　　　　—The West Point Hostess Cookbook, 1969

In an Army unit, the commanding officer is known as the
Six. Our arrival at West Point marked my official ascension

to "Household Six," she who rules the military roost. The dominant force in the domestic sphere. To quantify the anxiety this created within me, I relied on the "Pucker Factor"—the slangy military metric of how tight your butt will clench, on a scale of one to ten, from the anxiety associated with a given event. For me, becoming Household Six scored a Pucker Factor perfect ten.

The "where did you meet your husband . . . in a bar?" incident at the welcoming reception when we'd first arrived at West Point didn't help me relax. As an introduction, it set a lousy precedent. I had chosen my outfit for that occasion with great care; I wanted to look—and act—just right. When the colonel's wife asked me that fateful question, I imagined the sound effect of footsteps followed by a door slamming shut: Back. Away. Slowly. This was my first time being confronted by a woman "wearing her husband's rank." Her husband's rank was superior to Mike's, and there was simply no way she would have said what she did if the social position had been reversed. She relished her place, and wanted to remind me of mine. I just grinned with the chin-up resolve of a new recruit, clutching my little plate of Swedish meatballs. *Suck it up,* I told myself. *You're in the Army now.*

I hoped that none of my neighbors were as nasty as that woman, but getting to know them took a while, because the renovation of our quarters ran weeks behind schedule. For six weeks after we arrived at West Point, the entire New Brick housing area was cordoned off by hazard tape stretched over that Cyclone fence. We were forced to stay in the Five Star Annex, a run-down temporary lodging facility just down the hill. Every day, we'd trudge uphill and note the progress on the construction. The red brick Colonial facades on the duplexes looked very smart, and each modest rectangular backyard, separated by picket fencing, had a small covered patio. The duplexes were arranged in a neat row, about fifteen feet apart. Army posts are often referred to as "fishbowls." You live where you work, and everyone's piled on top of each other in apartments, duplexes, and houses on small lots. Post living offers many things—convenience, an instant community—but privacy is not among them.

We finally met our neighbors-to-be when we were flushed out of our dark, hot rooms at the Five Star by an enormous blackout that crashed the power grid of most of the northeastern United States. Everyone blinked at one another in the afternoon sun that shone into the small gravel playground. A Berliner who introduced herself as Maya sat on the concrete steps. She was married to Kevin, a geeky captain and Academy graduate with stiff posture and a prematurely gray crew cut with a cowlick in the front that made his hair stick up like a coxcomb. Kevin had an almost nonstop laugh and a tendency to interrupt. The two of them had just moved back to the states from Germany, where they had met and married. At the time, Maya was working for the German office of an American bank. Maya was extremely thin and quiet, but she seemed eager to talk, and I was glad that they would be living in the duplex across the driveway. Jorie and Dan were an older couple who would be living right next door to us in our duplex. Dan was a lieutenant colonel, assigned to a second stint on West Point faculty. They didn't have any children, but every day they walked over to the West Point kennel to visit their prized Norwegian elkhound, Ava. Jorie had a great husky voice and wind-burned skin. She seemed down-to-earth in her jeans and hiking boots and crew neck T-shirt. Stella and John were assigned to the quarters next door to Kevin and Maya. Utterly unfazed by the blackout, Stella handed her young son and daughter fruit strips while they climbed on the playground's painted rocks. Pondering the bag of frozen shrimp in her freezer that was bound to go bad, she announced that she had decided to make a shrimp salad for dinner, which marked her in my mind as a "lemonade from lemons" type of girl. John talked extremely loudly and appeared only too happy to let us know that he was West Point class of 1987, and an infantryman and Ranger, which seemed odd since no one else had downloaded his entire career history. He kind of sniffed when he found out Mike was military intelligence, like MI wasn't quite *hooah* enough. I knew I would remember the wives' names, but, less sure about the husbands, I assigned them each a nickname to remind me: Dan the Dude Man, because he was mellow; King Kevin because he seemed to like having the right answer for everything, indicating supreme belief in his brainpower. John, the tough guy, I dubbed Johnny Hardcore.

After six long weeks, the moving vans started pulling up on our block, teams of government-subsidized workers hauling boxes out of the trucks and in through the propped-open front doors. The wives were ready. When it comes to household detail, Army wives approach the task with impressive fervor, a little Patton (General), a little Stewart (Martha). I watched the women around me set up house with lightning speed. Have you ever passed a shopping mall parking lot or an open field where a traveling carnival has pulled in? It starts out as a bunch of trucks and trailers, then you drive by three hours later and there's a midway, a Ferris wheel, and a merry-go-round up and running with calliope music and blinking lights. It was like that—the mark of experience in a nomadic lifestyle is how fast you can get the tent stakes in and make camp.

I poked my head into as many quarters as possible. Soldiers, in their quest to reflect status, display coins, certificates, medals, and guidons (company flags). Officers' wives collect Polish pottery, crystal chandeliers from Karlovy Vary, and antique Bavarian sleds from years spent stationed in Germany—the quarry of all their travels during different assignments, plus a hookah that hubby sent from the Middle East.

Artwise, there was a detectable penchant for quilts, primitive country prints of cottages, hearts, and ducks, and military scenes. Nothing provocative—Stivers's *Christmas Raid*, yes. Picasso's *Guernica*, no. The comforting domesticity provides a perfect retreat from the battlefield's severity. If you are war-weary and homesick, maybe you don't want to park your butt in a hard plastic Eames chair and gaze upon the chaos of a de Kooning or the irony of a Rauschenberg.

By contrast, I had leopard-print dining room chairs and a hulking heirloom Eastlake Victorian bedroom set. I felt like a domestic bumbler. If you are married to a major, you are expected to have decent furniture, but between Mike's divorce and my horrible taste back when I was a stripper, all we had between us for the living room were his grody old blue sofa and my tacky custom purple velvet loveseat. I wouldn't let anyone into our quarters until we'd bought slipcovers.

Some of the husbands had their own strict sense of style. Mike and I went down to the housing self-help shop and picked out one of the seven Army-approved colors of interior paint—beige, the *other* beige, pale yellow, light blue, peach, pink, and hint-of-nausea green—to make over our powder room. When we got out of our car, Johnny Hardcore was out mowing his front lawn. He sniffed at our color choice. "My wife knows better than to paint any room in our house pink."

Mike smiled. "Yeah, well, I'm secure in my masculinity." *Zzzzzzzap!* Then he breezed up our concrete walk and through the front door, the smell of sizzling infantry flesh still hanging in the air.

* * *

Fortunately, Jorie and Maya turned out to be great neighbors. Together, we formed a blond pageboy trio, though hairstyle aside, we couldn't have been more different from each other. Maya was a wide-eyed newlywed, like me, and Jorie was a veteran Army wife seasoned with vinegar—she and her husband, Dan, had been married for eighteen years. Jorie was an avid bow hunter, I was an "only if it comes from the supermarket wrapped in plastic" meat eater, and Maya was a vegetarian. Jorie whipped out her gardening tools and potting soil and put her yard together like a landscaping pro the month she moved in; Maya put out some impatiens in window boxes; and I hung up some potted geraniums that promptly withered when I forgot to water them. I was obsessed with work, Jorie planned to take her time finding part-time work outside the gates in Highland Falls, and Maya didn't work because, she said, Kevin didn't want her to. But what we had in common was our recent arrival at West Point, and our dependence on each other for the day's kind word. Whenever I was lonely, I'd go into the yard and talk to either of them over the fence, like Tim talked to Wilson in *Home Improvement*. By going to the kitchen door and turning to either the right fence or the left, I could get whatever I needed at that moment—a pinch of sugar, a dash of salt.

Check Yourself Out. Look Sharp, commands a sticker on the mirror hanging near the door of West Point's Taylor

Hall, where my husband worked. At the military academy and throughout the Army, pride of appearance is imperative. Mike is bound by the Army Uniform Regulation (AR 670–1)—which dictates, among other things, that he must wear the appropriate headgear ("hat" to you and me) when he's outside, that he cannot walk or stand with his hands in his uniform pockets, and that, even in a downpour, he's not to use an umbrella. What, I wondered, did this emphasis on appearance mean for me, his wife, for whom the rules weren't written but implied?

As we unpacked boxes and hung up our clothes in the master bedroom closets, Mike schooled me on the hard-line don'ts. Both conversation and dress in military settings are pointedly apolitical—you keep your cards close to the vest. A peace sign T-shirt or a POW-MIA bumper sticker isn't going to raise an eyebrow—they're so commonplace they're not likely to be interpreted as politically loaded—but it's taboo to make waves. "If you showed up at the commissary in a Bush Sucks shirt," Mike explained, "the military police won't chase you down the condiments aisle and arrest you in front of the spicy mustard, but . . ."

I got the hint. On a federal installation, protest is illegal, and dressing or acting in a manner that is critical of the government or the Armed Forces is seen as biting the hand that feeds you—or worse—and it ranks high on the list of faux pas.

One evening, a clerk at the West Point gym approached me while I jogged on the treadmill. "Excuse me, ma'am?"

I pulled the iPod headphones from my ears. Was I over my time limit? Did I forget to bring a towel? "Is everything okay?"

"Yes, but ma'am, we have a rule here." By now he was blushing. "You're not allowed to wear a tank top in the fitness center."

This was no Juicy Couture sexy-thing tank top, with lace-trimmed cleavage, spaghetti straps, and something saucy spelled out in rhinestones across the chest. This was your basic Stanley Kowalski man's style undershirt, which I was wearing over a black industrial-strength jog bra that had all the sex appeal of a truss.

"I'm sorry," I said, baffled. "I won't do it again."

Soldiers march, wives walk. There are myriad ways to connect with other wives on post—scrapbooking crops, book groups, the West Point Women's Club, wives' coffees held in each academic department, religious groups, and gym classes. But also, we walk. We walk up hills and down, around Lusk Reservoir, past Michie Stadium, and loop around the Kosciuszko monument to Trophy Point. Sometimes we walk to the low, throbbing *chop-chop* rhythm of a UH-1 "Huey" helicopter flying overhead. We look up, watching as the black spots that speed down from the helicopter get larger and larger, then, way up high, parachutes bloom open, one after another. We marvel at the sight of the cadet parachutists drifting under their gold and black canopies against the brilliant blue sky.

Maya was always up for walking. Kevin went TDY a lot, and Maya especially appreciated the company when he was gone. We'd put on our sneakers in the afternoon and amble, talking about how little we knew about being married to Army officers. Were we or weren't we instrumental in our husbands' success? If we could help, then how much? That seemed to be anyone's guess. And what about the stereotypes of military wives that we confronted? We quickened our step, bracing for a steep slope near the cadet chapel, as we listed the ones we'd heard.

The first stereotype is that the typical military wife is a degenerate slob who's welded to the couch, watching soap operas, gossiping with other wives, and spending her husband's money, a big ol' freeloader who married not for love, but for free dental. A parasite in sweatpants.

The other is the uptight officer's wife, snooty and meddling, with a stick jammed so far up her butt she's got branches coming out of her nose. A Coach-purse-toting monster, she social climbs with the grim resolve of a Thackeray antiheroine. Becky Sharp with a DEERS card, she'll strike women from the coffee group invite list with impunity and cut the commissary line in front of a dozen cart-pushing enlisted wives.

Rounding out the retinue is the party girl who's practically itching for her husband to deploy so she can flee to the bar in booty shorts and a halter top and lure men back to her quarters for a night of sharing tequila and cooties. (You usually have to work in a snide comment about "tramp stamp" lower-back tattoos with this one.)

All three share the distinction of being mean to their husbands and backstabbing to other women. The Angel in the House is really a shark in the water.

Which stereotype would apply to me, I wondered? Such a rich bounty! Did I have to pick just one?

One walk brought us down to the Plain for a cadet parade review. We stood on the edge of the flat green field, waiting for it to begin. The band started up, and from the sally ports of the imposing granite barracks, the Corps emerged, all four thousand cadets in their toy-soldier uniforms and tarbucket hats, the feathers of the Firsties' shakos bobbing with every exact step. We stood entranced by this advancing force of youth and pomp and promise— the Long Gray Line, exultant. The call of the commands reverberating across the field, echoing down the valley and back through two centuries of history, and the drums, the drums, the drums. There were few moments in my life when I could recall feeling so full at heart. We were frozen in place while the Corps passed in review, each unit commander saluting the general officers' reviewing stand. Maya exhaled a German-accented "awesome." And it was. Not "kinda cool" awesome but hair-standing-up-on-your-forearms, blinking-back-tears awesome. Every nutty stereotype we'd have to unravel was worth it to witness moments like this. When the last of the cadets disappeared through the sally port, we walked on, wiping our eyes.

For West Point grads, the ring's the thing. So pronounced is the loyalty to the Corps, some graduates weld their class ring to their wedding band. When the Firsties, the fourth-year cadets, get their class rings, early in the fall of their senior year, the event is heralded by the tradition of Ring Weekend, with a formal and a chant that the underclassmen lavish on a Firstie who's brandishing his West Point bling:

> *Oh my God, sir!*
> *What a beautiful ring!*
> *What a crass mass of brass and glass!*
> *What a bold mold of rolled gold!*
> *What a cool jewel you got from your school!*
> *See how it sparkles and shines?*
> *It must have cost you a fortune!*
> *May I touch it, please, sir?*

Jorie's husband was an Academy graduate, but she couldn't be moved to play politics. "Oh, Christ," she said, rolling her eyes, "who cares about that ring-knocker bull-shit?" I was coming to regard Jorie as my bad-cop mentor—if we'd been in junior high together, she'd have dragged me off to the girl's room for a smoke. It wasn't very long before I noticed the subtle competition between the wives: Is your husband a graduate or ROTC? Enlisted or commissioned? What's his MOS? Like the Sneetches in Dr. Seuss, the mad dash to place oneself within the spousal hierarchy ended up a confusing mess. Who was a cooler-than-cool star-bellied Sneetch? Was I? Were you? How many stars did you need to be declared the winner? Or did the winner have no stars at all?

The tension between the wives of officers and enlisted soldiers was opaque to me at first. What, *more* hierarchy? Enlisted soldiers and officers aren't allowed to fraternize for professional reasons—threat of favoritism and potential undermining of officer authority among them—and this carried over to many of the wives as well. Seeing as how wives were already balkanized by the rank-based housing arrangement, this further factionalizing seemed like another obstacle to getting to know potential friends.

But I wasn't sure how friendly I wanted to be with some women. Gossip traveled thick and fast around the fishbowl. Jorie, awesome as she was, had a ransom of dish on the wives she hung out with in Ava's doggie playgroup, and she loved to share. You did not want to become the subject of gossip for having a lawn so long that you got a billet from your neighborhood mayor, or because you got sloppy drunk at an academic department tailgate party, or you hadn't put your nameplate on your house for three months after you moved in (the trend was to tag your house in the cutest way possible: The Potter Platoon, The Thompson Troop, Camp Carmichael). Mostly, the West

Point wives seemed to me like a supportive sorority. But sometimes, it was like *Mean Girls* with lawn ornaments.

My everyday life fell far outside the institutional thrum of the Academy, but I was confronted by it even within my house. Most mornings, I could hear the boom of the salute cannon followed by the bugler's reveille carried on a breeze from Trophy Point, marking the day's start as the honor guard raised the flag. Soon after, a pastor from the Protestant chapel roared by on his Harley-Davidson. I was often awakened by the early morning troop runs—hundreds of cadets barreling down my street, calling cadence, the noncommissioned officer running alongside leading the chant:

Here we go. *Here we go.*
All the way. *All the way.*
Every day. *Every day.*

Some afternoons, Jorie, Maya, and I would share a box of crackers on Maya's front steps, waiting to see what would come along next—a dozen cadets in camouflage and gas masks, for example, running down the street with another cadet on a stretcher, doing a practice drill.

And so many joggers—day or night, rain or shine, the re-flective safety sash clipped around their shoulder and waist. When the weather turned cold, the female cadets circled the post in thick, fleecy gray sweats while the male cadets chose to tough it out in gloves, pullovers, knit caps, and— *hooah!*—shorts.

Since cadets can't have cars on post until their senior year, they get around either on white shuttle buses or on foot. It's considered good form to offer them rides if the weather's bad or if they're facing a particularly long trek up or down one of West Point's many steep hills. I frequently hauled a carload of cadets down the hill from the PX to the library. A cadet once told me about an especially bone-chilling winter day when he'd been leaning against a retaining wall waiting half an hour for a shuttle that showed no sign of coming. A car pulled over—a colonel got out, told the cadet to stand up straight, got back in his car, and drove away.

Cadets, it turned out, lived in fishbowls of their own. Each day, tour buses pulled in to West Point and unloaded packs of people fascinated by the West Point mystique. They'd point at the cadets as if they were set-dressing, and corral them into posing for pictures.

"That must be kind of nice for you, though," I said to the cadet as we turned off Stony Lonesome Road. "You're sort of glamorous to them."

"I don't know, ma'am," the cadet said. "It's mostly kind of weird."

In the Army, everything has, or is, a number, even you. Everything a family member does within the DEERS grid requires reciting the "last four"—the last four digits of your sponsor's (husband's or parent's) Social Security number. It's how you're identified—the Army equivalent of your DNA.

But I'm not just defined and categorized by Mike's last four. I'm also a 31. In the Army, dependents are assigned numbers—children are 1, 2, 3, and so on, according to birth order. The first wife is the 30, and as Mike's second wife, this Household Six is a dependent number 31.

My 31-ness had never bothered me until, one day, I was in Keller Army Hospital for a routine physical and the receptionist called me by the name of Mike's ex-wife. "I'm sorry, that's not my name," I told her.

She glanced down at the chart, then glanced back up at me, confused.

I leaned over the partition and said quietly, "I'm the 31." She understood instantly and laughed so hard she almost dropped my chart.

"Just out of curiosity's sake," I asked, "how high up does it go?"

She glanced down at the form in the chart. "Hmmmm. 39."

"Holy crap!"

"I know, right?"

Why was I surprised? The armed forces are hardly divorce immune. According to a 2004 *New York Times* article, 20 percent of military marriages end within two years of a soldier's being sent off to war. And in a 2005 *New York*

Times article, John Leland reported that a soldier told him that 25 percent of the men in his unit ended up divorced during or after their tour in Iraq. (The official numbers are quite different. Per Army surveys, the divorce rate jumps from 9 percent to 15 percent after a GWOT deployment.) Still, for all those bummer percentages, the typical image of the military family is one that is happy, robust, and intact. Have you ever seen a published photograph of a military family aside from the glorious "reunion hug" photos, in which the wife sobs into the uniformed shoulder of her just-home husband? Maybe there's a kid or two in the joyous pile, and somewhere in the shot there's also a flag. It's military marriage, Norman Rockwell style.

I knew the odds against me: 45 to 50 percent of first marriages end in divorce, and second marriages have a failure rate of an alarming 60 percent. Add to that the fact that Mike had also been stationed at West Point with his first wife, which created a few uncomfortable moments for me. When Mike showed me around Thayer Hall, where he'd taught history, the head of the department came out and shook Mike's hand. Then he held his hand out to me. "It's nice to see you again!" *Awk*-ward!

Statistics, a whole new world, the shadow of the old wife and the old life: It was a lot for a 31 to handle.

Meeting a general is like meeting Madonna—it's hard not to be starstruck, and I say that from the experience of having met both.

When Madonna's *Sex* book came out in 1992, my friend Julie, who'd been in the book with her girlfriend Alistair, was hired to staff the book release party. Industria Studios in the West Village would be transformed into a sex carnival for the night, and Julie's job was to round up the freaks. She found dominatrixes and drag kings and drag queens in her social circle, but she was short a few blondes for the Madonna-look-alike charity kissing booth.

I got the job by sheer coincidence; I was living in San Francisco but happened to be in New York for a visit. The night of the party, the *Sex* freaks gathered in the photo studio dressing room. We slipped into our black leather, fishnets, and corsets, drawing on heavy black liner. A drag queen plucked my eyebrows to give them a more Madonna-like shape, and clipped a long platinum *Truth or Dare*–style ponytail into my hair. The two other Madonnas were a male and a male-to-female transsexual, so we had the gender spectrum covered.

At Julie's cue, we carefully wobbled our way in sky-high heels up the ramp festooned with red-black roses wrapped in barbed wire. Then we sat at the top of the ramp and tried to corral celebrities into buying kisses. Rosie O'Donnell totally blew us off. Billy Idol kissed my shoulder but didn't give me any money. We shrieked at Robin Leach when he came past, but he laughed, said "Maybe later," and headed toward the bar. We were having a heck of a good time, but as fundraisers, we completely struck out.

When Madonna showed up, the whole party froze; it was

as if the sun had come into the room. A clicking, whirring wall of black-clad paparazzi preceded her up to the second floor, the TV-camera lights casting a bright white beam over the entire slow-moving mass. Eager for a new photo op, the photographers started yelling, "Madonna, buy a kiss! Buy a kiss, buy a kiss!" The mass drew closer, and I could finally see her, this tiny woman in a low-cut, black Bo-Peep minidress, carrying a stuffed lamb under her arm. Her publicist, Liz Rosenberg, steered her our way.

Next thing I knew, Madonna was right in front of me surrounded by an arc of shouting, jostling photographers and reporters. I was seriously about to faint. The biggest pop star on the planet was standing within arm's reach of where I sat dressed up as her pale imitation.

I couldn't stop staring at her. I mean, at them. Her pores. I couldn't believe it—Madonna had huge pores.

Robin Leach showed up again and shoved a twenty-dollar bill at her. "Buy a kiss, Madonna!"

She looked confused, but at the crowd's insistence, she looked us all over—the three versions of her—and handed the twenty to Chris, the boy Madonna. "Ten, please," she said. He took her hand and left a trail of gooey red lip prints from her wrist to her shoulder.

She made a face. "Ew!" And then Liz Rosenberg grabbed her elbow, the paparazzi closed around her, and she was gone.

Had I expected her to be perfect in person? Of course. I'd been seeing her perfected image in photos and videos for years. Her stock-in-trade was bad-girl glamour, but in front of me, she was a woman with a great stylist and skin like any other woman in her thirties. Plus, she was so small amid that huge fuss, I was almost afraid for her. That the biggest star in the world was so very tiny in person put a lot into perspective.

Still, I was uptight at first whenever I was around the West Point superintendent, Bill Lennox. If we were in the same room, I'd watch him from the corner of my eye, tracking his every move. He was as exotic to me as Madonna herself. He was a three-star general, the only one on post, and the only one I'd ever seen. At a West Point football game, Mike introduced me to him; he swung his arm out toward me and gave me a handshake so forceful I felt it at the base of my neck. "How ya doin'?" he said with a grin. Under that almost papal shroud of authority, he seemed like kind of a friendly goof.

Army muckety-mucks value "leadership by walking around," that is, making yourself visible and accessible to your organization, as opposed to holing up in your office, clouded by an entourage, and issuing edicts from the royal throne. General Lennox took this to heart, and I often saw him as he made his rounds on post. His stride had a distinct forward pitch, as if he were bracing himself against a stiff wind, and when soldiers and cadets saluted him, he smiled as he saluted back. I dug him because he drove around post in a customized Go Army mobile, a homely old Dodge sedan the cadets handpainted for him with black and yellow spirit graffiti. When I'd pick up Mike in the moat of Taylor Hall, there, in the Supe's primo parking spot, was that ugly old hoopty. This thing looked like the dog's breakfast on wheels, but Lennox didn't care, he'd go putt-putting down Washington Road in his Go Army mobile, proud as if he were piloting a Rolls-Royce Silver Cloud.

In this suburbia-on-steroids, manners were paramount. If your neighbor took in your mail when you were out of town for a week, you bought her a thank-you gift, for which she sent a thank-you note. Like the Warner Brothers Goofy Gophers Mac and Tosh, repeatedly chattering, "After you!" "Oh no, I insist, after you!" the exchange of courtesies extended comically. I'm fairly certain that somewhere out there, two eighty-year-old veterans' wives are still swapping thank-yous from a poppy-seed cake baked in 1953.

When I was around other wives on post—at a "mandatory fun" event like a cookout at Mike's boss's house, or an impromptu chat in the PX parking lot—I'd find myself at the edge of the group, listening. I didn't have much to contribute yet. Their pluck rivaled the strength and resourcefulness of frontier wives. One wife whose husband was gone for a year had an inventive way to make up the lost time. Since her kids were saddened by the idea of Daddy missing holidays with the family, she stockpiled every holiday until he returned. He came home to a fully decorated

Christmas tree with gifts underneath, Easter eggs hidden beneath the couch cushions, the kitchen cabinets, and his sock drawer, and a chocolate valentine heart on the bed. After serving the Thanksgiving turkey dinner, she lit Fourth of July sparklers on his birthday cake that they toasted with New Year's Eve champagne. He opened homemade cards crafted by the kids for each occasion.

Liz, a woman who was married to a major in the English Department, had achieved some renown for pulling off the Army wife hat trick—giving birth to triplets while her husband was deployed to the Middle East from where they were stationed in Germany. The women who worked had portable careers—they were nurses, or teachers, or they started home-based shopping party franchises like Pampered Chef and Avon and even, there were some whispers, Passion Parties. (I'd have given a lot to mull over fur-lined handcuffs with a bunch of Army wives, oh yes.) Because most families move every other year or so, the first thing most spouses sacrifice is a steady career. One woman I met earned her bachelor's degree over the course of ten years and at four different colleges.

I knew I needed the approval of these women, and I craved it desperately. In the absence of family, they would be my family. In the absence of my mate, they would become my soul's support. But more than anything, they were fellow travelers who understood, where so many other people simply couldn't, exactly what I was going through. The relationship between Army wives is a sisterhood in the most practical sense of the word. I moved quietly among them, awed, and a bit intimidated, too.

What makes a perfect officer's wife? I was starting to see: a woman who is adaptable, diplomatic, community-minded, and expertly domestic. I sometimes imagined a pair of Big Daddy Patriarchy hands thrusting a fancy tea tray at me, with WIFE engraved on it in curly feminine script. Yes, being a military wife meant a measure of ma-terial security—predictable pay increases and free medical care till the end of time. Though I was thrilled to be mar-ried, inside I felt conflicted. As I met the other wives, so friendly and at ease with their casual wear and designer bags bought on discount at the PX, I thought, *I don't know if I can do this*.

Underneath his "more *hooah* than you-ah" surface, Johnny Hardcore, our neighbor two houses down, proved to be a pretty good guy. I could only take him in measured doses, however, because he turned almost every conversation into a sermon on the mount, and he was curiously devoid of "inside voice." Even though he hadn't been downrange since 1991, he still spoke as if he were fighting to be heard over generators and helicopter blades. He may have treated Mike like some lightweight at first, but I knew that Mike had impressed him sufficiently when, on the last mowing day of the season, Johnny pushed his mower clear through Kevin and Maya's yard, crossed our driveway, and cut our lawn for us. "Just squarin' you away, brother," he said, when Mike brought out a couple of thank-you beers for Mr. and Mrs. Hardcore.

After one of the football games, Mike and I joined our neighbors for drinks and chips in the Hardcores' driveway. I thought we had transitioned from formality to friendship, so I told them about how, a couple nights before, I'd stormed down the hill to the Five Star at 1 a.m. because a couple of guests were standing in the parking lot, talking so loudly they woke up Mike.

The neighbors found this hilarious, because—of course—what was the wife doing, storming down a hill to give a bunch of strangers a piece of her mind? That was the man's job.

"That's right," I said to the group, "that sound you guys hear is my *huevos* clanging together!"

The group went dead silent, and I sat there covered in Army-wife flop sweat.

Everyone I met was so friendly and sincere, it kind of freaked me out. Where was the sarcasm? Where was the edge? Did they just keep it private? Did any other wife look at her husband on a shaveless Sunday, with stubble growing all the way up his cheekbones, and say, "What's up, Al Qaeda?" Despite the deeper ironies of military culture, West Point appeared to be an irony-free zone. You could hang a cheeky "Eat, Drink, and Beat Navy" plaque in your kitchen, or pick up a sandwich called a Stinger Sub in a Grant Hall café called the Weapons Room, but for the most part, earnest endeavor was the name of the game.

One wife, in a heartbreakingly genuine effort to draw me in, said, "Welcome to the Sisterhood of the Traveling Camouflage Pants," and I was so overcome by cuteness I almost needed an airsickness bag. I'm all for a team building gesture, but the twee! The twee! It was overwhelming! From then on, whenever I encountered anything on post that was just too precious to process, I chalked it up to the influence of a phantom character I named Mrs. Army-Pants, a petty gesture that all but insured my spot in Army Wife Hell, but it helped me make sense of the weird.

The weirdest thing about West Point? No one discussed the war. West Point represented an eye in the storm of the Global War on Terrorism—since few people deployed from there, it was a place to breathe easy for a while.

In my "civilian" friendships, your opinion is like your fingerprint, a critical marker of your identity. We talked about the war all the time, pro or con. It was a political football tossed back and forth in constant conversational play. But at West Point, I never conversed about the political or moral ramifications of the war. Among the wives, we talked about where the war had taken our husbands, what it was doing to our families, our plans, our careers, our dreams, our psyches, our souls, and our marriages. One wife shared the devastation of seeing her toddler run up to strange men in camouflage, calling out "Daddy!" Another wife spoke about having to beg for a deferral on her husband's deployment date because she was on bed rest with a difficult pregnancy. Ten days after she delivered, her husband left for a treacherous mission in Afghanistan. The depth of candor surrounding the domestic ramifications of the current conflict was astonishing. But what we thought of the war itself? It never came up. Not even once.

I understood the silence as an extension of the soldiers' own protocol. They watch what they say and to whom they say it—the Army is supposed to be an apolitical organization, and soldiers aren't paid to express political opinion. That restraint applies to social settings, too. As a soldier, do you really want to find out at the neighborhood barbecue that you and your comrades hold totally opposing views? Editorializing threatens unit cohesion—in a life-and-death workforce like the military such divisiveness is unacceptable. To soldiers, personal opinion about the war is not a political football but a hand grenade. So the glue that binds the Army community is common experience, rather than shared opinion.

But that didn't mean that I was opposed to supporting someone's politics once they became known. One afternoon I came out into the backyard, looked over the fence, and found Jorie holding a copy of Bill Clinton's memoirs, which she tried to hide when she saw me.

"It's okay, Jorie," I called over the fence. "This is a safe space."

I bounced back and forth between West Point and New York City, which felt like a game of cultural ping-pong between the two worlds. My New York friends had married in their thirties and had kids late; my Army friends, with the exception of Maya, married in their twenties and many had kids who were already in high school. To my friends in New York, West Point was as exotic as an ashram or a polar research camp. They were paranoid about the conservative patriotism of the military, a prejudice that I exploited for my own amusement. I told them that after 9/11, the Polished Look, the beauty parlor where all the West Point wives went to have their nails done, had started calling the French manicures "Freedom manicures." I had them going for a long time. It was awesome. I also said that I had to salute my husband whenever he walked through the door in uniform. (One doesn't salute indoors. We genuflect instead.)

I'd find myself trying to explain my life to them in environments that were the exact opposite of West Point—for example, while sitting in the front row of my friend Jo's burlesque show at the Slipper Room.

When I told my acquaintance Billie that I was married to a soldier, she was shocked. A redheaded siren who was heavy on the glamour but not exactly overburdened with intellect, she wrinkled her nose and asked me, verbatim, "So is he, like, all right-wing and conservative and stuff?"

During breaks in the show, my friends and I caught up by yelling at each other over the taped recordings of Sonny

Lester and Slim Gaillard. What do you *do* up at West Point? they wanted to know. What do you talk about? And always, always, "What do Army people think about the war?"

I had no idea, I told them. They'd sit back in their chairs. "That's weird."

Yes, I explained to them: imagine living in the middle of a hurricane and never talking about the weather.

My friends weren't judgmental. Quite the opposite. They viewed me as a maverick adventurer, taking notes and making keen observations about the regimented pageantry of the military squares, man. But in truth, I was less a Jack Kerouac type, seeking self-definition within a regional identity, than a military version of travel dweeb Rick Steves, *ooh*-ing and *ahh*-ing across the surface, fanny pack in tow. When I'd get together with these old friends, I'd brandish postcard-size verbal dispatches from the exotic realm of West Point: the way the entire Corps of Cadets had to stand in formation before breakfast and lunch; how all 4,400 of them bolted down their meals in twenty-five minutes in the enormous, elegant mess hall; the fact that the mess tables had tablecloths and cloth napkins and identical condiment selections arranged by height in a pyramid shape—shortest to tallest to shortest again. They loved my recitation of the vintage Tuna Noodle Casserole recipe from the cadet mess, printed in the 1969 edition of the *West Point Hostess* cookbook my mother-in-law gave me: 200 pounds of noodles; 60 gallons of chicken stock; 85 pounds of butter; 135 pounds of shredded cheddar; 4 gallons of sherry wine; 100 gallons of milk; and, not to be forgotten, 163 pounds of canned tuna.

They asked, of course, about Mike's hours. He kept a pretty structured day—out of our quarters by seven in the morning and usually home by eight at night, which was a vast improvement over his deployment routine, when he worked twenty hours then slept for four. In addition to his duties on the superintendent's staff, he'd taken over the rear detachment detail for his former unit, which remained in Baghdad. Rear D meant coming home from the office to pull second shift addressing the unit's family concerns, including, in one tragic case, a casualty. From my spot in the kitchen, I listened, learning that the responsibilities of leadership include helping a grieving parent make sense of his only son's death. In the mania of bereavement, the man kept pressing for details. Was there a cover up? Was his son killed by friendly fire? I moved between the refrigerator and the oven, tears streaming from my eyes, as Mike patiently explained, over and over, the circumstances of the young soldier's death. The father spun out in rage over the loss of his son—he'd laid him in a cradle once, and now he'd laid him in a grave. What remained of his beloved child was the simple soldier's memorial of his boots with his upended rifle therein, and a set of dog tags hanging below his helmet balanced on the rifle butt. Mike hung up the phone and held his head in his hands. Placing a dish of baked chicken on the table, I understood why military wives keep an orderly house—it provides needed ballast for the tumult of loss. This knowledge was not for friends. I filed it away in the sad recesses of my own heart.

After a while, I didn't have much else to say, because, slowly but surely, I was losing my voice. I'd come of age in a community where Silence Equals Death, and now I lived in a milieu where I feared that saying the wrong thing might kill my husband's career—and my social prospects. I felt myself melting away, succumbing to a prefabricated role in a place where bonds and traditions are marked as much by what you talk about as what you don't.

9

The Whore on the Receiving Line

Early December is deer-hunting season at West Point. You can get a permit to hunt at various spots around post, and the deer sure as shootin' know it. Around the housing areas, where it's safe, you'll see plenty of does and more than a few bucks. One morning, I glimpsed a spike peering cautiously over the stone retaining wall behind the Catholic chapel. In summer, the deer are as tame as you can imagine, especially in the tree-dense streets near Lusk Reservoir. When you pass by, they look up as if to shrug and say, "Another pink ape. Whateverrrrr." But in winter they walk warily. They sprint for cover and blend into the branches.

Deer season meant holiday season, and since it was that time of year, old friends started checking in. When plying me about my life at West Point, their first question was: Do people *know*?

Know that I used to be a stripper, that is.

Answer: Folks might have known, but not because I told

them. I had nothing to hide, technically, but I didn't make it a talking point, either. I suppose an Army officer marrying a very former stripper might shock some people. But to me, the only shocking thing was that it had potential to shock at all. Nowadays, you can't watch a movie, TV show, or video without some reference to stripping, and every major publication features some cultural doyen rubbernecking at the collision of Porno and Mainstream.

It does sound funny, though: "ex-stripper turned Army wife." Kind of calls to mind a *Private Benjamin*–era Goldie Hawn tripping past the cadet formation in platform heels or boozily peeling down to a camouflage thong in the officers' club. But I didn't hit West Point like some flighty fish out of water. All appropriate courtesies were rendered: I dressed sensibly, chatted amiably, and could be trusted to make it through a receiving line without offering the superintendent a lap dance.

I could, in fact, have submarined the matter entirely if I hadn't published a book about my cross-country farewell stripping tour. But I can't take the book back, and, honestly, I wouldn't. It's my personal Pledge of Allegiance to the grrrlhood, and it gave me the freedom to explore how I felt about my involvement in a very complicated business. Then there was the small matter of the *Playboy* pinup. That I didn't sweat at all. Most of the fan mail I received was from—guess who?—military men. Thousands of e-mails—more than I ever could have imagined. The girlie/green relationship dates back to the first stag book and is as American as apple pie. My dearly departed friend, the burlesque legend Sherry Britton, was not only a popular World War II pinup, her likeness had once appeared as nose art on a bomber. And more than one dancing girl has stepped off the stage and into a soldier's loving arms. A turn or two at the shake shack and a couple of pinups aren't that controversial, really. Hard-core is much harder to live down. I ache for the repentant porn queens and the girls who go too far in spring-break videos. Heck, I even feel bad for Paris Hilton.

When pondering the complexity of how who I was squares with who I am now, men tend to laugh, but women tend to get agitated. It taps directly into a basic female social anxiety: that a woman's past will cost her a future. Indeed, in some cases, that does happen. (Hi there, Miss Lewinsky!) I did worry that someone might snub me when they found out, and though he assured me it wouldn't, I worried that it would reflect poorly on Mike. In the face of those fears, I tried to be Teflon Annie. Sometimes it worked.

Still, I didn't fret too terribly much, because I was learning that military people are sophisticated—more so than civilians assume. They understand what it's like to be judged unfairly. Sex work and soldiering are both flash-point vocations—rife with public misconceptions and stereotypes. When it comes to enduring negative projection, soldiers know the drill. I maintained perspective. For all the hell I might catch, nobody ever called me a baby killer.

Periodically, during that first winter at West Point, the seasonal blues made me sentimental for the good-old, bad-old days, when I was young and flossy and wild. Maybe I didn't love the job, but at least I knew the territory. I knew that I fit in, which was more than I could say about West Point. Sometimes I'd hear a great song on the radio and ache to be back in the strobe-lit clubs, raking in the cash with my patented brand of glittery, robotic, above-it-all dread. *Come one, come all, and join this spangled parade of sex-sex-sexiness! This is the path to excitement and thrills and hundred dollar bills!* Even though I should have known better, that carnival barker hook still got to me.

"The lady gets in for free."

In a fit of nostalgia one Tuesday night, I dragged Mike to a local strip club out by Stewart Air Force Base called Paradise Island. Paradise Island is a boxy joint, a single-floor place with funky-smelling carpet and dark walls. Totally nude, which meant they served no alcohol. The bouncer checked our IDs and waved us in. We gripped our five-dollar plastic cups of Diet Coke and tried to get into it.

Going to a strip club with your man is an interesting litmus test. We sat down at the bar. I could tell Mike was uncomfortable.

He leaned over to me and whispered. "I don't know where to look."

The girls worked their way down the bar. Shimmy-shimmy-spread. Shimmy-shimmy-spread. There's nothing exciting to me about seeing pink. Maybe I don't care because I've got that particular bit of equipment myself, so the sight is kind of like being in Bed Bath & Beyond and seeing the exact same blender that's in your kitchen at home: Oh, I've got one of those. Huh.

I fiddled with my fistful of singles, laying out five for each dancer who came by. I hadn't had a wad of cash in my hand this way in a long time. God, I missed the gambler's high of a good night, when you'd have so much money at shift's end, your fingers turned black from counting out the bills on the dressing room floor.

But this wasn't one of those jolly, adrenaline-pumping big money nights when the music was blasting and the impossibly hot, smiling athletic girls were sprouting hundred dollar bills from their garters. This was just another bum Tuesday where you'd have to rattle your can to earn enough cash to cover your utility bill.

The next dancer to stop in front of us on the bar startled me. I'm open-minded—you can pretty much float any fetish by me and get a thumbs-up—but Jesus Christ, I hate to see a pregnant woman working in a strip club! I know pregnant women can run 5ks and kayak and hike the Appalachian Trail. They're not glorified egg cozies. But still, when I see a woman popping a belly, however small (this woman looked like she was about four months), teetering in high heels and a silver minidress pulled down to expose her breasts yet cover her bump, I want to pick her up and whisk her away to a tropical island (not Paradise

Island) where she can sit with her feet up and be fanned with palm fronds and plied with virgin piña coladas fortified with extra banana. Get this lady a pedicure and foot massage, stat.

We tipped her twenty bucks. She smiled and looked grateful.

Starry-eyed cultural critics insist that in a strip club, the dancer has all the power. She's the one in control. It's a lovely fantasy—one that seduces even me—but that's never the reality of a service business. Sure, if the club is packed, the dancers are all busy, and everyone wants your fine, fine ass, then it's your racket—if one guy gets even a little out of line, you motion to the bouncer and it's "See you later, sucker." You know that customers are like trolley buses, there'll be another along shortly, and no one's going to get over on you. Every dancer I know had her bullshit tolerance lowered by this job. But your power is only as great as your demand. If you got no takers, you got no game. You're tempted to make compromises—put up with demeaning comments about your body, suffer through conversation with a man who's got roaming hands and raptor breath, let another customer get a little closer than the rules allow. When the money's tight, the pickings are slim, and the pressure is on, you eat crap or go home broke. You've heard the expression "Beggars can't be choosers"? Exactly.

Whatever beauty or sex appeal you've got, you rarely enjoy it when you strip, because there are a dozen sexier, prettier, newer girls pouring in every day. It's a constantly renewing source of Not Good Enough, a big chompy mouth gnawing its way through heaps of hot, writhing young bodies. Men show up hoping against hope that she's "into it." Most of the time, she isn't. Her motivation is the bottom line.

But catch her on a good night and she's into it, maybe even loving it. That's just enough juice to keep the machine humming.

There's something about dancing that sets you free, even if you otherwise feel like a slave to the job. In the smoke and neon and darkness, you have a sacred space on the stage where you can put aside the gender politicking and the power-jockeying and meld with the music. Yes, certain clubs make you dance a certain way—no bending over! no touching yourself with your hands! stay three feet away from the customers!—but within that is the simple joy of movement, of shedding clothes and inhibitions and feeling yourself grow huge and dramatic, walled off from silly judgments and Faustian bargains. The shy girl, the geek, the slut, the whore—whoever someone thinks you are doesn't matter because this is your song, your stage, your time. Even though your attractiveness is on the club's auction block, sometimes there's a song or two that's yours and yours alone. Like the caged bird sings, the dancing girls dance. It's not a ballerina's discipline or a modern dancer's stretching the boundaries of beauty. It's the harlot's hard bargain—here's what I've got, take it or leave it. But if you take it, know that you're not getting all of me.

This little piece, the beauty of this moment in the dingy spotlight, is my own secret pleasure, my own sweet escape, and it is inviolate. Whatever dirty business might happen in the audience, the performance stays pure.

That's what I was looking for when I dragged Mike out of the house, that singular show of female freedom and enjoyment, and I wasn't finding it here. The dancers all looked bored, and the guys did, too. Not that the dancers were likely to notice. The customers blend together and pass on by like a floe of porno slurry. A guy might want desperately to be flattered, to be seen, but in reality, he's just a wallet with a pulse. Maybe guys simply want the lie, the illusion of being acknowledged, indulged, and known. Curiously, in this callous business based entirely on mutual use, the saving grace is gratitude, rare as it may be. There's always that redeeming 10 percent of your customer base that's truly appreciative for whatever you give him—real or not—and that's what carries you through.

But too many times you're dancing for some clueless married yob rationalizing his loophole in monogamy. You don't know his story, so you assume the worst: that he's just some assclown. The relentlessness and repetition harden you to men—or at least "customer" types. Whatever you offer, they want what's just out of reach. The writer Elisabeth Eaves, in her stripper memoir, *Bare*, put it best, "These men want, simply, to see more. More body, more tongue, more tit and especially more pussy, as deeply as they could behold." They keep grabbing at more, more, more until, inevitably, there's nothing left. You burn out, and they appear not to care that you were harvesting the most private part of yourself for their easy consumption. The phrase "pearls before swine" takes on a deeper meaning.

Another dancer squatted down before us. I kicked Mike under the bar to get his attention without appearing obvious. He looked up just in time—she was trying to shift her weight to conceal a small but definitely visible hemorrhoid.

Maybe that's what it comes down to for me—apart from the gender inequality and burnout and crap working conditions and moral quandaries that can set your head spinning, one thing about stripping remains: This is a job where your privacy is so compromised, you can't even keep your hemorrhoids to yourself. As far as bottom lines go, I don't know that it could get more blatant.

I tipped her a twenty, too.

We rolled out of the club, thoroughly depressed. Mike started the car. "They used to have exotic dancers at Fort Benning, you know."

"What? Actually *on* the post?"

"I'm telling you, I joined a very different Army. When I started, in '88, it was in the days before political correctness. You'd go to the officers' club every Friday and drink until your eyes crossed. It's what was expected. Now at quitting time on Friday, you go home to your family. When I was at Fort Riley, all the officers of my tank battalion went to a strip club in Topeka together, except for myself and the battalion operations officer, who was the churchiest of the church-going. Our commander stapled his business card to every single."

"That's lame."

"He was trying to be funny."

"There's not a stripper alive who'd find that amusing. She'd probably hex the guy as she picked all those staples out of her tips at the end of the night." Nothing that makes a stripper's job more complicated is considered funny.

If you want basic indignity, stripping has it in spades. Sure, on some shifts, it's awesome. But mostly, it's Dilbert in spandex. Club management is often clueless at best and downright exploitative at worst—a girl can count on paying out a good chunk of her tips to the house, in the form of ridiculous tip-outs, "stage fees" as high as $200 a shift in some places, and bogus penalties, like being fined $100 for chewing gum onstage.

I don't miss the hustle. When I danced, I thought of the dough in aggregate terms—two hundred, three hundred, five hundred, a thousand dollars a shift. Only after I quit did I ever break it down: On a two-hundred-dollar night, ten guys paid me twenty dollars each to sit in their lap. Yet if a man at a bus stop had offered me twenty dollars to do the same thing, I would have spat in his face. Context becomes another form of compartmentalization. You learn to shut down. There's something very draining about taking the most personal part of yourself and doling it out in dollar-size chunks.

It's easy to self-mythologize as a stripper, to view yourself as some bantamweight badass, bucking social stricture, when you're really just a down-and-out art chick trying to support yourself in a way that gives you enough spare time to pursue your passion and also frees you from the corporate prison of pantyhose and spreadsheets.

On a preholiday trip to Los Angeles to do a reading at a Franklin Avenue gallery, I visited with two friends, Ernest and Nina, a porno power couple. Ernest has a lengthy résumé as a producer and director of fetish videos, and Nina, through her endurance, intelligence, and world-class backside, is one of the few adult actresses to obtain true legend status. In their chic Highland Avenue condo complex, they rented not one, but two apartments. They bunkered in Ernest's spotlessly clean place, with its extensive fetish art collection—original Olivia de Berardinises and Sorayamas—and impeccable Art Deco furniture. They were clever and funny, and swapping war stories with them was never anything less than delightful.

Nina and Ernest let me crash in their downstairs apartment, which appeared to be little more than a receptacle for Nina's wardrobe overflow and several towering piles of unopened fan mail, a shocking amount of which was from prisoners. In her expansive walk-in closet, I fondled her thousand-dollar handbags, sparkly skintight dresses, and

Lucite-heeled stripper platforms with envy. The shoes! My God, so many exquisitely trashy shoes—mules with red marabou poufs at each toe; metallic gold strappy sandals with sky-high heels; white platform go-go boots that laced up to the knee. On the floor, tossed as carelessly as a Goodwill sweater, was a brand-new Burberry tote, tags still attached. $325. The stab of envy I felt was profound. I *missed* this life, dammit. Ernest and Nina flew to Europe for the International Adult Video Awards and cruised around Hollywood in a late-model black Lincoln Navigator with custom rims, while I was toeing the line in military Mayberry. I was old and stodgy and boring now, and Ernest and Nina were still living it up as the fetish intelligentsia.

Ernest has never been a porn apologist, and I'm sure that's why I took to him as well as I did when we met years ago at an alternative lifestyles conference. He can draw a bead on the business in a way that most of his colleagues wouldn't dare. More timid souls queue up to talk about how wholesome the porn industry is, that it's like one big family at heart—no one is ever pressured to go a baby-step beyond their own limits—and it's their choice, oh yes, their *choice*. Ernest had a different take. In an adult fanzine interview he said, "Yes, there are award ceremonies where everyone gets dressed up and pats each other on the back and hands out trophies. But bear in mind that those trophies say things on them like 'Best Anal Scene.'" He knew that the machine would grind on no matter how much criticism was heaped on it. I have heard him say about the porn industry, "This is a business that traffics in human souls."

When I shared my gnawing envy with them over a sushi dinner, Ernest looked at me, incredulous. He put down his chopsticks. "Do you know what Nina and I say about you?"

I shrugged, popping a few edamame beans from the pod.

There was a significant pause. Nina picked up a spider roll. "We say you're the one that got away," she said.

"You made it over the wall and across the moat." Ernest stabbed the air with his chopsticks to emphasize his point. "You got out. Stay out."

I returned from Los Angeles with a lot on my mind—I didn't fit into the adult world any longer, just as I felt I didn't fit in at West Point. And I realized that deep down, I really was afraid of being judged for having been a stripper, more so than I might ever let on. I feared someone yelling, "Whore!" down the length of the frozen food aisle at the commissary, or seeing someone's smile drop when they saw me come into the living room at coffee group, like, "I know about you, and now you know that I know, and I want you to know that I don't want to know you." Even worse, I feared being excluded entirely: Pariah Wife. Just pin the scarlet letter on her now, so everyone knows she's an untouchable.

Eleanor Roosevelt said, famously, "No one can make you feel bad without your consent." Please. Like Eleanor Roosevelt ever worked the pole. That sounds good, but it's just not real. Anyone can make you feel bad if you have your guard down, and who wants to live life with a heart sheathed in Kevlar? Stripping makes people uncomfortable—pushes their buttons and challenges their boundaries. And when people need to reorient who they are in the face of what you've done, they can get mean. As if their disdain could undo what's already been done. As if it would change things for the better. As if you hadn't already heard it all before.

The stripper life is far behind me and recedes more in the rearview mirror day by day. It is, literally, not my business anymore. But the threat of sex-specific scorn wakes me up, reminds me of where I've been. When I hear of or read attacks full of fuming generalizations and analyses that are basically little more than finely honed hate, I feel moved to defend my fallen-angel comrades. These are people I know. These are people I love. On their uniform sleeve, combat veterans wear the patch of the unit with which they fought, even decades later. In a less visible way, I do the same: *Hey, haters, I served in the porno trenches with these people. Deal.* But if I didn't belong there, and I didn't belong at West Point, then where, exactly, *did* I belong?

That first West Point Christmas was a busy social season spent hanging up strings of colored lights, wrapping gifts, and picking out a tree. I sent more holiday cards than I had in every other year combined. Mike and I made the rounds of required holiday parties on post—we visited his boss's house, and the grand home of the chief of staff on Professor's Row. When we arrived at the Chief's house twenty minutes after the party's start time, the festivities were already in full swing. There is no "fashionably late" in the Army. Ribbon-wrapped bottles of hooch and other hostess gifts lined the hallway. I placed our tribute—a holly-and-pine tabletop arrangement—on a narrow ledge, then immediately wanted to kick myself because there wasn't a card attached. They wouldn't know it was from us. Ugh. Another Army wife formality foiled. On the ledge stood a clustered collection of miniature houses, each bearing the name of a duty station: Fort Leavenworth, Fort Drum, Fort Hood, Darmstadt, Germany. On a side table in the parlor, the Chief's West Point graduation portrait was displayed next to his plumed tarbucket parade hat. When I visited the ladies' room, I dried my hands on a holly-print towel held between the praying hands of plaster angel.

Still too shy and self-conscious to join the other wives in the holiday tradition of caroling for the cadets outside their barracks, I spent the night of the caroling party walking around post alone, my breath swirling out in frigid puffs that hung in the winter air. West Point regulations forbade outside decorating until thirty days before a holiday, so right after Thanksgiving, the blitz of Santas, sleds, and lights began. Entire streets now twinkled with Christmas trimmings. Along the icy, tree-dense streets, I'd see the shadows of deer shift then alight when they heard my footfalls. They'd disappear in the crackling brush. I never would have guessed, when I started stripping, that one day I'd be an Army officer's wife. And when I started stripping, I never could have guessed that so many years later, like the deer on post, I'd still feel hunted.

One winter day, I got an e-mail from a stripper asking if she should come forward about her night job—she's thinking of writing a book, maybe a play. I told her to consider the aftereffects, what life would be like with paranoia as a constant companion. But what about those of us for whom it's too late to cover up? Well, we make like the deer, dear. We step carefully. We learn to blend.

10

Taps

The "gloom period" settles over West Point in late winter, drawing everyone's spirit down with it. Gray uniforms, gray buildings, gray monuments, gray river, gray slushy snow. The storied West Point esprit de corps lies fallow as everyone on post drags along, restless and bummed, dreaming of summer and itching in their wool.

Sometime near the tail end of my first long winter at West Point, my dad, who was living in New Jersey with my mother, fell down in the driveway while shoveling snow. Unable to get to his feet, he lay there in the cold and ice until my mother happened to look out the window and see him, splayed on the ground and helpless. As she worked to lift him back to his feet, he told her that he couldn't feel his legs. Something wasn't right.

After a preliminary round of tests, the doctors still hadn't determined what was wrong. They booked him a series of appointments with a physical therapist and sent him home, where his condition worsened, the weakness traveling upward from his legs to the rest of his body. There is nothing quite as awful as seeing the man who taught you how to ride a bike slowly lose his physical ability. My dad—my strong, stoic bear of a dad—spent the next several weeks in and out of the hospital for additional tests. He started shuffling around the house with a walker, slit-open tennis balls jammed over the rubber feet so the walker could glide more easily along the floor. As the weeks went by, he began to lose the use of his right hand, and his elegant, martinet-sharp penmanship was reduced to jerky scribbles. His tools and workbench in the basement started gathering dust. It took him tremendous effort to turn a doorknob.

He went back into the hospital. Again with the tests. Mike and I drove to New Jersey to visit, bringing things that would distract him—magazines, bags of black licorice jellybeans, gumdrops covered in sugar, large-print crossword puzzles. We sat with him and my mother. Machines in the hallway beeped and whirred. Nurses walked by, orderlies pushing carts full of lunch trays. My father sat upright in the room's one chair, a pillow underneath him to cushion his now-bony hips. The sight of his pale legs poking out from under his hospital gown and bathrobe upset me. I kept having to look out the window. Still no answers, but he seemed to trust the hospital staff. I wasn't so sure.

By May, the snow had melted, the gloom had lifted, and it was spring again in the Hudson Valley. Graduation was coming up, and Mike was mentoring some of his former students who had chosen military intelligence as their branch. We had them over to our quarters one warm, sunny evening for a backyard cookout.

While I was stacking hamburger patties and hot dogs on a plate to take to the grill, two of the female cadets, Lia and Jennifer, appeared at the kitchen door. "Do you need some help, ma'am?"

Being called ma'am while out and about on post made me feel like the recipient of a charming, antiquated courtesy, but being called ma'am in my own home made me feel like the Crypt Keeper.

"Call me Lily. Please." They didn't. They couldn't—the protocol was drilled in too deep. Happy to have a little help, I started them chopping cucumbers and tomatoes for the salad.

Only fifteen percent of the Corps is female, and from the beginning, I felt a special appreciation for female cadets and soldiers. West Point didn't admit women into the Corps of Cadets until 1976, so in many ways, they're still a novelty. Certainly, there are plenty of old Gray Hog alumni who think the Corps should have stayed entirely male. I'm not on board with their indignation. We all know the famous girl-power quote "Ginger Rogers did everything that Fred Astaire did, only backward and in high heels." Conversely yet complementarily, female cadets and soldiers do everything male soldiers do, yet manage to maintain their femininity in camouflage and combat boots. Certain professional pursuits aren't open to women—namely, most of the combat arms branches (infantry, field artillery, engineers, air defense artillery, and armor)—but the other branches are fair game. Mike was pleased that these women had chosen to branch MI, and flattered that they'd turned to him for counsel.

I never got sick of interacting with the cadets. They're hard not to love. I started to feel some weird *ownership* of them, an almost parental pride, partly because they seemed so young to me, and partly because they'd pledged four years to the Academy and at least five years of service to their country after that. The years at West Point are grueling and the absolute inverse of the typical college experience. Cadets don't have the option of scheduling classes in the afternoon so they can sleep in, or lounge around playing Frisbee on the Plain in their scant off-hours. When the annual listing of the nation's top party schools comes out, West Point is invariably near the bone-dry bottom of the list. They seemed so superhuman in their dedication that when I'd see them in their civilian clothes, lined up waiting for rides off post at spring break, I had to do a double-take. Cargo shorts, T-shirts, flip-flops—they were just regular kids!

Lia was a lovely girl with blond Botticelli curls raked straight back into a bun and calm blue-gray eyes. After the barbecue, she asked if, by any chance, we could host her mom and dad for graduation week. It was only weeks away, and the local hotels had been fully booked for months.

Graduation week at West Point means a tidal flood of parents wandering over hill and dale. It's part of the spirit of the place to open your home to them, and the week with Lia's parents was pure hectic joy. I didn't know what to expect before meeting her mom and dad—were they quiet and orderly like Lia, or more forceful and flashy? I couldn't have guessed that they were hippie Hare Krishnas who drove buses for Seattle public transit.

Mike and I enjoyed their company. They filled our refrigerator with their own specially purchased vegetarian food, rinsed off their yogurt bowls and bread plates in the sink, and the father tried to convert Mike only once—"You know Krishna is the one true Lord, right?" They were clearly crazy about their only daughter—Lia's mother documenting every uniform change and graduation week event with her professional-grade SLR camera.

The commencement exercise is profoundly emotional, the capstone to a demanding life experience that edifies and transforms every single cadet who takes on the challenge. At the end, the graduates toss their hats in the air. The parents on post turn their young children loose on the field to scramble for a hat to keep as a souvenir and many cadets tuck a twenty-dollar bill under the label as a treat for the child who picks it up. Then the newly minted grads hurry off to pin on their second-lieutenant rank insignia—a single gold-tone rectangle called a "butter bar."

Lia wasn't just graduating that week; she was also getting married to one of her classmates at the cadet chapel just hours after the commencement ceremony. She invited us to attend, and we encouraged her to take as much time as she needed getting ready at our quarters, since she had already cleared her room in the cadet barracks. In our spare bedroom, her mother helped her into her gown. There was a soft knock at my bedroom door. I opened it. Lia was there with her bridal veil in hand. "Ma'am, do you have any bobby pins?"

What a difference a day makes: That morning when Lia woke up, she was a cadet. Then she was a West Point graduate. Then she was a second lieutenant. Then she was a bride.

From there, she and her new husband loaded their possessions into his late-model midnight blue Corvette and flew from the nest of the Academy and into the Army. Into the war.

The following afternoon, I crashed a wedding at the cadet chapel. Well, technically I was invited, but I didn't know the bride or the groom. The bride-to-be had e-mailed to tell me she'd enjoyed reading something I'd written about life at West Point, and she was dating a cadet and would soon be an officer's wife herself. During our short correspondence, she'd asked if I wanted to come to their wedding. Surely, it was the most unorthodox wedding invitation I'd ever received, but I readily accepted. It seemed the right thing to do. If I were a young woman marrying a soldier and had invited a senior officer's wife to the wedding, I'd remember whether or not she'd showed up, and I wanted to do right by the next generation of Army couples.

Having been at West Point for almost a year, I was still blown away by the social immediacy, that quick sweep-in to friendship: "Hey, you seem nice! Do you want to come over for coffee? Take a walk together? Come to my wedding?" I was almost compelled to attend on the basis of bridal chutzpah alone.

I dressed in a suit and heels, left Mike at our quarters to tend to our graduation week guests, and walked down to the cadet chapel. The wedding was intimate and elegant, dwarfed by the immensity of the chapel, which seats 1,500 people. The groom and his attendants came out in their dress blue uniforms and stood in line at the altar. Joe looked handsome and nervous, his blue eyes scanning the enormous church. The wedding march began and the guests stood. The chapel doors cracked open and afternoon sunlight streamed into the room in a long, holy beam. The first time I saw Robyn, a tiny slip of a girl with her brown hair swept up in ringlets, she was coming down the aisle, holding a red bouquet in one hand and her father's arm in the other.

Robyn and Joe were "two percenters"—part of the rare two percent of couples who stay together for the whole four years the cadet is at West Point. They were high school sweethearts in the northern reaches of New York

State before Joe came to the Academy. Joe had branched field artillery and they would be moving to Fort Sill for his branch training immediately after their honeymoon. Would they find humor in this frequently forwarded spoof of military marriage that made its way around the Internet?

Dear family and friends, We are gathered here today in the sight of God and the Department of the Army, to witness this exchange of vows, and see the love that these two dedicated, loving people have for one another.

Wilt thou, [groom], take [bride] (who will now be referred to as the "dependent") as your family member, to dwell together in so far as the Department of the Army will permit?

Wilt thou love her, comfort her, via the postal service or over the phone, make sure she knows where the commissary, PX, and church are, and what time she is scheduled to use the laundry room the day she arrives, wherever you are stationed?

Wilt thou attempt to tell her more than 24 hours in advance that you will be leaving for two weeks, beginning the next morning?

Wilt thou [bride], take this soldier as thy wedded husband, knowing that he is depending upon you to be the perfect (well almost) Army wife, running the household as you see fit, and being nice to the commander's wife? Furthermore, you understand that your life with your husband (little that you may have together) will not be normal, that you may have to explain to your children, not once, but twice, and more often in the same day, that mothers do have husbands, and that children do have daddies, and that the picture of the man on the refrigerator is not the milkman, but the same individual who tucks them in at 2200 hours, long after they are asleep? . . .

Joe and Robyn's priest kept it more conventional. When he declared them man and wife, they kissed and turned to face their guests. Laughing their way up the aisle in recession, they made the perfect cake-topper couple. They'd chosen to have military honors rendered with a saber arch. I made my way outside, milling outside the church doors as the saber detail formed, each saber bearer holding his sword high in preparation for the couple to come forth from the church. There they were. They joined hands and hurried through the gauntlet. As the bride and groom exited the arch, the last man on the line tapped Robyn's bottom with the sword and said, "Welcome to the Army, ma'am."

I smiled and applauded in the crowd of guests. I'd finally gotten the traditional military wedding I'd dreamed of, only it was someone else's.

* * *

Later that spring, the rest of Mike's batallion came back from Baghdad. (So did Mike's sneakers.) One of the soldiers from Mike's unit, Sarah, was getting married in Massachusetts. At the wedding, I got to meet some of the other soldiers from the unit for the first time. The six of them shared the slightly whipped look of the recently re-deployed—they'd only been home for a few weeks, and the fatigue in their posture was the same as Mike's when he came back. And all six of them were African Ameri-can (for the first time I realized that, compared with the rest of the Army, West Point is really *white*.) Of course I was curious to hear stories about how Mike was as a leader. What did his soldiers think of him? I was pleased that one of them liked him enough to invite us to her wedding, and delighted when, at the reception, one of the other guests from the battalion told me they threw Mike a surprise going-away party before he'd left Camp Udairi.

Watching Sarah smile demurely as she made her way down the aisle on her father's arm, her dress a simple ecru satin sheath, you'd never know from looking at her that she was good with a rifle. During the ceremony of this final third in my summer wedding triumvirate, I thought about the uniqueness of each bride—a just-commissioned offi-cer from West Point, a high school sweetheart, and a white-collar reservist—and what they all had in common: an utterly unpredictable life ahead of them. As Sarah and her new husband, a shy Englishman named John, exited the church amid a soft rain of soap bubbles blown by the guests, I wondered where they'd be in five years, and how this war would shape their lives together.

The reception was held at the Essex Peabody Museum in Salem, which her family had rented out. The wedding was one of those occasions that I wished everyone who bitched about the elite not serving in the military could see. If your parents can rent a museum for your wedding reception, and the financier Peter Lynch is one of your guests, I don't know how much more elite you could possibly be. For all her privilege, Sarah was no snob. She had put her own career in Boston's financial industry on hold so she could serve her country by deploying for a year, packing an M-16 and sleeping in a hot, sandy tent like any other soldier.

I met Sarah's mother during the sunset cocktail hour in the museum courtyard. A tan, lean blonde with flawless patrician polish, she brought to mind tennis, golf, sailing on the Cape, and wicker purses after Memorial Day. She held her full tumbler in her left hand and reached out to greet me with her right.

We spoke about what we had in common—knowing what it's like to have a loved one deploy. "Sarah was gone for so long," I said. "You must have been terrified. How did you deal with all that worry?"

She said nothing, just smiled wryly and pointed to her scotch on the rocks.

My father was admitted to the hospital once again. He didn't feel well. The doctors still couldn't diagnose him. His symptoms were uncommon and his brain scans were clean—they weren't sure why he had become partially paralyzed. It wasn't multiple sclerosis, it wasn't a stroke. Finally, they narrowed it down to transverse myelitis—a rare neuroimmunological disease that causes paralysis, with 30 percent of victims suffering permanent disability.

In early June, Ronald Reagan died, and at every presidential funeral, the cortège contains a unit from each of the four military academies. On June 9, Mike's fortieth birthday, he took a group of West Point cadets down to Washington, D.C. From the Capitol lawn, he called me at home, where I was watching the procession on TV. "How do we look?" he asked.

"You'd love the way the sun is catching the tops of their tarbuckets," I said. "I'm proud of you, this is so beautiful."

Mike came home the next morning. The morning after that, June 11, three days before Father's Day, my father died.

My father had had a guy crush on Mike. While my dad was not an effusive man, he had sent Mike several chatty notes while he was deployed. The respect, I saw at my father's memorial, was mutual.

I wore black and Mike wore his dress blues. Since my father was an Army veteran, we agreed that having a uniformed officer presence was the right thing to do to honor my father's service. There is no moment when I more acutely felt my husband's love for me than when he stood at my father's flag-draped cremains, came to attention, and gave his finest salute.

The days immediately following my father's death were such a blur, I could only recall them later through an unearthed blog post:

Haven't updated in quite some time, for good enough reason: My dad died June 11. He was 72, and had been dealing with a neurological illness since March. He'd gotten to the point where he could hobble around a bit without his walker. On, like, the 8th of June, he said he wasn't feeling well so my mom took him to the hospital again and they ran some tests. On the 11th, in the morning, a spot on his lung was diagnosed as lymphoma. "Highly treatable!" "Chemo and radiation" blah blah blah. He was on the phone with my mom and sister, and his colleagues, sounding chipper, that morning. By that afternoon, he just keeled over and died in his hospital bed. Apparently from massive heart failure.

Honestly, I think he thought Bad Heart + Transverse Myelitis + Chemo + Radiation + Being 72 = I'M SOOOOOO OUTTA HERE!!!

That whole Kubler-Ross thing? The separate stages of Denial, Anger, Bargaining, Dorothy and Toto, or whatever? TOTAL CRAP. What you get when someone dies is all those feelings ALL AT ONCE, warping and spinning around like grief's bad trip.

That night in his office we found his "wrap up" program, an Excel spreadsheet stating how to conclude his affairs, miscellaneous instructions and farewells. He'd started it in March. He knew he was going to die. With his one good hand (he had to switch to mousing on the left), he typed in all this stuff, so my mom wouldn't have to go crazy figuring out what to do on her own. My mom has a mind for research and random fact retention, but not so much for household minutiae, and, understanding this, my dad prepared. He knew to care for her even when he would no longer be there.

The memorial was the following Thursday. They had to close off the entire street (just across Route 10 from where Jeanette and I suffered high school together). The police chief came, the fire chief came, hundreds and hundreds of people—plus, all my dad's (5) siblings, and all us kids and in-laws. After my dad retired from corporate drudgery, he got into local politics and was elected mayor last year. He was big into land preservation and managed to save 300 acres from development, which is no small thing in North Jersey these days, where they're plopping down mini-mansions like pigeons drop turds.

Anyway, I had no idea my dad was such the Republican player (mayorship in a small community is essentially a volunteer job—it's not like you need a war chest to get elected, or, for that matter, amass one once you're elected). I was so f-ing glad to not be alone in grief—let me tell you, that is the biggest thing about death. You realize you really are just some insignificant speck on the face of an indifferent planet, and anything that makes you feel otherwise, even if it's someone you don't even know saying "I'm so sorry," well, it is great. In the midst of discomfort and awkwardness, people come out anyway, for no other reason than they want to pay respect. So even though it was hard, I wouldn't have missed the service and I'm very glad I went.

The next week Deb and I went to see Skinny Puppy. Her brother dates their road manager, MJ, and she got us VIP passes. After the show, Ogre, the lead singer, came over and MJ introduced him to Deb. He shook her hand and looked at me: "And who is this?" I said, "I'm the wingman." Ogre: "What's that?" Me: "You know, the sidecar. Just along for the ride. Anyway, my dad died last week and it was great to see this show and get the grief blasted out of me." He started asking me questions about my dad and said his dad died when he was 17 (Ogre was 17, not his dad) from cancer and he gave me this huge, thermonuclear-strength hug. Very strange. But I guess I am now a card-carrying member of the Dead Parent Club and from what I gather, the members sort of look out for one another.

The elemental kindness I encountered humbled me. Who knew that a latex-and-fake-gore-splattered industrial musician would reach out to console you? Who knew that people you went to middle school with would track you down to send condolences when they read your father's obituary? And who knew that inside that great, steel-hearted military machine, there were so many thoughtful people?

They came with flowers, they came with cards. The day after my father's passing, Mike's boss's wife showed up at the house with calla lilies elegantly tied together with strands of raffia. Maya stopped by with prepared meals, easy things I could eat straight out of the dish. Mike's secretary, Anne, bought a remembrance for my father at her church—a beautiful leather-bound diptych with Christ showing his radiant sacred heart. None of my neighbors went to the commissary without asking if I needed them to grab something for me. This wasn't passing due diligence up the chain of command—none of these people were subordinate to Mike. There was no political or professional advantage to their gestures. They did it simply because it was the right thing to do.

In my father's absence, I was left with his memory. I was a childhood ham, eager to stand out in a sea of five kids, and happy to perform any show-off stunt that might get some extra attention. The summer I was four, my father took me to the park across the street, where I quickly scaled the steps of a rather tall slide, with all the nimble daring of a monkey. Sweaty in the hot sun, I held on to the metal railings then let go with one hand. "Dad! Look at me!"

My hand slipped and I fell to the playground pavement with a sickening thud. My chin was on fire and I started wailing. The next thing I remember is my dad scooping me up and running—*running*—all the way back to the house. He was wearing a navy blue windbreaker, and I knew I was bleeding all over it. He didn't care, he just kept running, my chin stinging every time one of his feet hit the ground. A trip to the emergency room and ten stitches later, I was back in my bed, scabbed and shaken up, but no worse for wear, really. Even now, when I see the scar, a pebbled rut just under my jawline, I remember my father's rushed pace, ferrying me home.

With five kids, an overwhelmed wife, and a series of tedious and stressful middle-management corporate jobs, my dad wasn't exactly the paternal ideal. My memory of his heroism on my behalf is undercut by his frequent rages, his impatience, and the cigarette butts in the ash-tray as he worked his way through multiple packs of Kents and my mom burned through at least two packs of Carl-ton menthols each day. The seven of us collided under one roof in a mashup of temper tantrums, torturous *Sound of Music* sing-alongs, casseroles, intermittent geek misery (one sister pulled out her eyebrows and lashes under stress, another bit her knuckle and pounded her head on the pillow), and the ever-present curl of tobacco smoke.

Before he hit his retirement mellow and turned to local government, the only time my dad seemed truly at peace was when we lived in Michigan. His colleague, Pete, had enough land for an apple orchard and a large vegetable patch, which my dad tended every summer, planting row after row of squash, zucchini, and pumpkins. Once, when I was ten, he took me along with him and let me use the tractor mower. As I mowed around the orchard, I got a lit-tle too close to a low-hanging apple branch and didn't have the driver's reflexes to swerve, so I made a quick overhead grab and the mower growled off without me, ditching it-self in some tall weeds as I swung from the branch. I ran up the hill crying, afraid that I'd ruined the mower. My dad walked me down the hill, turned off the mower, and con-soled me as he tried not to laugh.

By fifteen, I was still a monkey. Okay, I was a bit of a nightmare—wandering to the edge of acceptable behav-ior and pushing it to the breaking point. I went to midnight showings of *The Rocky Horror Picture Show* and *The Hunger* at the Rockaway Mall, followed by a stop at the local diner for disco fries—french fries smothered in brown gravy and mozzarella. I took trips to Manhattan to haunt Danceteria, always sure to get to Port Authority by 1 a.m., in time for the last Saturday night bus back to Jersey. My parents tolerated my arty experimentation. They saw it as harmless, if a bit embarrassing—the hair dyeing, the two nose rings, the gloomster clothing. But when I went one step beyond and got arrested for shoplifting at Shoe Town in the Roxbury Mall, my mother was mortified. She showed up at the police station, stone-faced, and the police officers showed her the pair of boots I'd stuffed into an oversize purse. I was so ashamed. She scarcely spoke to me on the long drive home. When we got home, I went straight to my room and lay down on my bed, pretty much wanting to die and fearing that when my dad came home from work, I'd be doomed. As I heard his footsteps coming up the stairs, I turned over and buried my face in my pillow. He opened my door, but he didn't yell. Instead, he sat down on the side of my bed and pulled me up into a huge, wordless hug. I started sobbing. "It's okay, " he said. "It's really okay." Had my father ever hugged me like that before in my life? I couldn't recall. When I'd split my chin as a four-year-old and he ran to get me home, that was parental instinct kicking into gear. But this was different, this was a consolation of character. A more reasoned means of tenderness and a deep affirmation: I'd fucked up and he loved me anyway.

After my father's death, life went all lopsided. If my soul was a house, there were four cornerstones to the foundation: Friends. Husband. Work. Family. Now that family corner was chipping apart. The lack of balance became apparent, every moment queered by that crooked-house feeling. Oddly, I felt disentitled to grief. Part of it was the sheer shock at my father's sudden demise. One minute he had a hopeful prognosis; the next, I heard my mother's voice on the phone, saying, "Are you sitting down?" And in the course of the war, I had simply forgotten that people die of other causes. My sensitivity to loss was focused on the conflict. As the force with the most troops on the ground, the Army was taking the biggest hit. As I watched the death toll climb, the news of every soldier killed in action felt personal. And yet, I'd experienced a deeply personal loss and I had trouble grasping its magnitude. This was a bitter reminder that life and death—prosaic, unrelated-to-current-events death—go on. It wasn't a tragic demise, simply the sad end of a man's natural life span—his affairs in order, his suffering brought mercifully to a close. In the hierarchy of grief, death by natural causes seemed so unworthy.

Externally, I appeared functional. I kept appointments. I hit deadlines. But inside, I just wasn't *there*. I wasn't sad or angry or hurt or lost. I wasn't anything. My emotional life became a blank screen. I'd examine my face in the mirror, wondering if what I saw in the reflection was really me. I recognized my face—it was the family face. Basic, pleasant enough. Strong chin and cheekbones, with small, deep-set eyes passed down from my grandmother to all six of her children, including my dad. Squinty. Happy. I was grateful that I viewed the world through my father's eyes—it meant there was some connection to him left.

"Do you smell cigarettes?" Jorie's voice came around the wall between our back porches. She was in her yard with her doggie playdate friend from the next street over. Her friend's boxer was chasing Ava across the lawn. "Who is smoking?"

"Sorry," I called from my patio. "It's me."

Jorie poked her head over the fence. "Oh, I didn't see you there."

I'd taken to sitting on the small concrete patio in the afternoons, smoking Parliament Lights and working on my laptop while listening to the Tommy Dorsey CD my father had given me a few years earlier. At my father's memorial, I'd taken one of his mass cards—it had a photograph of a rainbow on the front, and the Twenty-third Psalm on the back—and tucked it in the clear inside pocket of my laptop case so I could see it whenever I took out my computer.

The dogs circled in the yard. Jorie went inside her duplex

and came back out with something wrapped in aluminum foil. "In case you don't want to go to the store." I peeled back the foil and smiled. It was a frozen chunk of venison.

"Thanks," I said. "I don't have much appetite." Jorie wordlessly unlatched the fence gate so Ava could run over and lie at my feet.

Instead of emotional pain, I was racked by a dull, physical ache. My entire skeleton hurt. My joints felt like they were grinding together under the skin. At night, my bones were so sore, the pain woke me from a dead sleep. I self-diagnosed it as "grief-ritis." Even my eyes hurt. Leaving the house was torture. When did the sun get so bright? Someone turn that thing off!

Day by day, I ached my way through this season of beginnings and endings, of weddings, graduations, and death. I chalked up the soreness to the vagaries of mourning, hoping that the pain would soon shift into a more bearable, recognizable shape—tears that could, with enough time and Kleenex, be brought under control, instead of the low roaring beast in my body that kept me up at night, Motrin be damned.

What I didn't know was that, as bad as I felt at the time, things were about to get so much worse.

II

Desperate Army Housewives

I can clearly identify the moment I started going nuts. Mike and I were at his family reunion at Round Pond, one of West Point's recreational areas just off the rural highway that runs past the cadet training grounds. There's a lake, campsites, and several picnic areas nestled in the leafy green woods. It was the highest heat of summer—broiling, overcast, and humid. I'd had my fill of shucking corn for the grill, tossing horseshoes, and batting the volleyball back and forth with various cousins. The two of us climbed into our Jeep and headed up to the rec area office to buy some bait for the younger kids who wanted to fish. On the way back, Mike held the paper bag of dried-up crickets on his lap while I drove. As I steered around the campground loop, two young soldiers ran by. The length and speed of their stride was impressive. Their shirts were off, and every glimmering muscle was a moving symphony of youth, vitality, and male entitlement. The only thing missing was the Olympic theme thundering up to match the force of their exertion. They looked so healthy; they looked so happy. I watched them through the Jeep window and said, extremely loudly, "Fuck you!"

Mike stared at me in disbelief.

I was attending the family reunion as the new wife, so new that a number of Mike's relatives hadn't even realized he'd remarried. The clumsy introductions typified my life of late. I'd slid into this new role sideways, and I was coming to realize that that might have been a sizable mistake. Usually the lifestyle jolt of marriage is gentled by the preamble of meeting the new family-to-be and being toasted at bridal showers and the wedding itself. An Army bride could educate herself about the military life by taking classes, on post or online. But I'd had none of that and the culture shock was kicking my ass. I'd always been a "sink or swim" type of person, so I said, Hey, throw me in. I thought I'd swim with ease but instead I was sinking. Fast.

In September when the weather turned colder, I saw them—the couple in the commissary. They stood side by side in front of the stacked canned goods and cereal boxes. The guy had a well-groomed blond afro, goatee and sideburns, aviator shades, bell-bottoms, and a black turtleneck sweater. A proud progenitor of white boy funk, he looked like the *Vice* magazine answer to the Mod Squad. His girlfriend towered like an Icelandic goddess, with knee-high fur boots, skinny jeans, a puffy down vest, and a huge gray fur trapper hat over her loosely falling, long platinum hair. This was no salon job—that was nature-given Nordic blond, the stuff of Valkyries and ABBA. Her outfit was the kind you can only wear if you're rail thin—it's so homely and odd, it serves as the perfect highlight for your wraithlike slenderness. In front of the displays of baked beans and juice boxes on special, they stood out like sore thumbs—the kind of arch juxtaposition you'd see in a Terry Richardson photo: hipster sexy in the land of olive drab.

I couldn't help myself. "What are you doing here?" I barked at them like an overexcited interrogator.

White Boy Soul said, "I used to be in the Air Force. We were driving through and we just thought we'd take a look around."

"Gosh, it's such a relief to see people like you around here." I pointed to myself. "I used to be you. I mean, I used to look like you."

Princess Ice smiled, her eyes glowing like pale aquamarines.

They were everything I wasn't—chic, ironic, and deeply amused by this formal military environment, whereas I was taking the whole thing so seriously, you'd think I was living for a grade, that I'd be beaten with a birch switch if I turned in less than a B+ performance.

Under their indie-rock mellow, I could tell they were like, "Okayyyyyy, crazy lady. Whatever you say."

For the rest of that fall, I'd sit at the computer and peck out a few paragraphs, maybe lay down a scrapbook page or two, then when Mike called to say he was on his way home, I'd start dinner. I went to football games, and cheered with everyone else on the afternoon when the Black Knights snapped their embarrassing nineteen-game losing streak by beating Cincinnati 48 to 29, which excited the Corps so much, all 4,400 cadets stormed the field, tore down the goalposts, carried one off the field, and threw it into Lusk Reservoir. I was honored with an invitation to sit in with a cadet creative writing group, and listened to them as they nervously read their essays and poems in a corner of the West Point library—except for the lone Plebe in attendance, who, per upperclassmen orders, was forbidden to speak.

The only time I had a good laugh was when my friend Michelle came to visit from San Francisco. The martial electricity of the Academy was so exciting to her that she stared at everything like a kid at a zoo exhibit. Overwhelmed by the cuteness of the cadets in their as-for-class uniforms, she leaned out the car window, hooting at them like she was on a Bike Week bender. Eventually, I was like, "Uh, Mrs. Robinson, do you mind? I kind of live here."

In the interest of keeping up appearances, I let Mike haul me to Philadelphia for the Army-Navy football game in December. When we got there, the stadium was almost empty, but everyone who filed into our section was wearing an earpiece and a Secret Service pin. It turned out that

Mike had managed to get us tickets for the superintendent's section, three seats down from President Bush. Karl
Rove sat right in front of me, so I spent the game having
a silent one-way conversation with the back of his head.

"Karl Rove's head, why don't you wear a hat? It's twenty-
seven degrees outside."

"Karl Rove's head, do you have dandruff? No, I see that
you don't. Good for you."

Mr. Rove brought his son with him, and at one point,
he asked him, in this singsong-y voice, "Andrew, do you
want some hot chocolate?" The kid shrugged. Rove may
have had the president in his pocket, but like any parent,
he was at the mercy of a bored teenager.

I made Mr. Rove take a photo of Mike and me. It came
out really good, but when I looked at it, the image of a
wholesome, rosy-cheeked military couple, I thought about
those two groovy cool cats I'd seen in the commissary and
wondered, "How the heck did I end up here? What happened to my life?"

And then came the babies. There's a tendency in the military to grow your family just after a deployment. Maybe
it's so the couple is together for the baby's arrival, maybe
it's a result of all the reunion "festivities," or maybe it's a
primal reaction to war—the realization that life is fragile
and precious, and you should create more while you have
each other. While you still can. On a regular post, after a

unit returns, you can set your watch to the postwide baby boom. The couples who had moved to West Point post-deployment were no exception. West Point is a wonderful place to have kids. Your risk of deploying from here is relatively slim, and if you can wrangle a permanent faculty position, your kids may actually graduate from sixth grade at the same school they started kindergarten in.

By now, the personnel who were new the previous summer had settled in, and the bumper crop of babies was making its appearance, right on schedule. I looked out the window of my home office one afternoon and saw no fewer than six new moms out together for a walk. I marveled at the squadron of strollers coming down the hill. I was in my thirties. Hormonally speaking, I was supposed to have babies on the brain. What was so wrong with me that I didn't ache to join the army of mothers? Not only was I unmoved by the urge to join them, I wanted to run away.

On one of our walks, Maya shyly announced that she, too, was pregnant, with her first child.

"Congratulations! Are you excited?"

"I am. We weren't planning it." She sounded as nervous as she always did. She had a trembling dog quality that made me cautious around her, like she had been treated poorly and needed extra care. She didn't like me to be alone with Kevin. When they came over, she wouldn't leave us in a room together. Something in me was alerted when we'd met and Maya said she didn't work because Kevin preferred her to be home. She never mentioned whether or not *she* wanted to work. So often, I'd see her just sitting and staring out her living room window at the street, looking lost and lonely and bored, and that worried me.

Like any soldier, Mike was fanatical about haircuts. Each week, he'd drop into the Top Brass barbershop in Highland Falls for a fresh shearing. The soldier's haircut has four different stages: Scalptastic, Velcro, Velvety, and Puppy Butt. The brief Velcro stage was the most amusing because, as the name suggests, things get stuck in the hair at that length—pillow fuzz, threads from pullover shirts; once I found a small scrap of paper like he'd been using his head as a bulletin board. Whenever his hair grew past Puppy Butt, he'd go in for a trim from Crystal, who understood the full zero-blade repertoire. One of our daily traditions involved me slowly rubbing Mike's head as we lay in bed, while he asked, "What stage is my head? Is it Puppy Butt yet?" The ritual became his favorite way to close out his long days.

But when he'd ask me now, I'd just pat his head and say, "I don't know. It's fine." His disappointment was obvious.

My day-to-day life seemed to have been overtaken by rules, rules, and more rules—there were rules that were printed in books and pamphlets, and invisible rules you absorbed as if by osmosis. Yet it seemed I had more questions than answers. Did Army wives listen to Rammstein? If I ran into the dean in the dairy aisle at a commissary when

I happened to be dressed à la Unabomber in a dirty hoody and my hair in a bandana, did that mean Mike wouldn't get promoted? I didn't know, but I felt as if there were eyes everywhere, watching and assessing my performance. If I made a mistake, I wasn't just failing myself or my husband—I was failing my country, too. It was a star-spangled guilt trip that I fell for as easily as a cultist spell, and, more and more, it gnawed away at me.

When I got too agitated to sit still in the house, I'd tell Mike I was going to the gym and drive around post, blasting Metallica's *Master of Puppets* as I burned up the blacktop at the government-regulated twenty-five miles per hour. I felt like I was suffocating in my marriage, like I was a prisoner in my own skin. Just as an animal would willingly chew off its own paw to get out of a trap, I'd have bitten clean through my ring finger if it meant relieving the pressure from that shiny Tiffany-style wedding band.

There is a Holiday Inn Express in Fort Montgomery, New York, not far from the Academy gates. The hotel occupancy rises and falls in rhythm with the West Point calendar. In fact, it seems that the place exists solely to manage the overflow from all the joyous occasions at the Academy—families coming for graduation, alumni returning for football games. I started fantasizing about killing myself there.

Every potential suicide has her exit fantasy: walking in front of a bus, feeling acutely the step of her foot off the curb as the exhaust and wheels screech up; teetering on a bridge as if poised for flight, arms out, wind blowing around you. For me, the dream was black, easy sleep, drawing me down like a powerful, sucking riptide. When Mike was at work during the day, I'd perfect my plan: Check in to the hotel and hang the Do Not Disturb sign on the door. Toss back a handful of sleeping pills, wash it down with vodka, and then lie down on the bed and put a plastic shopping bag over my head. Tie it all off with a length of extension cord, and relief would be mine. The only thing I couldn't figure out was how to spare the housekeepers the sight of my dead body.

Did my father's death have something to do with this? Maybe. I don't know. I guess it had to. I'd been faking "fine" convincingly for years, with dark spots of depression surfacing at unpredictable intervals, like black ice on a highway. Friends would wonder, *Why did you miss my wedding? Why do you keep canceling plans with us?* Editors would ask, "Why is this assignment late?" I never said: Because I was too depressed to move. Because I was trying to fight back the urge to blow my brains out. But now the depression was back, suddenly and worse than ever before. Maybe my father's death was the final turn of the jack-in-the-box handle releasing the darkness I'd been holding in. Maybe I didn't feel safe in the world anymore with him gone. All I knew is I was growing increasingly anxious, bordering on paranoid. People didn't like me. I couldn't get any work done. If we moved, my career would fail. No one on post would ever want to be friends with me, they just saw me as Mike's dumb childless whore wife, and my old friends couldn't relate to my new life as a military spouse. They'd go on with their lives, and I'd be left behind, stuck in this miserable, lonely, frustrating rut. I started viewing everything as a threat, and when I feel threatened, I withdraw. And then I attack.

I'd grin my way though a West Point social event with Mike, then at home, I'd vent my frustration about how I didn't feel like I fit in. The fights. My God, the fights. Always started by me, always over something insignificant, ignited by my insecurities. If I spare you the inane details of the row that ended with me storming out the back door of our quarters, yelling, "Maybe you should get a new wife!" don't feel cheated. Our neighbors, Jorie and Dan, who heard every word through those thin military-issue walls, can fill you in.

In the urgency to quiet the racket inside my own head, I reverted to a form of relief I hadn't visited in years—the blade. No one thinks of professional, middle-class thirty-something wives as cutters, but there I was, digging through my box of scrapbooking tools in search of the shiny silver X-Acto knife. I hunched over on the taxpayer-financed bathroom tile, drawing the blade down the outside of my calf once, twice, three times.

As counterintuitive as it sounds to someone who doesn't do it, cutting doesn't hurt. For me, there's just a sweet wincing sting, then the tremendous payoff: the little meteor shower of endorphins tingling down my limbs; the single-point focus of the dazzling razor edge; my once-churning mind as quiet as a city banked in snow. As stress relief, one cut is as good as a thousand screams. All the chaotic motion stops and it is still and silent for a time. I knew that the emotional dragons would roar back up momentarily, but for an all-too-brief window: Peace. Quiet. Bliss.

Mike received a glowing OER (Officer Evaluation Report) and subsequent confirmation that he was promotable to lieutenant colonel, the highest rank he had hoped to achieve when he was first commissioned as an officer back in 1988.

There are few things more moving for an Army wife than seeing her husband get promoted. Sixteen years of service had led up to this. West Point's chief of staff (Mike's boss's boss) led the ceremony, and the Academy adjutant general read the Army officer's oath as all the soldiers involved in the proceedings stood at attention. Mike shared a few words, and his new rank insignia, a silver oak leaf, was presented on a velvet-covered tray. Traditionally, the soldier's new rank is pinned onto either shoulder board by his loved ones. Even with the aching tension in my heart, I was able to celebrate his success. Attaching that silver oak leaf was one of the proudest moments of my life.

Dozens of Mike's colleagues and friends and family members came past on the receiving line to congratulate us. I shook each hand and thanked everyone for coming.

What nobody knew was that just hours earlier, I'd taken my place on the bathroom floor once again and drawn the X-Acto down my calf, cutting three more thin lines from knee to calf. Three was the magic number. At first, the cuts were white, invisible to the eye, but they slowly filled with blood, beading up and welling red. The cuts looked like a swipe from a bear's paw or the mark of a tribal rite, but no one at the ceremony could see through the dark brown tights I'd worn to match my brocade suit and heels.

The wounds were shallow and scabbed up quickly, a trio of crusted mahogany-colored trails. I worked assiduously to hide my leg, changing clothes in the bathroom and getting into bed only after the lights were off. But one night Mike came into the kitchen unexpectedly when I was wearing my gnarly old green bathrobe, which only came down to my knees. He was stunned at the sight of my leg. I tried to appease him with the "I cut myself shaving" excuse, but he didn't believe me. I could see the shadow coming over him. He had no idea that such a dark depth existed inside of his outgoing, adventurous wife. When I told him I felt bad—I didn't fit in, and I didn't feel well and I didn't know why—he said, hopefully, "You shouldn't feel bad! Everyone here loves you. Everything will be fine."

I started reading the post newspaper, *The Pointer View*, with an eye toward salacious detail. It became my own personal scandal sheet. Not every week had juicy news, but now and then there was a nugget that kept me bringing the paper off the front step as a faithful reader. A cadet who had kiddie porn files stashed on his computer. An officer who was caught masturbating over the sleeping adolescent guests at his daughter's slumber party. See, these people weren't so perfect. They were crazier than me. What started out in my mind as military Mayberry was looking more and more like military Mayberry crossed with a Tom Perrotta novel. On these quiet streets lined with minivans were back yards, basements, and closets full of dirt.

The strain on Mike was becoming obvious. He wanted more than anything to get back to Happy Us again. His every assurance said, in essence, "You're making a big deal out of nothing. You've got nothing to worry about. Just relax." He even relayed the sentiment in greenspeak: "Stop tripping over mouse turds." And I, in my angry, deafeningly mute way, screamed back, "I can't!"

He'd ask, over and over, "What are you angry about? Why are you so sad?" But I didn't know how to explain that I wasn't angry *about* anything. I was just angry. I was just sad.

He started to get the point on the night I swung my foot back and kicked a hole through our living room wall. Correction: I kicked a hole through Uncle Sugar's living room wall.

The following afternoon, Jorie's husband, Dan, was trimming the grass on their front walk. When I came out the front door of our quarters, he stopped the trimmer. "Hey, how's it going?"

"Good, Dan. How're you?"

"Fine, thanks."

He scrutinized me closely. "You sure you're okay? Because if not, I want you to know you can tell us."

I froze. I knew what he was trying to say. He and Jorie had heard all the racket and they thought Mike was beating me.

Mike and I started couples therapy the next week.

Army couples can get free counseling through the post mental health department, or with a post chaplain. It's a nice perk; however, I'd have sooner burned in hell than talk to an Army counselor. It would be like a pig telling the butcher he didn't care for bacon. So I turned to the resource I had at hand: the Yellow Pages. I didn't feel tremendous confidence that I'd find someone to save my marriage in the same place I might find a dry cleaner or an all-night car wash, but I didn't dare ask around for a personal referral. News of marital strife would race through the fishbowl with the speed of a tsunami wave.

It turns out that angels live in yellow books. We got lucky on the first try. We found a therapist named Patti, a Ph.D. who specialized in treating children and couples. She walked into the waiting area dressed in a baggy loose-knit sweater, corduroys, and clogs, looking like she had just picked leaves out of her hair after rolling around the fields at Smith. Her office, in the hamlet of Warwick, resembled a fantasy closet—in addition to the standard couch and doctor's armchair were a miniature table and chairs for small people, a sandbox, shelf upon shelf of toys—knights, lions, cars, dinosaurs—and a wall full of gloomy drawings by her young patients that looked like Pictionary played by wounded souls.

Mike and I sat next to each other on the slightly saggy office couch and unpacked our story—how we'd met, married, and gone through deployment, redeployment, and moving to a new post within a year.

Patti crossed her legs, raglan socks showing under her clogs. "That's a lot of change for a couple to go through in such a short time."

We told her that it was typical for an Army couple, nothing out of the ordinary by military standards. I laid out what was bothering me—that I felt aggressive and anxious. I was sleeping even more poorly than usual and I couldn't concentrate. I'd started cutting myself again for the first time in years. I was preoccupied with morbid thoughts. When I told her my father had died after a lengthy illness, she seemed very interested.

By the end of the hour, Mike and I were both convinced that we were in good hands with Patti. But the modern modality for couples therapy is to work on the marriage together, and then as individuals—a shrink for you, for me, and for us. Therapy times three. *How much would all this sanity cost us?* I wondered. Mike opted for a therapist who

was covered by Tri-Care. He felt he could find someone ad-
equate enough in network—his concerns about himself
were minimal. He wasn't the one crashing his boot through
drywall. I, however, knew I was going to have to find someone industrial strength, which was going to take some time.

I found another Ph.D. therapist in Warwick, an earnest,
silver-haired woman named Casey who also taught yoga
and didn't take insurance. She seemed smart and appropriate in her concern—she didn't hit the roof when I told
her about my history of cutting (maybe a dozen times,
mostly when I was a teenager), viewing it as a compulsion
more often born of intense anxiety than some outsize mental illness. My skepticism about mental health practitioners was deeply held—I had tried therapy in prior times of
stress, and I'd even tried Wellbutrin for a couple of
months, which only made me more anxious, so I carefully
tapered off. Over the years, I had seen, and summarily
dismissed, a shrink who had me look at a bank of flashing
lights while chanting affirmations, another shrink who
seemed to think that my wearing high heels and makeup
to our appointments was a sign of underlying pathology (as
if wearing flats and ethnic beads mean you're a paragon of
sanity?), and one who believed I'd benefit from "rebirthing."
By comparison, Casey's approach of guidance through evaluation of my emotional response to events seemed utterly
sane. What I was not prepared for was the cost. I had mental health sticker shock—the $150 an hour out-of-pocket

expense blew my mind, especially since she recommended that I come in twice a week because I was "in crisis."

Therapy, and all that came with it—driving to therapy, writing out checks for therapy, seeking out the right practitioner—became our new part-time job, Mike and I both pulling second shift on the couch. I wasn't getting much better. During one session with Patti, I spent the hour seated next to Mike in a non-verbal state, combing my hair with my fingers until I had a lap full of broken bleached strands. At the next session, I told Patti: I will make you a deal. I will trade you promise for promise. I will be totally honest with you if you promise to never send me away to a mental hospital.

I have always had a great fear of being institutionalized. When I was in grammar school, my family lived in Ann Arbor, Michigan, for a few years, and we were friendly with another family who lived out past the state psychiatric facility. We'd travel the highway at night after a visit. I could see the red glowing letters that spelled out "Mercywood" peering through the naked tree branches, like evil eyes watching me, and I'd shiver in the backseat of the car. The place had a psychic scream to it that I could sense coming out of the windows. Eventually, I refused to even look at the sign when we drove by, holding my breath as I did when passing a graveyard. I can tell you the name of every mental hospital in every area in which I lived as a child. At seventeen, I watched the movie *Frances,* about the tortured life of Frances Farmer, and I regret it to this day.

When her family couldn't deal with her, they sent her away to some wretched hellhole where she was strapped naked into ice-cold hydrotherapy tubs for hours. Later she was lobotomized. I still can't watch movies plotted on mental illness. I walked out of *A Beautiful Mind* after half an hour.

Patti made me that promise, so I told her that starting at the age of four, I'd refused to let anyone brush my hair. The knots hurt too much and I didn't want to sit still while someone tugged at my scalp with a comb soaked in No More Tangles. I was, admittedly, an angry, combative kid—reluctant to go to school, uncooperative. Because I had terrible insomnia, I rarely awoke in time to make the school bus. I'd fight my mom to stay in bed. When my mother brought me to my first-grade classroom at McKinley Elementary, I'd run back to her car and lock myself in, demanding to be taken home. Once the vice principal came to the car and dragged me into the building kicking and screaming. I was terrified to be away from my mother, and all I wanted was to go home. Home, home, home, take me home. Once, in a moment I can only remember with the deepest shame, I wanted out of school so badly that when my mother walked me to the classroom door, I kicked her in the shin in front of my entire second-grade class. I can still hear her wounded, embarrassed yelp in my ears as the kids stared at me. I took off at a run, and it's safe to say, I've been running ever since.

* * *

Though I never connected the dots, the year I started acting out as a little kid was the same year I had a babysitter who would shake the shit out of me. When I first started getting shaken, my feelings flew out of me and I went numb right away. What was I, three and a half at the time? I was sometimes dropped off with babysitters up the street, an older couple my dad knew through his work. The wife had a collection of perfume bottles on her dresser top, sparkling colored crystal and glass that enchanted me. One afternoon, I reached for one and the husband came in and caught me as I held it in my hand. Did he think I would steal it? He grabbed me by my shoulders and shook me back and forth, using words I'd only ever heard when my dad was pissed or when the older kids were hanging out playing four-square and kick the can, trying to scandalize each other. When my mom picked me up, I didn't say anything about what had happened, because I didn't want her to know I'd been messing with someone's things. Plus, I was scared of this man—if he'd hurt me, maybe he would hurt her, too.

I only went to their house a dozen times or so, since my older sisters or brother could usually watch me, but on the rare days when everyone was busy—usually because my mom had Girl Scouts with my sisters—there I went. Every time I got dropped off, the man got pissed at me for one reason or another—once he got angry because his wife fed me a piece of coconut cream pie he'd been saving for lunch. It seemed as if he was looking for any excuse. He'd

stare at me as if searching for infractions. I was only allowed to watch television if I was sitting on his lap or next
to him in his recliner, where he'd hold me to his side like
I was a fugitive who might escape. He had that fusty old
man smell, like dusty cloth and ointment, and his attention to my "naughtiness" had a whiff of creepy fascination.
When his white-haired forearm brushed against my leg
as I sat on the recliner with him, I flinched and tried to
move away.

Grown-ups encourage kids who are mistreated to "tell
an adult you trust." Are you kidding me? Do you think a
violated kid trusts *any* adult? Kids aren't stupid—I know I
sure wasn't. He convinced me that I was a troublemaker,
so telling would only get *me* in more trouble. Keeping the
secret was a practical survival decision. I did not believe
the "truth would set me free." The truth would detonate
a bomb in my life, opening me up to the added humilia-
tion of embarrassment and trashed privacy, and everyone
would know I was a bad kid and a thief, whereas if I just
kept my mouth shut, it would pass. People who take advantage of other people—perpetrators of any harm or violation—know this. They count on it. The convenience of
secrecy is the climate that allows them to thrive.

Besides, kids don't tell with words. They use simpler,
more physical language to alert you to what's going on.

At some point when I was in second grade, the McKinley mandarins sat me down in front of a psychiatrist, some
rent-a-shrink they moved around the school district to

meet with troubled kids. He stammered nervously and had a Yiddish accent and thick Kissinger glasses. I sat in front of him in a conference room and bawled about how I didn't trust anyone. The shrink had only one Kleenex, which I used and shredded through almost immediately. I thought later, *What kind of shrink only has one tissue?* I came out of that session with one clear message: They think I'm freaking crazy and this is how they choose to tell me. If I don't act right, the next stop is the loony bin.

That night, I sat on the toilet in our pink-tiled bathroom and worked the snarls out of my hair for good and I was never late to McKinley Elementary again.

At the start of third grade they trotted out the gifted child test. Puzzles, word games, plying me for random facts. How tall is the average man? I thought about Shaun Cassidy. He was five-ten, so that was my answer. Who discovered America? I was like, Duh, Amerigo Vespucci, who doesn't know that? (Well, to be fair, kids who don't have four significantly older siblings who like to babble off facts.) I impressed them enough to be taken out of class twice a week with six of my classmates to do things like genealogy projects and photography with Mr. Helveston, who wore platform shoes, flared slacks, short-sleeve button-downs, and wide, diagonally striped ties. I got the hint: Be smarter than the average bear and you might avoid the cage.

Outwardly, my marriage to Mike appeared perfectly nor-mal. If you didn't know any better, you'd think that I was a bit aloof, but otherwise, things were fine. Deb came to West Point for a visit with her nephew, and I hosted a lunch where Mike did all the talking. Molly drove up for a tour with her husband, Matt, their newborn daughter, and her mom and stepdad, who were in from California. I smiled and laughed as Mike and I toured them around the sites of the Academy—the parade field, the cadet mess with pigeons that had flown through the open doors zooming overhead, and the Old Cadet Chapel and graveyard, with its monument to Molly Corbin, whom the DAR celebrated with a ceremony at West Point every spring. I still wanted physical closeness with Mike; I liked having him near me. But any stimulus beyond hanging out with him alone or working by myself in our quarters freaked me out. So I did my best to stay distracted and mentally just out of scene, an actress in the nonstop, low-action drama known as My New Married Life. I was like a 1950s housewife zoned out on Mother's Little Helpers, only my drug of choice was dissociation—just tuning out and smiling. Then, when our guests would leave, I'd flip the script completely, getting bitchy and agitated that I wasn't a better host. I had a withdrawn, numbed-out low, and a cranky, stress-fest high, and I couldn't find a peaceful middle ground. Through it all, the only thing that was consistent was my desire for everyone to go away and leave me alone.

I felt safer telling this to Patti than to Casey—maybe because Patti worked closely with children and understood their unique response to pain. She was very patient as Mike and I tried to puzzle things out. Not knowing what was wrong with me was terrifying, as was the process of looking behind the numbness into the black hole of my heart, and seeing how much hatred and anger were in there. And wild, wild fear—terror beyond what sane people could fathom. I was afraid that I was angry enough to kill myself, and terrified that I might succeed. Most heartbreaking of all, I realized that I was scared of my husband—that his love for me was contingent on my performance as a wife, that if I messed up, it would be over. We weren't two friendly but sovereign nations coming to therapy to make a peace accord, we were twined together. It was the most threatening thing I could imagine—truly being dependent on someone. If I put my life in his hands, I believed, then he had the power to destroy me. *You will turn on me*, I thought. *You will turn on me, I know it.* I was supposed to be his battle buddy, and in my fear, I turned on him. He had become the enemy.

Once Mike started talking to Patti about some of the terrible things he'd seen in the Army—deaths, injuries, accidents—he transformed into someone almost unrecognizable. He came home one day with his head shaved clean to the scalp on the sides and just a stubbled whorl on top. His weight plummeted. During a tense moonlit drive along a remote road coming back from Patti's, I saw a wet patch of road and braked suddenly. This startled Mike so much, he completely flipped out. "Why did you do that?" he asked me, after I corrected the car out of the swerve. His voice sounded strange. Small, flat, as if coming through a funnel.

I kept my eyes on the road, unsure what to do. "I saw a dark patch and for some reason I thought it was flooded or something and . . ."

He cut me off. "If you do that, they can see you. Because the moon is so bright, they can see you. One hundred percent illumination." He went on like this for several minutes, completely oblivious to anything going on outside his own head. I finally realized he wasn't *there*. He was having a fully actualized flashback. He was in the Kuwait oil fields, at night, with the thousand-meter sight line, in full view of the enemy. "One hundred percent illumination night. They can see where we are." His face looked waxy and stiff, with dark hollows under his eyes, which were opened wide and not-seeing.

My thoughts accelerated, my confused mind struggling to make sense of what was happening: This is a joke, right? He's messing with me. In a few seconds he'll stop and say, "Just kidding!"

My heart was in my throat. What if he tried to hurt himself or jump out of the car onto the busy highway? I checked to make sure the doors were locked.

Not knowing what else to do, I kept driving, saying to him, "No one can see us. We're going home now." Quietly. Calmly. "You're safe now. There's no one here but me." Over and over again until we reached the West Point gate.

By the time we were handing our military ID cards to the security guard, Mike had come back to himself. I drove slowly along the curved road near the central post area, pointing out Trophy Point and the Great Chain. "Do you see where you are now?" I asked. "You're back at West Point. We're almost home." He had no memory of what had just happened. In our quarters, I helped him into bed and lay beside him, shaking. Exhausted, he passed out right away, and I watched him as he slept.

Thank God that was Mike's only flashback; even his therapist was confident he wasn't in any danger, that it was just an isolated incident of post-traumatic stress from his combat experience, shaken loose by the tremors in our marriage. He felt a profound loss of control so the memory of when he was at his most vulnerable leapt from that void. Certain he was making great headway in his own battle, he wanted to aid in mine. Moonlight glinting off a wet road may have triggered Mike's PTSD, but close proximity to an authoritative person who was supposed to care for me sent me into a tailspin of my own.

In the way that a blessing can also be a curse, the trait that makes you fall in love with someone can be the very trait that makes you want to kick them in the neck later. I had that lovely paradox within my marriage. Mike is Decision Guy (military wives in the house, holla if you hear me); he wants to get things done. And Decision Guys usually suffer a chronic case of Do Something disease, so he really wanted to Do Something to help me snap out of my funk. No hand-wringing, dithering, equivocating. Lay out the items, make a bullet-pointed list, and start checking things off. If I was wound up at night and wanted to leave the house for a walk alone, Mike would hop in the Jeep and drive around post trying to find me. When I started self-lacerating, calling myself a whore and an idiot and a failure, he would try to argue the point.

To Decision Guy, helping equals love. He wants nothing more than to see you reach a happy resolution on anything; your satisfaction is his success. When options A through Q don't tickle your fancy, he drives on, offering options R through Z, with thirty-six addenda, which he presents to you during your bath time, drives to the mall, and on leisurely, romantic walks through the woods. "How about if you . . ." Out come the pep talks, ideas, strategies, stopping short only at drawing up a PowerPoint presentation. He wants an end to the tortured moaning, the indecision, and the doubt. But sometimes I didn't have a way out of how I was feeling. I just had to sit with it, and the best thing he could do was just listen.

I know he meant well, but the help he was offering wasn't helpful. He was a trained leader, doing what he was meant to do, Army Strong style. Almost twenty years of training had turned reacting aggressively, assuming control, and moving to save and protect into instinct. I couldn't fault him for that; still, there was a rigidity to his dealing with the situation that didn't seem healthy—almost compulsive, as if he couldn't tone down the Do Something urge even if he wanted to. Sometimes, I just wanted to yell, "Stop with the officer's counsel. I'm not one of your soldiers, I'm your wife!"

Then I'd step out of myself, as if watching from afar: Wow, what a bitch. He's just trying to help. He loves you. What's your problem?

In session, Patti pointed out, gently, that while Mike was of true heart, his tendency toward solving and fixing suggested he was codependent. I balked. I mean, seriously— has anyone been codependent since 1997? If the desire to save someone was an indication of codependence, the ramifications were staggering. ("This just in! Entire Army declared codependent!")

The textbook codependent dynamic is a system of compatible, but destructive, neuroses. One falters while the other rescues, the neurotic partnership summed up by the phrase "the horns on his head fit the holes in mine." But in our case, the conditions were a little different. We both had horns, and they were locking.

Confessing my anger to Patti made me feel like a narc in my own marriage. I expressed my idiotic envy that Mike was getting better faster than I was. His therapist said she believed that he was "very emotionally resilient," and she was confident that he would be fine. We'd been seeing Patti for six months, and his own therapist cut him loose with her blessing after only half a dozen sessions. Damn, he'd seen thousands of exploded bodies and miles of twisted blood and guts and metal, and he's up and running already? What the hell? It made me feel worse about myself—how this was possible, I didn't know. Then Patti steered us back to the subject of my childhood, the point of constant return. Toward the end of a session, I tended to zone out so I wasn't paying attention when she said something about post-traumatic stress. I thought she was talking about Mike. But she wasn't. She was talking about me.

Post-traumatic stress disorder is a dissociative disorder caused by a traumatic event involving death, the perceived threat of death, or serious injury to oneself or others. It can also be caused by living through a series of small negative events that, taken individually, are relatively minor but, over time, add up to very significant trauma—sort of like death by a thousand cuts. Trauma usually results from not having any control over the events and not being able to help ourselves no matter what we do. When we are threatened, our normal response choices are fight, flight, or freeze, but when we are traumatized these responses go off-line. We become stuck. So we fight—getting angry all the time. Or we attempt emotional "flight"—constantly trying to avoid or run away or withdraw. Or we freeze—becoming numb or depressed. Or we do all three by turns. The neuro-emotional cycle becomes a misery loop, dooming us to repetition as we try to undo what happened to us—an army of Chicken Littles under a sky eternally falling.

Public awareness of post-traumatic stress disorder is mostly related to war—military combat is one of the stressors that causes the disorder, but it can be caused by many other events: violent assault, rape, vehicle accidents, natural disasters, seeing harm done to another person, or learning that someone close to you is in danger. Many experts believe that the terrorist attacks of 9/11 and Hurricane Katrina left tens of thousands of people with varying degrees of PTSD. The recognized symptoms of PTSD include, but are not limited to, uncontrollable crying, nightmares, insomnia, depression, dissociation, difficulty concentrating and completing tasks, intimacy avoidance, and flashbacks. There is no time limitation on when symptoms can appear. They can show up almost immediately after an event, or years later, and they can pass quickly on their own for some people, while others may need extensive therapy to find relief. The elephant in the middle of the room that has everyone creeping around on tiptoe is that for many people—raising my hand to be counted among the guilty—the number one telltale symptom is near-constant agitation. When I couldn't withdraw or hide, I got stressed out, and the alchemy of stress turned me into an unbearable, uncontrollable jackass.

PTSD means, in "talking over beers" terms, that you've got some crossed wires in your brain due to the traumatic event. The overload of stress makes your panic button touchier than most people's, so certain things trigger a stress reaction—or, more candidly, an over-reaction. Sometimes, the panic button gets stuck altogether and you're in a state of constant alert, buzzing and twitchy and aggressive (pretty much where I'd been for the past year). Your amygdala—the instinctive flight, flight, or freeze part of your brain—reacts to a trigger before your rational mind can deter it. You can tell yourself, "It's okay," but your wily brain is already ten steps ahead of the game, registering danger and sounding the alarm. So you might say, once again, in a calm, reasoned cognitive-behavioral-therapy kind of way, "Brain, it's okay" but your brain yells back, "Bullshit, kid. How dumb do you think I am? I'm not falling for that one again!" By then, you're hiding in the closet, hiding in a bottle, and/or hiding from life, crying, raging, or ignoring the phone and watching the counter on the answering machine go up, up, and up. You can't relax and you can't concentrate because the demons are still pulling your strings. The long-range result is that the peace of mind you deserve in the present is held hostage by the terror in your past.

With the four letters P-T-S-D spinning before us, Mike and I stumped forward as best we could, Mr. Can-do and Little Miss Do It My Way. We were both experts at performing under stress. The difference between him and me was that I didn't know how to exist without it. Relaxation was so foreign to me, it may as well have been the moon. The serene domestic safety of West Point made me feel smothered. There was so much peace and quiet there, I was choking on it.

* * *

Mike and I somehow made it through Christmas, New Year's, and into the depths of the 2005 gloom period. In February, West Point hosted the Royal Military College of Canada for the annual exchange. The West Point/RMC exchange weekend is one of the longest-standing academic traditions in North America, dating back eighty-plus years, and the festivities include sports exhibitions and debates and formal dinners. Mike and I were honored to attend a dinner in the cadet mess with the superintendent of the Academy and the commandant of the RMC. The tables were clustered in view of the poop deck from where, in 1962, Academy graduate and five-star general Douglas MacArthur delivered his famous "Duty, Honor, Country" speech:

> In my dreams I hear again the crash of guns, the rattle of musketry, the strange, mournful mutter of the battlefield. But in the evening of my memory always I come back to West Point. Always there echoes and re-echoes: Duty, Honor, Country.
>
> Today marks my final roll call with you. But I want you to know that when I cross the river, my last conscious thoughts will be of the Corps, and the Corps, and the Corps.

Once Mike and I found the calligraphied place cards with our names on them, we rocked it old school, conversing with the person to our right during the appetizer, and the person to our left during the main course. The crystal stemware glistened under the dim glow of the chandeliers, and the light gray uniforms of the Academy cadets blurred into a perfect background for the bright red and black uniforms of the cadets of RMC. Afterward, we went over to the Holleder Center where we had the unique experience of watching a hockey game while decked out in evening wear. I put on a happy face for the couple from RMC whom we hosted in our quarters, a Navy commander and his wife, who were lovely guests and couldn't have been better company. I used to adore the military academy's ceremonial fuss and fanfare; I even loved the word for it: *punctilio*. But after RMC weekend, Mike could no longer entice me with the West Point punctilio. I greeted spring in deep seclusion. Mike did his best to try to engage me. Did I want to go to another hockey game? Another formal dinner? A debate? No. No. And no.

In an article I'd read in *The Pointer View*, a soldier was quoted as saying, "When the going gets tough, the tough get going." Oh, Army, dear Army, you with your endless up-by-the-bootstrap salvos, as if all of life's challenges could be transcended with an inspirational, instructional slogan.

Dear Army, Bite Me.
How does that slogan grab you?

* * *

Finally fed up, I packed an overnight bag one April week-day while Mike was at work, preparing to check into a local motel. After the hours of couples therapy and inconclusive talking, talking, talking, I needed some time alone. I'd hoped to make an inconspicuous escape, but Jorie caught me sneaking my suitcase down the back walk. Underneath her crusty demeanor, she had proved to be genuine, maybe even a kindred spirit. She certainly had her own independent way about her—many times that winter, I'd looked out our back window to find her and her husband dressing out a deer she'd shot earlier. As much as I liked her, I kept my distance this morning, because maybe, deep down, she was One of Them, the perfect Army wives, because after all, she'd had her house decorated and her yard meticulously landscaped within two weeks of moving in.

When she saw me, she said hello, asked what was up. She wasn't deaf, so there was no sense in either of us pretending that there wasn't trouble in paradise. She heard the racket coming through the adjoining wall of our duplex several nights a week. So I was straight with her: "I'm leaving for a little while." She knew I wasn't talking about a vacation. How did I expect her to react? Did I think that she'd switch into Mrs. ArmyPants mode and judge me from her perch of perfection? "I can't *believe* you would leave your husband when he so clearly *loves* you." She didn't. Instead, she leaned on her gardening rake and said, philosophically, "You know, you're not doing anything that every Army wife hasn't dreamed of doing at least a thousand times."

Suddenly, I saw Jorie clearly. A West Virginia farm girl eager for Dan to retire from the Army so they could return to the land, she was biding her time as best she could. As a neighbor, I loved her—salty and open-hearted, she always kept an open door for me and Mike. We shared many happy times with her and Dan in their back yard, roasting marshmallows in their clay kiva and playing with the dog. Her harsh, gossipy edge made me wary, but I could now grasp it as a defense mechanism. Being married to a military man is a consuming way of life—if you're in it, you're in for all of it, and when forced up against the pettiness and pageantry, Jorie turned sharp and sarcastic. She was at her happiest at home. I held the vivid imprint of her absorbed in the task of taking a knife to the chest of a whitetail hung by its back hooves in their shed. Maya, with her animal loving-stance and stubborn morning sickness, watched with disdain from her back fence, her hand over her mouth. "Mein Gott, what is she *doing*?" Jorie looked serene, unperturbed, like she did during the hours and hours she spent working on the landscaping in her yard. Those solitary hours of planting and pruning and grooming kept her sane, grounded by the good earth. With every shovelful of soil, she was digging her way to freedom, and with what she'd just said to me, she was inviting me to do the same. I walked down the driveway, opened the back door of the car, and flung my suitcase onto the seat.

When the going gets tough, the tough get going. And I was gone.

12

It Ain't Easy Being Green

IF YOU ARE GOING TO WIN ANY BATTLE, YOU HAVE TO
DO ONE THING. YOU HAVE TO MAKE THE MIND RUN
THE BODY. NEVER LET THE BODY TELL THE MIND WHAT
TO DO.

—*General George Patton*

I didn't want to go home. I didn't. Go home, that is.

Wild as I was, I never ran away from home as a child. Well, maybe once—I was probably six or so, and in a little kid tantrum, I packed up some saltine crackers and peanut butter in a bandana, and made it maybe four blocks before the lure of the familiar and the fearsome enormity of the big, bad world had me beating a hasty retreat through the kitchen door, where my mom welcomed me back. My life on the run lasted ten minutes, tops.

The desk staff at the Middletown Marriott Courtyard never questioned why I kept extending my stay every few days, even though my registered address was less than ten miles away. It's bloody amazing how much you can get away with if you've got a credit card and good grooming. They simply smiled at me and swiped my card.

Even though I was on the run and coming unglued, I tried to make an orderly day for myself. Every morning I woke in the hotel's brand-new, scratchy poly-blend bedding. After my complimentary breakfast of yogurt and dry cereal, eaten while avoiding eye contact with the other guests, I made myself hot tea in a Styrofoam cup and sat in the big cushy swivel chairs in the business center, looking for sublets on Craigslist. My mood was almost buoyant—being alone made me more cheerful than I'd been in months. In the afternoons, I visited the hotel's bright and empty fitness room and jogged on the treadmill while watching *Oprah*. It seemed critically important to not be home.

I still drove to Warwick to meet Mike at Patti's office for therapy. The second I sank into her saggy couch, I started to feel small and panicky again. One day, I simply started sobbing. "I want to be alone. I want to be alone. I want to be alone."

Mike wrung his hands while Patti sat looking at me with a calm expression on her face.

"I can't do this anymore," I panted. "I am trying and it's not working and I can't do it."

Mike turned to me. "What are you saying?"

"I don't want to be married anymore. I can't do it."

Once that bomb was dropped, the rest of the hour had

to be dedicated to controlling the damage. Patti spent a lot of time assuring Mike that this had nothing to do with him, but at no point did she say to me, "I think you should reconsider." Mike followed me to the parking lot, using any line of reasoning he could think of to keep me from going. I stood next to the car, keys in hand, ready to open the door. A light rain began to fall. I left my poor husband standing in a parking lot wondering what the hell had just happened. We had come to couples therapy to strengthen our marriage, and without warning, I'd announced that I wanted to end it.

My overly air-conditioned hotel room felt like a tomb. For some reason, I'd brought my Gucci purse with me when I left West Point. I think I'd convinced myself that I might drop down to the city to take some meetings with magazine editors so I could scare up enough freelance work to get me through any troubled times ahead, and the purse completed my business look.

Stylish and severe, the purse resembled a small brief-case. It was made of a low-sheen black leather that I loved. I had bought it at deep discount in a fit of optimism when I was twenty-seven and certain that astonishing professional success was just around the corner. Eager to make a good impression that might mask my deadline-induced paralysis, I brought the purse with me to every editorial meeting I had, the inside lining covered with the adhesive-backed visitor nametags of major media outlets like stickers on a guitar case or steamer trunk. This would be the first of many designer purses to come, I thought, furnished by funds from my own hard work, lined up on my closet shelf in their chic flannel sleeper bags.

It wasn't. When I started freelancing, my writer's block was so bad, I could barely produce. My first assignment for *Esquire* was to pay $10,000, but I totally choked, despite multiple deadline extensions. I knew why I had taken the bag with me when I left West Point. It represented everything my life had become—a cheaply acquired front of achievement with nothing inside and no place to go.

Instead of phoning editors, I sat alone in the room of this gleaming, efficient commuter motel—a woman with a Gucci purse and a death wish.

Part of me, the hopeful heart of me that married Mike, had died. I closed the curtains and balled up on the bed, my knees under my chin, rocking back and forth with my eyes squeezed shut. I heard several sets of footsteps outside in the hallway. "Did you see it?" The voice was excited. "Come look at it. The rainbow!"

I grabbed my plastic key card and walked out into the hotel parking lot. Spread across the sky over the dark green foothills was the most vivid, majestic double rainbow I'd ever seen. I thought of the mass card in my laptop case and whispered to myself, "Dad." Auguries and omens seemed like wishful thinking to me before, but now that I was cranked open and coming apart at the seams, anything seemed possible, including my deceased father sending

me a sign that he knew I was suffering and that he wanted
me to know that things would be okay.

I turned around and who should be taking in this glorious sight but the commandant of the Royal Canadian
Military College. Jesus Christ, what was that guy doing
here? The urge to run seized me. I was afraid he'd see the
insanity radiating from me like an aura, and know right
away who I was: crazy Army wife on the lam. He didn't
recognize me. "Lovely, isn't it?" I said, and slipped past
him.

The following week, I found an apartment that looked
good. It was way out of my budget, but I wanted to move
fast. In *Eat, Pray, Love*, Elizabeth Gilbert describes working her way back from depression and the depths of marital despair by traveling alone to Italy, India, and Indonesia.
In that same spirit, I took off for the decidedly less glamorous locale of Hoboken, New Jersey. I couldn't save my
marriage and save my own life at the same time. I needed
to howl in the dark for a while.

When I showed up in Hoboken, Deb dragged me to dinner. "I didn't want to say anything," she confessed over pad
thai, "but when I visited you up at West Point, you looked
so deflated." Then she dragged me to yoga. Our tattooed
instructor came around during the relaxation portion of
the class to adjust every student, and as he rubbed my
temples, tears streamed from my eyes and gathered in the
cups of my ears. Not even the esoteric realm could offer

an escape from my military life; yoga class had three different warrior poses.

I went downstairs one hot afternoon in June and found a fat legal envelope in the mail. I sat down at the desk and unfolded the papers: under the seal of the state of Pennsylvania, in big black letters, was printed, "Petition to File for Divorce." A yellow Post-it note was stuck on the lower right-hand side: "I'm sorry. I love you. I didn't want things to end up this way. Mike." Because soldiers move so often, the government allows them to choose their state of residence; Mike had been a Pennsylvania state resident since he'd moved there for grad school. My estranged husband was living in New York, I was squatting in New Jersey, and our divorce papers were drawn up in Pennsylvania. Eighteen months ago, we'd gotten married in a Maryland courthouse, and now our marriage was breaking apart across three different states. Welcome to divorce, Army style.

I drifted into the bedroom, numb and cold from shock. I was on the verge of divorce—a milestone so horrible yet so typical. I thought about statistics, how 50 percent of marriages fail. So 50 percent of adults would know this blowout, this anguish. I sat there pulling loose threads out of the bedspread for three hours. The arithmetic of heartache was purely staggering.

When you're separated, the price of freedom is not eternal vigilance. The price of freedom is about two grand a week, once you factor in the apartment sublet, gas, tolls, groceries, yoga classes, and great gobs of therapy. Since I couldn't concentrate well enough to work very much, I was surviving on credit card cash advances and prayer. This nervous breakdown brought to you by Visa.

By any external indicator, I wasn't a failure—somewhere in the midst of this chaos, I'd even found a publisher for the novel I'd slaved over while Mike was deployed—but I couldn't stop my brain's nonstop editorial commentary: Failure, failure, failure. Loser. Idiot. Stupid whore. If I didn't know any better, I'd have guessed that my own brain was trying to kill me, that it had decided that destroying me was its evil brain duty, and therefore must keep hectoring and degrading and abusing until I finally hurled myself over a cliff.

I drove two hours each way to Warwick to keep up my appointments with Casey. She rested her pedicured feet on a hassock during our sessions. "The point isn't to avoid the pain in life," she told me. "Life is full of pain."

By now I was looking at her like, *Oh, ya think?*

"What you have to do is to find a way to soothe yourself."

Well, no shit! I wanted to yell. A part of me stood apart from the proceedings and I said to myself, *I'm paying $150 an hour for* this?

I didn't need someone to point out what I needed to do. I needed someone to help me do it. Talk talk talk talk. I was so bloody sick of my days being nothing but an endless loop of misery and talk. I was sick of talking to Casey, who wasn't helping, and I was sick of talking to my husband who was trying to make me feel better but only made me feel worse.

When you're stressed and pulled apart, people say, "Get help," as if doing so was a simple, one-step directive, like "Buy a gallon of milk," or "Touch your toes." Getting help is easy. Getting *good* help is like punching your way out from the center of a rubber ball.

I stopped going to see Casey.

The weeks went speeding along. I'd been gone since April and now it was mid-July. Panic set in—I was losing precious time to this crisis and life was passing me by. Then I remembered something Casey had said during one of our sessions: "You have plenty of time to do whatever you want with your life," she said. "At this point, the only thing out of your reach is professional gymnastics." That, I had to admit, was worth $150 an hour to hear.

The divorce papers sat folded up and unsigned on the living room table for weeks. I couldn't even look at them. Soon they were buried under magazines and junk mail. Mike and I barely talked on the phone because every time we did, he'd start giving me the Army officer pep talk, and I'd start to cry, feeling like a kid at the feet of a stern parent. But I begged him to wait for me, told him I didn't want to go through with a divorce, that I didn't know what I was thinking when I said I wanted us to split. I sounded insane and I knew it, but I also knew that I meant it: I did not want to lose my marriage.

* * *

I've never been a "drugs are Jesus" type of person, but I thought maybe some antidepressants would help. I couldn't afford to pay out of pocket for a psychiatrist or for antidepressants, so I made an appointment at Keller Army Hospital at West Point. The receptionist referred me to family medicine. Internal medicine would've been better. The family medicine waiting room was full of little kids with runny noses and parents in their Class Bs. I felt like an island of broken in a sea of all these intact families. When the nurse called my name, I bolted up and followed her. I couldn't get out of that waiting room fast enough.

The nurse practitioner I saw, Colonel B., snapped her nicotine gum and nodded sympathetically when I talked about the abuse I was dealing with in therapy. She considered my litany of woes—sleeplessness, depression, anxiety, feelings of dread and dissociation—and prescribed the lowest possible dose of Zoloft. Sertaline, a.k.a. Zoloft, is widely regarded as the first go-to drug for treating the emotional symptoms of post-traumatic stress disorder. It seemed to be a sensible choice. She didn't demand that I plead my case—she understood that the symptoms I described aligned with a PTSD diagnosis, and I wasn't trying to use it to get out of a criminal conviction, for gosh sakes. I wondered if Army medical personnel were trained to be supportive and nonjudgmental, knowing how incredibly difficult it is to get soldiers to ask for help with mental health issues.

Colonel B. entered the script into the clinic computer. "You'll be fine," she said in her ex-smoker raspy voice. "I had a woman in here last month whose husband left her after thirty years. I got her on Prozac and now she's doing great."

In the pharmacy waiting area, I pushed the button on the ticket machine so I could get on line for my meds. The machine spit out my ticket and I sat staring blankly at the Food Network. My first step into the military psychopharmacological complex.

With my brown bottle in hand, I popped my starter pill and began the drive back to Hoboken. Within an hour, my mind was positively racing. Jibber-jabber, jibber-jabber, jibber-jabber. I could feel the speedy chemical wash rinsing over my brain. I pulled into the food court on the Garden State Parkway and bolted down two double cheeseburgers and king-size fries in the front seat of the car. Jibber-jabber, gobble-gobble. I felt no real taste for food, yet I was ravenously hungry, this hyperalert, incoherent vessel of need with no direction, just insatiable drive.

I couldn't sleep worth a damn. At about five o'clock in the morning, I looked around the apartment: What whirlwind tore through this place? Clothes, dishes, and papers everywhere. This was not a ramp-up period. Since I'd tried Wellbutrin a couple of years prior, I knew from ramp-up periods and this was not that. This was borderline mania, a full-on blast into hyperspace from a pharmaceutical launchpad, and this wasn't going to cut it.

I called Keller the second they opened that morning and

told them I was coming back. I turned off of Route 80 and merged onto the Garden State. I didn't yet have an EZ-Pass to speed me through the highway toll plazas. I dropped thirty-five cents into the hand of the toll taker, who turned out to be a mentally challenged young man. The mania must have screwed up my face because he said, "Don't worry, I don't bite." Somewhere in that welter of polluted brain, I felt terrible. But I could only mutter something that I hoped was a "sorry," mash my foot to the gas pedal, and speed away.

Dr. B. said my reaction sounded unusual but she'd be happy to prescribe another medication. No way, I told her. No more pills.

Since our every phone call ended with me dissolving into guilty tears, Mike and I switched to e-mail, conducting a cautiously navigated cybermarriage. Since I left, he'd gotten "custody" of Patti in our separation, and I was glad. He liked her and since he did indeed seem bound by some psychological quirk to play savior, maybe she could help him relax that urge. The call to save seemed to have an almost irresistible pull for him; like his cleanliness, it was another character trait of questionable origin—was that the Army training or just him? He sent me e-mail after e-mail suggesting possible treatments: support groups, medication, different types of therapy. He'd researched post-traumatic stress disorder and found a technique for treating it that was used successfully on thousands of traumatized people, including soldiers and survivors of sexual abuse: EMDR. EMDR (Eye Movement Desensitization and Reprocessing), is a form of psychotherapy that combines elements from both traditional and cutting-edge psychology (including the latest research from brain science) with the unique use of alternating left-right brain stimulation such as eye movements to "de-fuse" traumatic memories and their subsequent effects on your behavior. At first, it sounded like some kind of goofball New Age quackery, like sitting under a glass pyramid to channel healing energy from "The Universe." I looked into it. I discovered that the American Psychological Association, the International Society for Traumatic Stress Studies, and the U.S. Department of Veterans Affairs and the Department of Defense considered EMDR a legitimate and highly effective trauma treatment.

I checked out the EMDR International Association Web site to see if there were any qualified practitioners nearby. There was a woman twenty minutes away from me in Montclair. Her name was Victoria Britt.

A few days later, I drove over to Victoria's office. She met me at the door. A tall brunette with a long, somber face, she looked like a beatnik Anne Bancroft. Her dark eyes were ringed with thick black liner, and peeking out from her sensible flat sandals were plum-polished toenails. Her voice was deep and steady. I liked her instantly.

Seeing a new therapist meant I was stuck with the therapeutic formality of unpacking the childhood baggage. Oh, how I hate unpacking my childhood. There are few things I like less. During the first few sessions, I just talked, because I had to fill Victoria in on my background so we could figure out how I'd gotten to where I was today.

As an adult, I scarcely talked about the weirdness in my childhood because I didn't want to be pitied. To me, pity is just condescension in its Sunday best, and I didn't want the horrible parts of my early life to be interpreted as the driving force behind every life decision and creative product: Child Abuse—the relationship motivator! Child Abuse—the artistic subtext! Child Abuse—the musical! I couldn't deny that it had happened, I simply wished to continue my life as if it hadn't.

"When I was a kid, I never told anyone what happened," I said to Victoria in session. "I don't know why."

She raised an eyebrow. "Oh, you were telling people, all right." I know shrinks are supposed to keep a neutral face, but I was gratified to see that she was clearly disgusted on my behalf.

Deep down, I think I was reluctant to talk about the abuse—as a child or as an adult—because I was afraid that people would think it wasn't really all that bad, and that I shouldn't complain. Or, even worse, I was afraid that people wouldn't believe me.

When I said this to Victoria, she said decisively, "I believe you."

* * *

My EMDR sessions started with Victoria asking me to identify a painful memory and then to locate a corresponding unpleasant sensation in my body. I had a constant, clutching knot in my upper chest, and sometimes a choking sensation at the base of my throat, or a stomachache. Once I identified these things, she'd hand me a pair of headphones and a pair of small vibrating disks for my hands. The disks were connected to a small box with dials on it that controlled the speed and intensity of the vibrations. She'd start playing a CD with a rhythmic pinging that alternated from my left to right ear. Left *ping*, right *ping*, left, right, left, right.

After about a minute she would stop the machine and ask what I was experiencing. The revelations were profoundly stark. I'd say things like, "You know what pisses me off? I never had a fucking chance as a kid," or "Grown-ups are idiots. Why are some people even allowed to care for kids if all they do is make it worse?" I rarely cried or broke down. It felt more like I had pulled the curtain on what had really been making me so anxious, mistrustful, and prone to depression all these years. After several weeks, I was able to admit, "I believe I am responsible for the abuse. It was my fault." "I didn't deserve protection." "I have to give people what they want in order to survive." "I really thought this guy was going to kill me." I said these things as plainly as "The sky is blue," or "I need oxygen to survive"—they were my basic, core-warping destructive beliefs.

The sessions themselves felt pretty neutral for me emotionally, but in the twenty-four to thirty-six hours afterward came the big thaw, when the panic I had been feeling subsided and, in its absence, I was left in a pit of despair. This was what I'd been hiding all along under the buzzing and bitching and raging—pitch-black hopelessness and grief. It was as if someone had taken a seam-ripper to my soul and popped every stitch that had been keeping me together my entire life. The emotional agony was so great, I could not move. I'd sit cross-legged on the floor of my bedroom, staring at the carpet.

I told Victoria, "I can't take that much pain. It's great that the work is opening me up, but we've got to close everything again before I walk out of here."

At the end of every EMDR session, we would do breathing exercises and acupressure work to quiet my nervous system and put me on a more even keel. Since I had such a strong post-session reaction to the therapy, we stopped the EMDR portion much sooner and extended the breathing/acupressure part. Letting me get too low and then sending me home alone was too dangerous.

After the third or fourth month of EMDR, I started to feel more relaxed and less prone to panic. I'd managed to make more progress in a handful of EMDR treatments than in all my previous talk-therapy sessions combined. I had the distinct visual image of my brain rewiring itself, so the triggers no longer set off my panic button. The overwhelming feeling was of profound relief, like I'd been swimming against a current for most of my life and I could finally see a shoreline.

* * *

During one session, I asked Victoria, "What are the odds of Mike and I both being diagnosed as having post-traumatic stress disorder?"

"Unfortunately," she said, "rather high." About five million people in the U.S. have PTSD (roughly 3.5 percent of the population), and among war veterans, the estimates range from thirty to as high as ninety percent. Any mental health practitioner with military clients is on the lookout for signs of the disorder—Mike's flashback being a dead giveaway—as is a trauma expert like Victoria who is used to treating clients with abuse and/or neglect in their background.

She explained further: "Experts in the field are trying to establish a distinction between shock-based trauma, like combat or rape or a mugging or car accident, and developmental trauma, like a perilous childhood or a sexually or physically abusive relationship." The distinction was useful to me—it helped me see how our reactions could be quite different, as well as our recovery time. "But what both types have in common is that the person doesn't feel safe in the world. That's the first thing I look for. A person saying they don't feel safe, so they find they're bouncing between an amped-up high and a dissociated low."

The timing of this breakdown mystified me. Shouldn't my marriage have staved off the stress? A husband was supposed to represent a haven. I pondered this aloud in

Victoria's office. "I never had this problem with anyone I was with before."

"Well," she said, "you didn't marry any of them."

Point taken. I had been under lot of stress—my father had recently died, and within a single year, I had moved twice, sat home alone while my husband was at war, and entered a totally alien community, but it was becoming a wife, being with someone who was actually supposed to take care of me, that was the biggest trigger. I had put my life in Mike's hands, and that terrified me. I could not trust that I wouldn't be hurt, abandoned, manipulated, exploited, or just plain screwed. My marriage wasn't a loving refuge, but a threat. And another show in which I had to perform just right if I wanted to survive.

It occurred to me that stripping, for me, and the whole adventure of those years may have been the ultimate game of Survivor: Trauma Edition. Already dissociated and cynical about humanity, I undertook stripping as the female equivalent of a kind of Special Forces training—the physical discipline, the focus on *en pointe* performance, the thrill-seeking, the playing with fire and going into dark or taboo places most "civilians" don't go. The exaggerated gender typing, the special outfits or uniforms that mark, again, a defined break from civilian life, the pervasive sense of danger or limit crossing.

"Stripping—" says Elisabeth Eaves in her memoir, *Bare*, "in competition with acting and espionage—is the ultimate job for someone whose instinct is to present different facades of who she might be. There is nothing more illusory than a woman pretending to be a sexual fantasy for money." Granted, I first started in the sex industry for practical purposes—I needed money. But once my financial obligations were met, stripping became another way to hide. Sex work fortified me financially, but my cynicism only deepened, proving that, paradoxically, self-preservation and self-destruction can have an identical job description.

I was so used to doing my *who-do-you-want-me-to-be?* dancing bear routine, I didn't know how to be real without feeling like I was inviting trouble—no tips, no applause, no safe cover, no future. By marrying Mike, I saw myself in a new role—as half of a performance art duo, Lieutenant Colonel and Mrs. Duty First, bound by toxic perfectionism. "The Army comes first," I was told from the start, and in the interest of showing my own commitment to spousal selfless service, I had almost wiped myself out of the picture entirely.

My marriage wasn't just a trigger because I had to trust my husband. Somehow, the peacefulness of married life had set everything off screaming. In the chaotic environments that marked my youth and early adulthood, I felt alive. Alert. Capable and in control, at times in danger but somehow above the danger, too. When I was a teenager walking down isolated city streets late at night by myself, or a twenty-year-old in the sleaziest Times Square peep show, or when I drove around the country researching strip clubs all alone at twenty-nine, I felt at ease. If a situation got dicey, I was poised to react—I'd start seeing everything in slow motion, ready to take on anyone who might mess with me. The attraction to risk was almost addictive, and I felt oddly at harmony with my sketchy surroundings, like the outside and inside matched. But once I was married, and every night I was nestled into the safety of my own bed, in my own home, with my own family, that's when the shit hit the fan. I looked at the green lawns and weekend barbecues and the cheerful lives of order on display and realized that everything was being drowned out by the jet-engine scream inside my head, *Get me the bloody living hell out of here!* I started swinging out at everything, even my own husband. I wasn't just a wreck—I was a wrecking ball.

I had never considered my memories of being shaken or yelled at to be "flashbacks" because they were perfectly accessible in my memory bank. They didn't show up in nightmares that woke me up screaming, and they didn't pop up during stressful situations, like a Hollywood movie montage. They sat there like grim pages in a childhood scrapbook that held a fair share of happy memories, too, like ballet class, and swinging on the swings with my sisters, finding Easter eggs, and starring in the third-grade class play. There was no emotional charge. The image of the man's face as he held me by the upper arms and shook me like a rag doll was flat as a photograph. I could feel my head flop back and forth and the stiffness in my neck as I tried to hold still, but no fear, no alarm. But one day, as I was putting away some clean clothes, I had a twisted kind of flashback: I didn't see his face as he shook me; I saw mine. My bottled-up terror face as he squeezed my arms to my sides. I didn't cry, I didn't scream. I had the face of the guilty: If I weren't a bad kid, this wouldn't be happening. I remembered the terror that traveled down my limbs to my toes as he got right in my face and said, plainly, "If you do that again, I'll kill you." Imagining how frightened I must have looked opened a deep well of fear and pain. I dropped to my knees in my laundry pile.

This vision opened up a floodgate of sensory memories that I took to Victoria: The damp, musty smell of the basement rec room where he'd trap me next to him in the big recliner with the scratchy upholstery. The terrible stomachaches I got over the course of the year that my mother took me to the sitter's house. And the tingling heat in my face as I clung to my mother's leg when she dropped me off, begging her not to leave.

"Oh, she just doesn't like to be away from Mommy is all," I remembered the old man saying as his wife took my hand and led me inside. Her skin felt papery and warm. "She'll be fine."

I looked at my nursery school photos from age three and four. At three, I was a slyly smiling imp in a black and white checked smock, with a twinkle in my eye and an open, curious expression. At four, my face was pale and vacant. I looked exhausted, my hair matted against my head because I'd started avoiding the brush. The difference that a year made was startling. I had only been to this sitter's house maybe a dozen times, but I had the face of a child who'd been through hell and back. At some point, I must've complained convincingly enough to my mother to not bring me there, because she started asking the teenage girl who had moved in around the block to come to our house to watch me instead.

It doesn't take much to traumatize a child—all you have to do is shake her and say, "I'll kill you." Make her think that what you're doing to her is her fault: You're a bad person. You deserve it. And if anyone else knew what awful things you had done, they'd agree. Maybe *they'd* punish you, too.

When I hear of some incident of horrific abuse of children, I'm disgusted but never surprised. I've known all along that grown-ups do all kinds of terrible things to kids. It's everywhere. And abusiveness is not unique to men. Women abuse and boys get abused, too. There's plenty to go around. It's actually a subset of my thoughts, playing "Spot the Abuser." *Oh, that celebrated community leader over there? I bet he beats the crap out of his kids. That officer who went on a solo tour in Korea for a year? I'm sure he was out in the juice bars with a different underage hooker every weekend.* One of the primary symptoms of PTSD? Hypervigilance. Though I didn't identify it as such, I was seeing perpetrators everywhere.

Even though my recovery had become my life, I didn't talk about it much. I didn't tell my family anything more than that Mike and I were having some troubles, so I'd moved out, and everyone else I knew I kept strictly on a need-to-know basis. I'd go to Brooklyn to visit Molly and we'd lounge around her apartment, treat ourselves to nine-dollar sandwiches from the charcuterie across the street, and take her daughter for walks in her stroller. When we were together, I didn't have to be this big bag of crazy. I could get away from it for a while.

Privacy was key. My "thing" is being seen as capable, so I didn't want to share the news that I was having a breakdown. Even hearing the diagnosis "post-traumatic stress disorder" float my way made me recoil: I'm sorry, are you implying that I don't have my crap together? *I* don't have a problem. The people who shoot up schools with AK-47s have a problem. This PTSD business? Please. It's not like I dive under a table when a helicopter flies overhead. Those among us who are almost vain about their functionality—especially in stressful situations, which we somehow covet as if to prove ourselves—are not exactly easy to help. (In this regard, I can see why treating tough-as-nails soldiers presents a particular challenge for mental health professionals.)

People dearly want to help, oh, they do, proffering in good faith solutions that verge on silly. "Have you tried affirmations?" they ask. "Have you read the Abraham books?" I wanted to get better; that is, I wished to stop being suicidal. But to me, getting better did not mean devolving into some cloud-chasing bliss ninny. Even some of the suggestions that Victoria offered seemed goofy, like when we were doing EMDR, I was supposed to replace my negative emotions and memories by going to a "happy place" in my mind, perhaps, she suggested, someplace in nature. My "happy place" has never been in nature. Nature is full of ticks, mosquitoes, and mud puddles. I'm no princess, still, my happy place will always have indoor plumbing.

But I drummed up a happy place nonetheless: the yoga class that I went to in Hoboken because the instructor, Jeff, used Single Gun Theory as background music when he taught and he played bass in a band. I was like, "OK, I can trust this guy to bring a sense of serenity to my life because he has a giant scorpion tattoo, plus, he *is* a Scorpio and has occasionally thrown a Scorpionic bitchy-fit in class." I could let my guard down there because of the One of Us factor. Jeff's teaching style was spiritual but it wasn't mellow. Mellow to me is toxic. Mellow to me implies someone whose life is an easy slope. Mellow to me means someone has taken his eyes off the road. I do not trust the mellow.

I had to get serious about self-care, making sure I slept enough and ate properly—a box of Chips Ahoy! for dinner didn't count. I dabbed on unguents and downed herbal tinctures. Cut me and I bled Rescue Remedy.

The reason I was wound so tight, and thus, so mellow-averse, is because I knew that control is an illusion and safety is merely mutually agreed-upon fiction. Truth is, as we PTSDers have learned the hard way, life is full of fucked-up shit, and if you're not braced and on the lookout for fucked-up shit, that's precisely when another big Acme safe full of fucked-up shit will fall from the sky and crush you like the Wile E. Coyote under its Life Is Random weight.

"What would your life look like if you didn't feel you had to perform to survive?" Victoria asked me. An interesting question, considering I was already living my worst-case scenario: broke, alone, debt spiraling upward, mentally fried, and almost helpless. I barely recognized myself, and what few bits I could identify, I hated.

My original Hoboken sublet expired, so I rented a small studio of my own, a disaster pit that smelled like mildewed carpet and was in the front of the building on the first floor, so whenever someone entered or exited the building, the slamming of the front door shook my table lamp so hard the shade tilted. In the hallway, I met a neighbor who lived upstairs, an Australian woman who was pushing her young daughter in a stroller as she waited for her husband. She said, helpfully, "You should meet your neighbor across the hall. She's also a single girl!"

The studio was too small to fit my old full-size bed, so I borrowed an old camping cot from Mike. The cot was pretty comfortable, but the top right corner had a small tear. One night I turned over in my sleep and was awakened by a loud *rrrrrrrrrip* as the torn fabric pulled away from the sides and I sank to the floor, caged by the cot's aluminum frame. In my rudely awakened stupor I thought, *You know, I think this might just be my lowest low.* How much lower could I go? I was already on the freaking floor.

The next week, I sucked up the exorbitant rental agency fee, terminated my lease, and rented a minuscule but clean and quiet one-bedroom on the corner of Second and Adams streets. I called a moving company to meet me at West Point. If I was going to build "my" life, I needed my things, and Mike and I had to be materially divested.

The yards around West Point were decorated for fall—mums, football flags, scarecrows made of cornhusks. As a favor to me, Mike had started boxing up my things. I hadn't been in our quarters for months, and when I opened the door, the eerie sight of the exposed floor space around towers of moving boxes gave me a hollow feeling in my chest. The last time these quarters looked like this was two years ago, when we had just moved in, excited about starting our life as a military couple, finally together after being separated by the war.

I wondered how much our neighbors at West Point knew. Who was I kidding? They must have known everything. We could tell each other's work schedules by the number of cars in our driveways, could identify any major purchases by the big boxes pushed to the curb on trash day, and knew someone had declared a kitchen strike when the Chinese delivery guy pulled up for the fourth time that week. At our quarters, there was one car in the drive where there used to be two, and Mike was no longer wearing a wedding band. In the fishbowl, the slightest change can broadcast big news.

The movers sucked. Two of the men didn't bring photo identification with them, and the guards wouldn't let them onto post, so we had to reschedule for the following day. The lead guy kept asking why I was moving: "Military move, huh? With your husband? Is your husband an admiral?" I finally told him, my eyes leaking tears, that I was moving out alone (and also, that the Army doesn't have admirals).

I decorated the new apartment in soothing earth tones and painted a wall of shelves gold, filling it with figurines from different religions to make an altar—I doubted the existence of God, but I paid homage just in case. There may be no atheists in foxholes, but there was an agnostic in Jersey. I did yoga. I meditated. I went to a goth club and danced to Lords of the New Church till 5 a.m., like I was in the movies, feeling up and feeling groovy. During the revision stage of my novel, I renamed the biggest jackhole character after a critic who had taken a high-and-mighty hatchet to my earlier book, proving handily that while I may be thirty-something in my bones, it's always sixth grade in my heart.

I spent hour upon late night hour listening to the music of my teenage years. I wasn't reminiscing about lost innocence or happiness. I was pretty damn miserable back then, too. But teenage misery is so much easier to bear—you always expect to grow out of it. You don't yet know that it's not "just a phase." I plowed through boxes of old cassettes. *Floodland*, by Sisters of Mercy. Peter Murphy's *Deep*. Tears for Fears' *The Hurting*, which I realized, lo these many years and tubes of black eyeliner later, was a disc-long lament about child abuse. I steeped myself in the pain of this music. Sad, sadder, saddest. Mad, madder, maddest.

Oddly, this wounded place was a sentimental retreat. Back to who I once was. I wasn't going to revert to my blond and beautiful toddler "inner child." That little girl was history, snuffed before she knew what hit her. So I settled on my teenage years, the next best, most hopeful, innocence-adjacent time in my life. I was punk as fuck, and I felt like I could change the world, rather than bow down to it. Defiance was at the core of my identity, as was pain: the expectation of pain; the disappointment of pain; and finally, the artistic rendering of pain as a salve. I had made a friend of pain then, and that soundtrack was my sidekick now. My marital separation had become Exile in Emo-ville.

My survival depended upon living in the moment. When I felt suicidal and afraid I might do something to harm myself, I told my brain, "Well, let me take a nap first." I'd wake up, still miserable, but still alive. If I thought even ten minutes ahead, I'd freeze. I'd force myself to focus: What's good *right now*? Even if it was just one thing. My reliable car. The sun on the sidewalk. The arc of blue lights over the Virgin Mary in the courtyard next door. Ginger chicken with green beans and brown rice, eight bucks a dish at Precious on Washington Street. When you're young and physically healthy, with gas in your car and a novel on the way, it seems ridiculous to admit that the only thing you could think of to look forward to was a few chunks of white meat chicken with shaved ginger, but I was desperate.

In all this, the war had slipped below the fold in my life's big news, bumped by the headline *Rookie Military Wife Has Meltdown*. But I still remember the moment on October 25, 2005, when I was walking through downtown Manhattan with Deb. We'd been at Janovich on Broadway, trying to choose between brown or bronze velvet curtains for her living room, when we came out of the store and saw on the newsstand the covers of *The Post* and *The Daily News*: U.S. casualties had reached two thousand.

The symptoms of PTSD were coming under control, the trigger-strings being cut, one by one. I wasn't flying toward the polar extremes of pissed off or checked out. The ghosts of my past no longer called the shots, and I was relieved to find that fixing the problem took less energy than fighting to keep it all in.

But the depression refused to budge. Socked with overwhelming guilt for leaving my husband, I felt like some spoiled brat peeling off to "find herself" in an early midlife-crisis indulgence. Intellectually, I knew I needed to be alone to recover, but I also knew that Mike was suffering in ways he was unwilling to express. Until I could get my head and my heart into agreement, I couldn't be with him, and it tore me up inside.

Surely, I thought, I was made of tougher stuff than this. My paternal grandmother, widowed at a young age, raised her six children on a modest schoolteacher's salary. My maternal grandmother, who had my mother at seventeen, divorced her drinking husband and became a successful accountant in an era when it was rare for a woman to do either. And my own mother, who managed to get two master's degrees on either side of bringing up five kids, was now stoically grieving the loss of her lifelong mate. I'd tell myself to snap out of it and move on. I'm of strong-willed stock. What's the hold up?

I was convinced that I was squandering some legacy of female resilience. But the reality is, telling a depressed person to "snap out of it" is like parking someone in front of a stove with an extinguished pilot light and saying, "Start making pancakes, bitch." It's not laziness. There's no will because there's no way.

I was fully, voluptuously miserable, and though I wouldn't admit it to anyone, I still dreamed of suicide. I guarded this secret, sweet as stolen candy. I could kill myself at any time. The only thing in my life that seemed entirely within my control was the ability to end it.

13

BOHICA

BOHICA: Military acronym—Bend Over, Here It Comes Again

Former *Tonight Show* host Johnny Carson built his comedic reputation on "How [blank] was it?" stories. He'd bait the audience with an opener: "I went to a party that was so boring . . ." and the audience would gleefully shout back, "How boring was it?!" Then Johnny would bring it in for the kill. How depressed was I? I was so depressed that I turned down Mike's invitation to come to West Point for a formal dinner at Quarters 100, the superintendent's house, held in honor of Sandra Day O'Connor. Justice O'Connor was only the second woman to receive the Association of Graduates Thayer Award, which is given to an American whose service and accomplishments in the national interest exemplified personal devotion to the ideals expressed in the West Point motto, "Duty, Honor, Country." The award ceremony includes a full cadet parade review and the recipient "troops the line," performing a ceremonial inspection of the Corps. Justice O'Connor's escort for the ceremony, the class of 2005 cadet first captain, was only the third female cadet first captain in the Academy's two-hundred-plus years. Seeing Justice O'Connor rolling along the Plain in a Humvee with a female cadet right beside her was the ultimate Chicks Rule moment, and I was too messed up to make it. Which isn't really a funny, Carson-like story, but it paints a clear picture of how sorry things really were.

Sorry had become the operative word for my life, my constant refrain. I'm sorry. Sorry sorry sorry. I am so sorry. I'm sorry. I just can't. Sorry.

I had chosen Hoboken because it was close enough to Mike, close to my dearest friends and my favorite city, but also because there wasn't a ghost of a chance that I'd run into anyone I knew from the Army. The best thing about my little apartment was that I could shut the door and feel the world go away. The fishbowl effect was replaced by good old reliable urban anonymity. I had privacy. I could get as crazy as I needed—or wanted—to. No one was watching.

Every other week or so, I'd push a grocery cart down the aisles at the Hoboken ShopRite. I bought new dishes and cookware in the home goods section. Most pathetic was a tiny copper-bottomed Revere Ware pot. I'd cook all my meals in it; it was just big enough to heat up a single can of soup, a box of macaroni and cheese, or a small paper carton of leftovers. If something didn't fit in that pot, or in the apartment's minuscule microwave, I didn't want it. How my life had changed since I'd married—and my perception of what it meant to hurt. Rolling through a store feeling exposed and alone because your husband is deployed is painful, but it doesn't come close to the agony of shopping when your marriage is hanging by a bloody thread. When a woman is alone because her husband is at war, she's Penelope pining for Odysseus, prepared to wait an eternity for her beloved's return. When a woman is alone because she and her husband are separated, she's just some anonymous schmo wondering if she should sign the divorce papers from the law offices of Loser, Dumb-Dumb, and Wank. It's the difference between epic longing and epic failure. There's no heroism to it, and certainly no romance. Shopping becomes soup for one, milk for one, personal failing of colossal proportion for one. One who used to be the optimistic half of a whole.

For Mike, the consequences of our separation exceeded regular old heartache. His domestic situation was upended as well. The Army doesn't really care why your wife moved out—if you're living alone in family-designated quarters, you have to vacate them. Rules are rules. I was losing my mind, and now my husband was losing his home. The guilt of leaving was damning enough; now I'd made my husband homeless. This started happening right as Mike was up for reassignment, and if he received orders to move to another post, he would pack up and be gone. If he had to move, I would not go with him. Divorce would be inevitable. Our marriage would be lost to the martial rhythm of the military. Instead, Mike's boss was deployed, and the superintendent asked Mike to take his place. Mike could move up in the world without moving out of my life. By some miracle, God (and the Army) held us in place.

Mike did what he should have done—he looked for a house off post. But the idea of him buying a house without me upset me tremendously. But then again, what didn't? "You and I had a dream of owning a home together," he said. "Even if you're gone, I still need to get as close to that dream as possible." Then, he did something that really pushed me to my limit—he got a dog. Our dream dog, a yellow Labrador. A man who worked on post had listed the dog, a four-year-old male, on the West Point bulletin board, because he was divorcing and could no longer give the dog the attention he needed. Mike sent me a photo of the most gorgeous, lunk-headed Labrador ever born. A massive, web-footed beast, he weighed a hundred pounds. This wasn't a Labrador, but some hybrid strain of cuteness and gigantism—a Labrasaurus. The sight of the dog romping in the yard of the home I used to live in made me cry. My husband was living our ideal life without me, which, in my twisted mind, translated to: He's moving on and leaving me behind. I took this news to Victoria, bubbling snot and tears exploding off my face. "It doesn't matter what you do. It doesn't matter how hard you try to get better. It doesn't matter. You're still *fucked*."

Victoria put down her notepad and said, "I think you should reconsider medication."

Attempt to obtain proper medication, Take 2. This time, I sought help, once again courtesy of Uncle Sugar, but not from a general practitioner at Keller Army Hospital. I went instead to West Point's mental health clinic, where I could speak to someone more experienced. I didn't have the cover of "just going to the hospital" this time. It was hard to step over the threshold of self-consciousness and walk into that clinic. Here I was, a mature woman married to an officer who was just made an Academy directorate head, and I'd placed my mental state into the hands of some kid who sounded like Sergeant Peachfuzz manning the West Point mental health office phone line. "Ma'am, can you come in next Wednesday at thirteen-hundred?"

In one of the more compassionate moves of West Point design, the Community Mental Health Clinic is tucked discreetly at the end of a quiet winding hallway in the back of Building 606, which abuts a steep rock promontory. From the civilian parking area, you descend a long concrete staircase, then hop the elevator to floor 3M. Bless the symbolism of it—it's faster to rise than to descend. Inside the door is a plaque that says Mental Health, with an arrow, as if mental health itself could be found simply by following the signs.

There was another person in the clinic waiting room with me, a soldier. A young major. He looked like he totally had it together—boots in good shape, nails trimmed, fresh haircut. I wanted to put my hand on his arm, and ask, "So, what are you in for?" but I could feel *don't even look at me* radiating from him in invisible waves. We tapped our boot toes, read sweat-withered copies of *The Army Times*, looked at ESPN without seeing. We stared at the wall. Here we were together, the best and the brightest, admitting we just couldn't cut it. Funny, I never felt any self-consciousness about seeking therapy when I was a single writer. Neurosis is expected in the art world—writers go to therapy when they get a hangnail. But as a military wife, I was ashamed to admit I needed help. In my head, I heard the clucking disdain of Mrs. ArmyPants: "Couldn't hack this, huh? You know, in World War II, women would go for years without seeing their husbands, and *they* held it together. And what about the legendary Liz D., whom you heard about when you first got to West Point? Her husband was deployed when she was left alone in Germany giving birth to triplets and *she* got along fine! Some Army wife you are!"

Within the military, there is a tremendous taboo against admitting to, and seeking treatment for, mental health issues. Soldiers are known for strength—and admitting you're less than 100 percent mentally okay can be seen as a sign of weakness. And in a culture like the Army, in which one strives for a "zero defect environment," weakness is

anathema—a situation further aggravated by the Army policy that requires a soldier's commanding officer to be no-
tified when a soldier seeks counseling. In addition, there
can be very real negative career repercussions (no matter
what the official party line might be) if you're perceived as
enfeebled. The joke is that whatever a soldier's ailment, the
Army hands him a bottle of Motrin and tells him to walk
it off. Similarly, wives are expected to be just as stoic—well,
girly-stoic. Vulnerable on the surface but steely at core. A
good cry and a deep talk with a girlfriend, and everything
will be A-OK. Suck it up and drive on. Lather, rinse, repeat.

I was given a standard form to fill out while I waited. It's
alarming to sit down with a government-issue forty-point
mental health profile that ranks your incidence of dark, depressed, and destructive thoughts on a scale of Never,
Rarely, Sometimes, Frequently, and Almost Always, and realize you want to circle Almost Always on virtually every
one. "Don't you people have an 'all of the above' box on this
bitch?" I wanted to ask the receptionist.

These are the items for which I circled "Almost Always":
I tire quickly. I feel no interest in things. I blame myself for
things. I have thoughts of ending my life. I feel worthless. I
feel lonely. I feel hopeless about the future. I am concerned
about family troubles. I have difficulty concentrating. Disturbing thoughts come into my mind that I cannot get rid
of. I feel that something bad is going to happen. I feel something is wrong with my mind. I feel blue. I feel nervous.

Finally, it was my turn to see the Army shrink. I looked

around his office, which was filled with corny decorations like figurines of golfers, collector's plaques, plates from European countries with U.S. Army posts—Germany, Italy, Belgium—and a cluster of paperweights. He had a standing shoe buffer in the corner—if he was that fastidious, I thought, I bet he's pretty good at his job.

The zero-affect Colonel T. took notes while I spoke. He asked a few questions and listened with a *hm*. Not even a *hmmmm*. Just *hm*. He wasn't skeptical of Patti and Victoria's professional opinion that I had PTSD—I was just another abuse survivor and sad old sucker crawling from the wreckage of a busted military marriage. I told him about the nightmarish Zoloft experiment. He said he would have a discussion with Victoria about my case, and proposed that in the meantime, I start taking the antidepressant Celexa every day, and the sedative Klonopin when the anxiety got too much for the Celexa to quiet.

He e-mailed the prescription to the pharmacy at Keller, and I drove over to pick it up. Klonopin is a controlled substance, Xanax's lightweight cousin; I had to wait so long for the bottle, I thought they might keep it locked in a triple-locked underground vault. When the pharmacist appeared, I asked, "Did you have to go to a street corner to get this stuff?"

"Practically," he said, smiling, as he pulled the prescription bottle from the pocket of his white coat.

Back in Hoboken, I popped a pill and said a prayer for Mike and a prayer for our shared future. At our last session with Patti, he had taken off his wedding ring and handed it to me. Now, in my tiny apartment, I tied our wedding rings together with a pale pink ribbon, my ring fitting neatly inside his, and tucked them away in my wish box. I kissed the box's inlaid wooden lid. Would these rings ever be on our fingers again? It was in God's hands now.

A couple things could cut through the cynicism and rage I felt, releasing the pain in its purest state. Christian pop radio was one of them. From time to time, I'd listen to it on the drive back from Victoria's and find myself weeping with envy. The clean dedication and trust of these songs was so foreign to me—"Open the Eyes of My Heart"; "Word of God, Speak"; "Back in His Arms Again." These people of conviction and purity, singing the songs of the faithful, knew that God was there and that they were his children, as sure as they knew their own fingers and toes. Their fealty to the Lord was the opposite of what I felt in my own numb and blighted heart: No God. No hope.

Watching animal rescue shows on Animal Planet was even worse. The mere sight of a neglected dog started the rolling wave of sadness and grief. The poor things came into the shelter shaking, flea-bitten, and terrified. They pressed their bodies to the wall, or quivered in their cages, and then suddenly lunged forth snarling and snapping. They weren't bad; they were simply too scared to be socialized. Since they were too damaged to save, they had to be destroyed. Neglect and abuse had made them that way. Their haunted eyes and shaking legs left me heartsick for hours afterward. They never had a chance. Where was God for them?

The very worst was going to Molly's. On nice days, we'd take her daughter out to the park. She'd just started walking and to her, the world was huge and exciting and magnificent. I'd watch her as she tracked back and forth across the grass with her hilarious drunken-sailor steps and think, "Who the hell could hurt a child like that?" Other kids climbed on the benches and begged to be pushed on the swings. They were so innocent and so, so small. What kind of sick person would pick up one of these little humans and shake the hell out of them? And is there anything any one of these children could do to deserve it? Do you have an answer for me, God? Because I'd really like to know.

After a month on Celexa, I started to see a lot more light under the door. Deb and I spent an evening out in Manhattan at the grand opening of a yoga studio. David Life, who had hired me to manage Life Café so many years ago, had, along with his partner Sharon Gannon, become something of a yoga celebrity since opening Jivamukti Yoga in the late '80s. Deb and I used to practice with them in a claustrophobic basement on Avenue B, but over the years, they changed venue and polished their practice, becoming so popular among celebrities, people started calling the studio "Pradamukti." After years on lower Lafayette Street, they had moved to a new location on Broadway near Union Square.

The downward-dogging elite turned out for the event, which was kind of silly and kind of cool. I'd never been to a party at a yoga studio that had a velvet rope and paparazzi outside. We took off our shoes at the studio door and milled around the space. Everyone was buzzing that Sting was there, but I was more taken by the sight of Kimora Lee Simmons. She was palling around with her ex, Def Jam Records impresario Russell Simmons, whom I'd seen in class a couple of times doing asana practice on a mat placed immediately behind some impossibly thin, gorgeous model he'd brought with him. (If a guy's aiming for transcendence, may as well enjoy the view along the way, right?) Unlike the rest of us, Kimora did not leave her shoes at the door, probably because they were $800 Chanel pumps with pearl-tie ankle straps. Instead, some guy followed her around the party all night, holding her shoes for her. He appeared to have no other purpose. I know I shouldn't have kept staring at them, but my spiritual evolution is stalled at the level of the E! Channel.

When we left the party, I said to Deb, "You know, I think I could've avoided the whole emotional crisis of the past year if I'd only had my own Shoe Bitch." And at that moment, I knew I was healing for real.

I realized that when I felt overwhelmed, I didn't automatically think of suicide. As low as my thoughts could go—really, about as low as humanly possible—they didn't go that low anymore. There was a margin of pause between me and the ledge, a moment of calm reflection. There was no magic bullet or divine intervention that led me to this hopeful place. It was the unremarkable combination of drugs, time, and therapy. When I finally felt that things were getting better, I invited Mike out on a date, on my birthday, March 30.

He drove down to Hoboken from West Point and I met him on the corner of Second and Adams so I could direct him to the parking garage. The sight of him driving down the street brought back the old familiar butterflies. He stepped from his car wearing the new camouflage, the Army Combat Uniform (ACUs), which, with their digitized camouflage pattern, looked foreign to my eye. An era had ended—no more trips to the dry cleaner to ask for heavy starch in the old woodland pattern battle dress. The machine washable ACUs, designed for wear under body armor, were loose-fitting and lightweight, so they resembled very hardcore pajamas. I figured I'd come to love them in time—camo is camo after all, and it still had a hold on my heart. We parked the car and walked up Second Street together, holding hands. I felt that "I'm with the rock star" feeling I used to get whenever I was with him in uniform. I'd missed it. I gave him a tour of my apartment—which took thirty seconds. He looked at the gold wall with my altar on it, and sat on my Target mocha loveseat to test out the cushions. "You did a good job with this place," he said. "I like it here." I introduced him to my darling Italian landlord, who was very impressed to meet a soldier who was a fellow Neopolitan. He kept pumping Mike's hand, "Nice to meetcha! Nice to meetcha!"

Mike changed into civilian clothes and we took the PATH train into Manhattan. We went to Chat-n-Chew for meatloaf and baked mac and cheese, then tried to bowl at BowlMor but left because we were being deafened by Sister Sledge and the Weather Girls. He told me that he had stopped going for therapy with Patti because she was too far away from the new house, but that he was seeing a woman in town named Linda, who did EMDR.

My strong, hypercompetent husband was doing EMDR. "I realized I had unfinished work of my own to complete," he said. "Now I know that I don't have to take on responsibility for everyone around me. I can let some stuff slide."

As he talked, I could practically see that the core of rigidity inside of him had softened. He wasn't holding everything in place; he wasn't casting about for the perfect solution. I felt a wave of compassion when I made the connection: Hypercompetence was his version of hypervigilance. And now, after more than a decade on duty, Decision Guy had at last been dismissed.

We compared notes on our PTSD. Since he had experienced shock trauma and I had experienced developmental trauma, there were some notable differences in our responses, but plenty of similarities: We both had nightmares. We'd both accepted responsibility and blame for misfortunes that neither of us could help. I tried to avoid situations that made me panic, while he tried to control them. And we talked about how the "gotcha" factor messes with your head. When we were braced for danger, we could handle it better. But when we were taken by surprise and emotionally ambushed, that's when the trauma set in.

"I remember when I was drawing up on the Basra Highway," Mike said, "I'd prepared myself for what was coming, you know? I said, this is war, you're going to see some fucked-up things. So I was ready. But a couple days later, we were going around abandoned buildings looking for weapons caches and unexploded ordnance, and I wasn't thinking about casualties because there was no one around. My driver and I went into this building to do a search, and I opened the door and saw this dead guy, decomposed and covered with maggots. He was decapitated. He was just this headless torso, then I looked closer and saw his head was hanging off by a bloody piece of sinew.

"I was totally not prepared for that. I shouted and ran out of the room, saying, 'Not another one. Not another one,' over and over. I leaned up against the wall and I couldn't stop shaking."

The memory haunted him for months. When he came back home, his mother threw him a huge "welcome home" barbecue right away. Uneasy with all the people around him, and the noise, he bit into a hamburger and promptly vomited in front of everyone.

I tried to match his candor with anecdotes about my abuse, but I kept crying. Another difference between us: He could recall things for me in an unemotional manner, while I couldn't talk about my stuff without weeping until my face swelled up. But the key difference between the two of us was that he could remember a time in his life when he was calmer and less consumed by worry, while I, who had been wounded so early on, could not.

"I want you to know something," Mike said. "I finally understood what you'd been going through when I started doing EMDR. It made me realize that everything you've accomplished in your life, you did with one hand tied behind your back, and it shows just how amazing you really are."

That broke through the final dam of resistance inside of me. After all this time, he'd gone from helping to understanding, which was the type of help I'd needed most.

We rounded out the evening walking the streets of the West Village. The air was unseasonably warm, and under the lights of the shops and brownstone-lined cobblestone streets, the city felt like it was ours. It was the best birthday ever.

On June 1, 2006, I gave notice on my apartment and began packing up my things so the movers could put them in the truck for the drive north. Before I packed my wish box, I took out our wedding rings, still tied together with pink ribbon. I untied them, knowing that soon, I'd hand my ring to Mike and he'd slip it on my finger. We'd start a totally new marriage off post, with the lessons of the old one to guide us.

We started seeing Linda together for couples work based on a protocol called Neuro-Emotional Technique. Unlike EMDR, which felt to me like crude—if wonderfully effective—surgery for my nervous system, NET, which focuses mostly on relieving stress through manipulating acupressure points, was like a brain spa. After each weekly session, we'd trip out of Linda's office feeling relaxed, connected, and two thousand pounds lighter.

Mike and I became Us again. It took four therapists, two attempts at medication, dozens of EMDR sessions, the complete and total surrender of my life as I'd hoped it to be, and more than a year of time I'd have much preferred to have spent being happily married, but it was worth it. I was $30,000 in debt, but it seemed a fair price to pay to get my life back—well, maybe not on the days the bills came in.

It's not like getting to Better is like getting to Toledo, with a clearly defined route and once you're there, you know you're really there. The borders aren't so well-drawn, but you look for any You Are Here sign with the same longing for your destination, and like any weary traveler, you're so, so glad when the end of the road is finally in sight.

14

Embrace the Suck?

Every senior leader in the Army knows that the demands of military life have turned many once-strong marriages into rickety, barely standing structures, so when Mike told his boss, the Academy's new chief of staff, that he needed a day off because he and I had reunited and the moving van was bringing my things to our new house, the chief clapped him on the back, shook his hand, and said, "Well, that's a good news story!"

Mike and I been separated for the length of an extended deployment—fifteen months—and we were lucky to have survived. The mission was complete and our marriage was intact with the original constituents still in play: Mike, me, and the military makes three, with the wolf of the war still circling our feet.

I didn't have much anxiety about moving into the house Mike had bought off post—as busted-up as it was, it felt like a clean slate. I did, however, knot up inside when I thought about returning to West Point. It seemed almost like visiting the scene of a crime. But Mike was the head of an Academy directorate now and I couldn't beg off of shop functions because of "work" or "other commitments." I had to show up. Might as well start practicing right now. I started with an easy exercise—visiting Maya.

I turned onto our old street and parked in front of Maya's duplex. Of course, the quarters that Mike and I had lived in next door had been reassigned to another family. New window boxes hung from the wrought-iron porch railings and a vintage blue milk can with WELCOME painted on it stood next the front door. Did the new occupants live there peacefully? Did they notice the clumsy plaster patch on the living room wall over the spot where I'd kicked it?

Maya's BMW 325i was in the driveway, with a baby seat in the back. Christ, the kid had to be at least six months old by now—I didn't know the baby's name, gender, birthday. Nothing. *Mrs. ArmyPants would've brought a gift,* I thought, *and here I am, showing up empty-handed.* I banished that self-recrimination—*Take a hike, Mrs. Army-Pants, you are relieved of duty*—and knocked softly on the front door. Maya pulled back the curtains, and when she saw me standing there, she hurried outside and opened her arms.

After our hug, we entered her living room. There was a Pack 'n Play in the corner and toys littering the floor. "I don't want to alarm you," I said. "But it appears as if you might have had a baby."

"Hannah Jade! I put her down for a nap a while ago. You want to go see if she's up?"

Hannah was a skinny baby with rosy pink skin and huge gunboat feet. Maya gathered her up and smelled her neck. She turned to me. "Walkies?"

We strapped the baby into her stroller, loaded the diaper bag, and rolled down the hill toward Washington Road. We walked past the parade field and the entrance to Flirtation Walk, the path that represented two centuries of romantic hope, young lovers walking this secluded trail, stopping now and then to profess their heart's longing and smooch among the rocks.

Maya seemed interested in getting caught up, so I unpeeled the layers of my separation for her. I was never going to be the perfect military wife, and pretending that I was had nearly killed me. What did I have to lose at this point by being honest with my friend?

As I talked, she unconsciously pushed her wedding ring up and down her finger. "Was it scary?"

"Uh, *yeah* it was scary! I thought I'd be living in a refrigerator box within a week."

"Oh. But it helped, though, right?"

"I'm sure. There's no doubt in my mind that if I hadn't left, I'd have gone completely mental." The sick irony of it was, the separation saved my marriage. And my life.

"Well, things haven't been so great around here."

"Baby stress?"

"Not really," she said.

I stopped walking. "Well . . . ?"

Oh, Internet, your browser history is such a tattletale. Maya had discovered a MySpace page that her husband had started a year or so before. There were photos of him posing in his uniform, and some with another woman on his lap. His relationship status was listed as "single." Nice.

"Do you know who she is?"

"She's a soldier. I looked at her profile and it says she lives in Clarksville, Tennessee, which is outside Fort Campbell."

"How can you tell anything from the photos? It might just be some old friendly Army buddy stuff."

"Um, she posts messages on his page like 'Miss you'? And 'See you soon' with a Jessica Rabbit cartoon? What kind of *friend* posts like that?" She squeezed her water bottle, the plastic making a crackling sound. "And then I check her page and see that he's left her messages back, like, 'I *love* that picture.'"

That's never a good sign. If he doesn't even try to hide it, then he doesn't see himself as having anything to lose. Did he love this other girl? When a soldier strays downrange, he or she sometimes blames the bad behavior on "deployment goggles." Did Kevin strap on a pair a "temporary duty goggles" during one of his numerous TDYs? If so, it was a connection he was keeping alive, scarcely hidden from view.

"I know what's going on," Maya said. "I know. You just *know*."

She told me he'd done it before. Shortly after they'd

married in Germany, she returned to their quarters and found him banging a cake decorator from the commissary bakery. Well, damn, no wonder she got weird whenever he was alone with me for a few minutes.

Her wedding ring is like mine, a simple unadorned band. If this were a movie, this would be the scene in which she vowed to take back her power and threw the ring in the river. She'd start a spousal mutiny with other aggrieved wives, and as the credits rolled, they'd do an empowerment dance down the street as they headed off into their bright, shiny next phase. But this isn't Hollywood, this is her life. And the Army, too, is her life. If she divorced Kevin, the door would close behind her and seal shut. No more benefits, no more free medical. There are no half-measures when a civilian splits from a soldier. Once you're out, you're out.

Hannah started fussing, so we turned back toward Maya's quarters, walking in silence, past the Great Chain and the crowd of tourists taking photos of Trophy Point. Maya probably wouldn't have told me this two years before. But she knew that I'd been through my own flavor of hell and was in no position to judge. There's a bitter blessing in that, and I welcomed it. I'd pushed "suck it up" to the lethal extreme, and I didn't want to see her pitch over the same cliff.

Maya sighed. "It's bullshit."

I agreed. There was nothing else to do but agree.

Who would have thought that with the punishing operational tempo of back-to-back deployments, the constant moving, a war with no end in sight, and boundless uncertainty, the biggest threat to a military marriage would be the Internet? E-mail, instant messaging, and webcams offer couples some semblance of togetherness during a deployment, but temptation and intrigue are available at a mouse click. The Internet giveth, and the Internet taketh away.

So what would Maya do? Take their kid and move to Highland Falls and get a job somewhere around here, trying to support them as a single mom? Move with Kevin to Fort So-and-So, get couples counseling, and try to work it out?

I didn't have an answer. At that moment, neither did she.

The Army loves the Winston Churchill salvo: "If you're going through hell, keep going."

But where to, dear Winston? Where to?

There's an upside to the Army's high turnover rate: Half the people whom you embarrassed yourself in front of a year ago will be gone when you return. The Academy had a new chief of staff and a new superintendent, and Mike had a new job. Which practically gave me a new start.

Sometimes, the only way to be sure that things have changed is to do all the things you used to do and find out they feel different. I learned this at the Army homecoming game. The West Point motto is "Duty, Honor, Country." The recreational priority is "Football, football, football." Which is fine—what college doesn't have a sport in which it invests its institutional pride? West Point football has long been a showcase event, so much so that up until the early 1970s, wives were prohibited from dressing in slacks for the games. They had to wear skirts or dresses. (Decadence overtook the Academy in my absence and now we're even allowed to wear tank tops in the gym.) The religiosity of football is lost on me, but I had to admit that the rompy fever that overtakes West Point's Michie Stadium in the fall was impressive—the cadets in their camouflage hollering from the stands, the Army mules on proud display in the end zone, a yellow Army "A" shaved into their rump. Alumni drive in early on game day and set up tailgate parties in parking lots around the post, the wives bundled against the cold with black and yellow striped mufflers wrapped round their necks. In the social order that is high school, the Jocks are the natural enemies of the Freaks, and for that and other reasons, I never warmed up to the sport. I only watch the Superbowl for the commercials, but I forced myself into Michie. My secret? I was only in it for the food. I love stadium cuisine—hot dogs, popcorn, Cracker Jack, and any heavily salted, starchy goods. I couldn't care less about the game, but I feigned interest, pumping my fist in the air now and then, yelling "whoo!" around a mouthful of mustard-covered hot pretzel.

I didn't know what to expect when Mike introduced me to his new boss during halftime. Turned out the new chief of staff was half-Bubba, half-*paisano*, the product of the rural coal-mining country of Pennsylvania. He had a birding dog and drove a truck, and the first thing he did upon occupying his office in Taylor Hall was nail up the skin of a bear he'd shot. He squeezed my hand when we were introduced and made fun of something he'd read in a story I wrote. His wife was similarly easygoing, smiling at me like I was an old friend. When we were introduced, they knew only one thing about me—that my husband and I had been separated. And they drew me in anyway. They say that in relationships between military people of differing rank, "senior never remembers and junior never forgets," and I will never forget their automatic extension of friendship.

We sat down to watch the game. Dan, my neighbor who had so carefully asked if I was "okay" on the front walk of our shared duplex back before I moved out, saw me from a few rows away and waved. I also saw Maya sitting next to Kevin, who held Hannah in his arms. She'd made her choice—at least temporarily—to try to salvage the wreck.

In his book, *Love Is a Mix Tape,* rock journalist Rob Sheffield writes about how nice people were to him after the sudden death of his young wife, how people would go out of their way to remember her to him, to share a nice memory, to cut him breaks that might make his black days of mourning a little easier. "You lose a certain kind of innocence when you experience this type of kindness," he says. "You lose your right to be a jaded cynic. You can no longer go back through the looking glass and pretend not to know what you know about kindness. It's a defeat in a way." After seeing how sweet and welcoming people were when I came back to West Point, I was losing the battle to maintain cynicism myself, and I was so happy to no longer have to gird myself to fight.

The experience of war is referred to in the military as the Suck. To resign oneself to the less-than-savory conditions of the plight is to Embrace The Suck. S-U-C-K: Be it a verb, noun, or adjectival descriptor, this versatile four-letter word is the millennial military shibboleth. And, of course, to "suck it up" means to forge ahead in trying times. It's a fire-crackin', boot-strappin' good rallying cry.

In theory, anyway.

In the absence of embracing their deployed husbands, military wives, too, are embracing the suck, sucking it up, and doing their best to cope. Still, there's no denying that being in a military marriage can prove mind-bendingly difficult for those on the home front.

We know that during and after time in a war zone, soldiers may suffer a range of psychological ailments, from generalized anxiety to full-blown post-traumatic stress. Throughout history, there have been numerous terms for these infirmities: "combat stress reaction," "battle fatigue," "shell shock," and, in the Civil War era, "nostalgia" and the poetic "soldier's heart." But what to call the pain of those at home who hurt by proxy—with their own symptoms of depression, exhaustion, chronic worry, and anger? The clinical diagnosis is "secondary traumatization," but my own personal shorthand is "post-traumatic spouse disorder."

What troubles me is the fact that some distressed wives, rather than turning to each other, turn against each other. Robyn, the young woman whose wedding I attended in 2004, got back in touch with me, and in her status update, she told me that other wives in her coffee group at Fort Hood said she had no right to complain about missing her husband when he deployed because he had left three months later than the rest of his unit—and he was called away for twelve months instead of fifteen. She was stunned—seeking support, she was met with rebuke. Log on to an anonymous military spouse Web site like TrueMilitaryWivesConfessions.com, and you can see this dynamic played out every day.

The posts on this site, and the comments they elicit, make a potent anthropological study. Regardless of what someone posts, it's inevitable that some poster lobs an all-caps SUCK IT UP. In fact, the "suck it up" sentiment emerges so frequently it becomes a sort of damning cybercadence. Husband just left for his fourth tour in six years? Suck it up. Tired of moving every two years? Suck it up. Crying because you're saddened by the Christmas displays at the PX? Suck it up!

And heaven forbid if your husband hasn't seen combat.

If your man is "light on the right"—that is, if the right sleeve of his uniform is absent a combat patch—you might as well be married to the janitor who sweeps up after the elephants at a clown college. Inevitably, some peacemaker type enters the fray to say that every soldier, sailor, airman, and Marine makes a meaningful contribution (which is true), but the stubborn divide remains—those who believe that deployed troops are the real troops (and therefore, that they themselves are the *real* wives) will not be persuaded otherwise. Inevitably, someone ends the thread by dropping the hammer: Unless you're in the military yourself, you are a civilian, so quit with the stupid, divisive branch-bashing bullshit and get a life. Then the thread dies, only to resurface in a nearly identical form a few days later.

An odd form of one-upmanship has emerged, not so much wearing your husband's rank, but rather, using his sacrifice and your resulting privation as a bargaining chip for bitching rights. (One military spouse I know slyly refers to this competition as "deployment poker.") My friend Terry at a post out west told me that before an aerobics class, she observed a conversation between a Special Forces wife and an NCO's wife. The SF wife's husband had deployed fourteen times, but the missions were only weeks long, while the NCO wife was left alone for two yearlong deployments. The talk became tense. Each woman had shown her hand, but it was unclear which one was the winner. Does it really matter if a mission is twelve weeks or fifteen months, or that some deployments are ostensibly riskier than others? Whether your husband is kicking down doors outside the wire or toiling on a forward operating base, his absence is still a legitimate point of lamentation (and of pride). Duration or location, it doesn't matter. Gone is gone.

In a venue like a spouse's group or a Web site purportedly accustomed to sisterly carping, a response like "suck it up" and its close cousin, "You knew what you were getting into when you married him," seem annoyingly tone-deaf. I'm not sure which bothers me more—the lack of compassion or the finger-wagging Bossy Boots tone. Tea and sympathy are not among the perks of military service, but that doesn't mean kindness should be dashed from the spousal ranks. And I'm unclear on the prize for placing first in the Suck It Up Olympics. What does the winner get— a medal? An ulcer?

I once asked Victoria about the stress blowback for the military families, and she said, yes, secondary traumatization is as real as can be. "It might only be a 'small t' trauma, but it's still trauma." When you're married to someone, you're connected at the heart, soul, and mind: What hurts him bleeds over into you. How can it be any other way? The well-intentioned advice to distance yourself from negativity has its limits. How do you avoid the bad news of the day when it's on the television in the appliance store or glaring out at you from the headlines on the Yahoo home page? What if the negativity is in your own home, zoning out for hours with Xbox and waking up screaming, covered in sweat from a nightmare and then snarling over his breakfast toast?

I wonder if the competition is a response to stress. I know firsthand the struggle of trying to locate ownership for all those awful feelings that being a military wife can call forth—anger, worry, outright fear. Does it not make sense that the confusion and tumult could be forged into a spear, hurled verbally at some woman whose husband is on an aircraft carrier or a forward operating base? In a vertically structured organization like the military, it's rank rank rank all the time, every day and in every way. A bullshit force of habit, but still, we instinctively rank our entitlement to grief, to complaint. Perhaps we're seeking acknowledgement of our own pain when we belittle someone else's. I try to be patient, but if I read another response to a Web-site post, saying, "Put on your big girl panties and deal with it," someone's going to pay.

Being a military spouse is one of the last remaining bastions of old school wifedom. We're to present ourselves as (s)heroic figures possessed of zipped lips and oven mitts. But I'm skeptical of sucking it up as the default coping strategy. Neither soldiers nor their spouses want to advertise the fact that they're falling down on the job, but in a culture of assumed hypercompetence, we can become prisoners of our own image of capability.

* * *

At the chief of staff's holiday party, I spent a lengthy amount of time having a great conversation with a woman bedecked in flashy rhinestone jewelry. We started talking when I complemented her on her perfectly painted long red nails. Our chat roamed easily from our summer vacation plans to how the Army might better address the BOG (Boots on the Ground)-to-dwell ratio so soldiers wouldn't be so stressed out by the crazy GWOT deployment cycle.

She excused herself to freshen her drink, and I headed over to the buffet to sample the chief's Mexican venison dip. Mike joined me. "I saw you talking to Colonel Davis."

"She's a colonel?" I scooped up some dip with a Frito. "She didn't say anything when she introduced herself."

"Her husband was killed by an IED in Iraq last year."

The spicy dip soured in my mouth. This news brought into acute focus the reason we don't editorialize about the war in social settings. How foolish would I have felt if I'd found this out after flopping my thinky thoughts about the war out there like a stinking fish in a market stall? Opinions are ephemeral. Gone is gone.

At the tail end of the party the chief of staff brandished a humidor and hustled all the cigar enthusiasts to the porch for a smoke. He passed through the kitchen where I was sitting with a bunch of other wives. "Anyone want to come out for a cigar?"

The wife of one of the other colonels asked, "Maybe. Do you have a small Cuban?"

Once the chief was out of earshot, one of the other wives joked, "No, but I have a large Irishman you're welcome to."

Her daughter, who was home from college, howled out, "Oh my God . . . Mom!" She cupped her hands over her ears. "Therapy! Therapy!"

The wives stayed in the kitchen making noises about helping the hostess clean up. When I stepped onto the front porch, I saw the husbands, these masters of the military universe, enjoying a moment of quiet repose, the wintry lights of the Academy shimmering on the Hudson. Witnessing this richly deserved moment of leisure, I felt a sting, knowing that while I admire and enjoy the company of these men so much, with a single set of orders and a stroke of bad luck I could lose any one of them to a war. (Curiously, I rarely think this way about my husband. Denial-n-me? Oh yeah, we're tight.)

But within that poignant tableau, I caught a glimpse of what might file down some of the harsh edges of the relationships between military wives: less ironsides coping, more chilling. In that moment, the women were laughing together in the kitchen, and the men didn't have anything to prove, to themselves or to each other. If officers are expected to model good judgment even in after-hours, I'd say they were setting a fine example, one that stressed-out wives would do well to follow. We deserve the chance to slip the traces of stoic propriety and relentless composure sometimes and let it all hang out.

Sucking it up has both its place and its limits. The satisfaction of sniping is short-lived and pales in comparison to the slower-yield payoff of compassion, a sympathetic ear, and an un-self-conscious moment of joy. If not in this charitable season, then when? And if not with each other, then with whom? While the lip-zippers say "suck it up," I say bring it on.

15

The Terror Bride

As a card-carrying Army wife, of course I support the troops. Except, in this moment, for Mike, whom I wish to see rolled in breadcrumbs and savaged by hungry ducks. It's nothing personal. It's just Boggle.

Since Boggle is the only board game I can stand, it stokes my competitive spirit. I'm too impatient for Risk. (There is no hope for me as a dictator. I'd be the first autocrat who'd bail mid-coup to watch *Seinfeld*.) Monopoly bores me to tears: The only thing I like about the game is getting to be the little top hat. But Boggle games last for only three ferocious minutes, and your brain is occupied the whole time as you search for words in the lettered dice. Joining Mike and me for our Boggle tourney are our new neighbors, Nate and Alena. Nate and Alena became our friends when our dog, Chief the Labrasaurus, dug up Alena's daylilies. She had just planted them in a tidy row along the fence in front of their house, and Chief wasted no time burrowing into the fresh black potting soil when he and I stopped during one of his afternoon walks. I was forced to apologize for my impertinent rooting hound, who ended up with a soiled face like a boxcar bum, but both Alena and Nate were very understanding. Digging, they understood, is what dogs do. Nate, a gifted painter, teaches art at an elementary school in Westchester, while Alena flies to Chicago every week for her work as a process manager for PepsiCo. Nate, that rebel, drinks Coke.

Prior to our separation, Mike and I often talked about settling in the Hudson Valley, and when we were apart and West Point hadn't shown any signs of letting Mike go, he had scoured the nearby river towns, trying to find a place with personality—the inverse of bland Army housing. On a busy street in Beacon, a former factory town being reclaimed by artists and young families priced out of the city, he found a small folk Victorian built in 1888. The house had a good soul but every surface needed to be redone. The floors sloped, the wallpaper had greeted the turn of the last century, the ceiling sagged with the weight of plaster split from the lathe, and the windows rattled in a slight breeze. But Mike and I shared an enthusiasm for charity cases, and I had only one response when I finally saw this structure of desperate need: It's perfect.

It wasn't the fishbowl effect that made me eager to set up house off post; it was the funerals. Our quarters on West Point were right up the hill from the Academy graveyard. General Custer is buried there, as is Daniel Butterfield, the Civil War general who wrote "Taps." I wondered: Did Butterfield know, in his posthumous state, that his song colored my days? As the War on Terror progressed, and my private grieving further rattled my nerves and my marriage, the cycle of funerals at West Point increased. Every day it seemed, "Taps" came wafting up the hillside. The mournful bugling penetrated closed windows and walls, haunting me until I'd hide my head under a pillow, or turn up the radio real loud. The war in Iraq, declared "Mission Accomplished" in 2003, was killing more and more people, and annihilating my peace of mind right along with it. The arc of the war seemed to trace the path of my feeling of madness—both were escalating, with no clear end in sight.

After a time, GWOT casualties were buried in the southwest section of the graveyard, close to the side of the road. Going to the gym or the ATM meant driving past plots of freshly turned earth and temporary wooden headstones painted white with the name, rank, date of birth and death of the fallen, often with a final line reading "We miss you, Daddy."

The ramifications of vowing "for better or for worse" in a military marriage are heightened—I'm attached, by law and in spirit, to my husband, and by association, to the institution and the national populace he serves. When the news of the atrocities at Abu Ghraib broke in April of 2004, I felt so acutely pained, I was almost physically ill.

Here it was—every negative punk rock stereotype I held about the military come true: They were goons and thugs, flouting the Geneva Conventions and shattering souls on the public's dime. The Man gone mad. "For worse" was in my face—on the Web, on TV, detail upon detail of hoods and leashes and dogpiles of stripped and quivering prisoners. Is this how we "bring democracy?" The image that haunted me most was the one that became so iconic: Satar Jabar atop that wooden box, draped in black, a pointed hood on his head and a ragged blanket cover, arms dangling from wires like a gruesome marionette or a faceless Halloween ghoul. The more information that came out, the worse it got. Even though I knew better, I was forced to wonder: Was my husband capable of such evil? I was familiar with his relaxed, fair-minded, at-home persona, but his combat-self was unknowable. The shock had rendered me paranoid. Everyone was suspect.

Abu Ghraib upset me in a way I couldn't have imagined. If you've ever had someone cheat on you—the feeling was the same. The hot shock at the moment of discovery. The immediate disbelief—"Oh God, this can't be happening"— followed immediately by a frantic search to scare up more evidence. At first, you can't even be mad, you're just so stunned and hurt. All you can think of is your world ending as your heart breaks. Then it's so fucking painful, you can't believe it's possible to reel so much from the hurt, and suddenly, you want to know *everything*. The hunger for knowledge consumed me like a craving sickness. I started patrolling Web sites, wire stories, televised news reports, each story a nail driven deeper. *No, no, no!* I'd end up with an ache in the middle of my chest that made it impossible to sit up straight. Nothing but nothing tops the agony of betrayal, and this was the first gross violation of my carefully placed trust in the military. It was a uniquely shattering pain.

I looked at Mike. How did this happen? *Why* did this happen? When he saw the pain and confusion in my face, he could only say, "I wasn't there."

While I knew that Commanding General Janis Karpinski bore most of the responsibility in allowing the exploits inside the prison, Lynndie England emerged in my mind as the poster girl for the wrongdoing. I couldn't shake the image of her pointing at some blindfolded guy's penis and giving a big thumbs up, a cigarette clenched between her teeth like Tony Soprano with his gangster Macanudo. I work hard to be a compassionate, forgiving person, but I had trouble with this one. On behalf of Army wives, hardworking servicewomen, and every woman who gave a damn how the military came across in the eyes of a trusting public, I wanted to slap that smile right off of her smug little moon face.

War is a profoundly human event that often has a dehumanizing effect. Under tremendous pressure and strain, soldiers find themselves doing things that they would never otherwise do. That's what my philosophical self says, anyway. In my heart, I was less able to make sense of the horror. I grappled for some semblance of understanding for SPC England. Maybe she felt so lost in that hellhole that she wanted to do something to create a semblance of belonging, to show she was one of the guys. Something crass and vulgar that stretched the limits of good-girl behavior.

Honey, couldn't you have just made a sex tape instead?

I naïvely expected that the news of Abu Ghraib would explode at West Point like a bomb, the details dominating every conversation. I could not have been more wrong. In fact, the entire war remained, as before, an almost spectral presence—topic non grata. I'd search the faces of the people on post—does this bother you, too? Do you also fight the urge to cry and scream? Does it make you want to just *run*? Am I the only one who wants to march down to Washington and give Donald Rumsfeld a hundred-decibel piece of my mind?

I could, of course, deny any outrage, opting instead to duck and dodge any controversy with the ol' Household Six hand-wave: "The Army is a wonderful institution, and I'm so proud of my husband because he is fighting to defend our nation's freedom. Thanks to him, we're entitled to our opinion and to our free speech!" La la la la, can't *hear* you! Plenty of Army wives default to this speech. For some, the sentiment is sincere. Others believe discretion is a necessary professional courtesy—why rock the boat when your husband is on it? Still others, well, maybe they'd give you an earful of opinion, but they don't want to engage. They just want to hustle the groceries into the car and get home. Regardless of her motive, when a wife shields herself from controversy, the strength of her buttressing is bulldog tough. It's not a Green Curtain. Sweetie, it's a brick wall.

And there, within the silence, the rounds of "Taps" accelerated, the lone mournful bugle rolling up the hill to my front door. After the bugle came the twenty-one-gun salute comprised of three volleys from seven rifles. In the heart of the Army's glamour bubble, the grim reach of this war was unavoidable. Yet amid the burials and the news of the human-rights violations, family life on post continued as before. Troops were dying, innocent men were being terrorized by attack dogs, and Wheat Thins were two-for-five dollars at the commissary.

I realized that I might do better if Mike and I put some space—metaphorically, geographically—between the Army and me.

In November, Mike came home waving a couple tickets in the air: "It's that time of year again!" The first weekend in December, we bombed down to Philadelphia for the annual Army-Navy gala and game. Army-Navy, dating back to 1890, is one of the oldest, and most bitter, rivalries in college football, and the manic enthusiasm surrounding the game is infectious enough to captivate even the most football-averse individual (me). The gala was the predictable cocktail-hour/mingle/dinner affair, punctuated

with athletic displays by the Army's cheering squad, the
Rabble Rousers, that paled in comparison to the acro-
batics that the attending officers laid down on the dance
floor later that night. You really can't comprehend the
scope of God's humor until you see military brass rocking
out to Kool and the Gang's "Celebration."

The next morning, we rose early for the game and piled
into a van as part of the superintendent's entourage. Since
it would be a long, frigid day at Lincoln Financial Field,
Mike had bought me a ticket to the VIP warming room
where I could hang out with the other wives, and, if need
be, escape from the chill in the stands. Shortly before kickoff, the warming room filled with injured veterans from
Iraq and Afghanistan, bussed up from Walter Reed Medical Center to watch the game. Some came in on crutches,
others rolled through in wheelchairs, men and women
missing arms, legs, a hand, some scarred ear to ear. Each
of them heartbreakingly young. I stood near the bar watching the whole scene when I heard a man talking in a low
voice: "She's about five-foot-six, with long hair and this
tight sweater and . . ." I pivoted, ready to scowl and maybe
offer a searing word of correction to the tool bag who dared
turn the military academies' most revered athletic event
into an ogling opportunity. But when I turned, I saw that
the man speaking was a Marine officer in dress uniform,
leaning over the shoulder of an injured jarhead with a
jagged scar zigzagging over his entire scalp. One of his eyes

was just a fleshy, empty socket stitched shut, the other fitted with a glass eye emblazoned with a skull and cross-bones where his pupil should be. He sat listening intently as his friend described the hot chick he would never himself be able to see. In an instant I shifted from offended to deeply touched. As far as I'm concerned, if you'll check out women for your war-blind buddy, you don't deserve a lecture. You deserve a blessing. God bless you, you knucklehead. God bless you and your ever-loving red-blooded American male heart.

Before kickoff, I took my seat in the stands. Rubbing my hands together to keep warm, the winter wind biting clean through my lined leather gloves, I looked over my shoulder to the row behind me. Well, what do you know? There sat Donald Rumsfeld, with his wife, Secretary of the Army Francis Harvey, Army Chief of Staff Peter Schoomaker, and a small tribe of Secret Service agents. The game hadn't yet started, and everyone in the VIP sec-tion had that early-to-the-party vibe, glancing around try-ing to grope their way into some time-killing small talk. I had wanted so badly to give Rumsfeld a piece of my mind, and here was the perfect opportunity. So many options, where to begin? Maybe with a comic opener:

"Hey, Sec Death. I mean, Sec Def. Wassup?"
"Boy, this cold weather is *torture*, isn't it, sir?"
Or maybe I'd be more to the point:
"What kind of monster are you?"

* * *

I glanced from Secretary Rumsfeld to his wife, a hand-some woman bundled up against the cold in gleaming black mink. What was it like, I wondered, to sleep next to a man who was now regarded as an architect of evil? What manner of opinion did she keep under *her* hat? I stamped my feet to get the blood circulating, trying to bring some warmth to my toes. I wasn't just cold; I was numb with shock, standing an arm's length away from the man who couldn't even be bothered signing the Killed in Action letters sent to families of fallen veterans—he used a signature stamp instead. The man who, when confronted by a soldier who stood up at a press conference in Iraq and asked why he and his comrades were forced to dig up rusted scrap metal to cobble together protection for their unarmored vehicles, said, "You go to war with the Army that you have, not the Army that you might want." Shifting back and forth, I weighed the possible outcome of saying something to her husband, and no matter how angry I was over the hell that Rumsfeld and his crew had wrought, all I could envision were my words casting a long, dark shadow over my husband. For all my fury and indignation, I would not win this war with a personal attack, and by putting Rumsfeld on the spot I would be serving no one but myself. What he did to our country might be unforgivable, but so, too, would be turning a football game into my own personal bully pulpit. My husband committed to a vocation of selfless service and sacrifice. I would match his sacrifice with discretion. For the first time in my loudmouth life, I chose impassioned silence.

One of the men in my husband's shop came up to me, holding out a camera. "Lily, will you take my picture with Secretary Rumsfeld?" When I was finished, he said to Mike, "Your turn. Come on, you two." We clustered together—and I never, ever thought I'd say this—hubby, Rummy, and me. The shutter clicked. In the photo, I am smiling.

Okay, so what did Abu Ghraib mean—to the Army, to West Point? Over the months after I came home, I'd pick up the matter and put it back down again, like a troublesome book I didn't really want to read but felt I must. I was wearing grooves in the mental floorboards over it. Was this regarded as the huge letdown I thought it was, or was the official attitude just something akin to "Oops, my bad"?

What I wanted was the view from above—some authoritative perspective on the situation. I wasn't interested in the bloviating of a parlor general or an agenda-pushing pundit. In idle moments, I'd read political journals and books, and jab my way around military Web sites, searching for critical comment. On the West Point Web site, I saw something that made me look twice: a layout on leadership and its responsibilities. The text was laced with images of the torture at Abu Ghraib, as well as the My Lai massacre. Clearly, someone was making a connection. The page be-

longed to the Commandant of Cadets, whose principal
duty is the military, physical, and moral-ethical leadership
development of the Corps, General Caslen. I'd met him a
number of times at various West Point parties, and once,
when the Army chief of staff was entering a room we were
both in, I turned to General Caslen and said, "The boss is
here. Guess we'd better act busy." He'd stared at me as if I
were the biggest idiot on earth. A devout Christian who
nonetheless looked like he could pierce through your femur
in one clean bite, he intimidated me more than a little.
Renowned for athletic rigor and plain speech, he wasn't exactly regarded as a glad-hander. In short, he'd be just the man
to ask for a reality check. He was a very busy man, and I
didn't want to waste his time or risk making a fool of myself
before him again, so I kept my inquiry brief. Who I was, and
what I wanted to know: How is Abu Ghraib regarded, in
your purview as a key leader and mentor at the nation's military academy? I stayed up late, writing and rewriting the
e-mail, then finally hit send, wondering if he'd even bother
to reply. His response to my 2 a.m. e-mail was swift and to
the point:

> The message is simple. As a result of the posting of
> those photos because of the acts of these soldiers, we
> have killed many Americans. The number of foreign
> fighters who joined the jihad as a result of those pho-
> tos will never be known, but it is significant. From in-
> terviews of captured foreign fighters, most said they

decided to join the jihad from what happened in Abu Ghraib and Guantanamo.

The message is not only tactical but hugely strategic. The amount of ill will America received from many countries after Abu Ghraib was significant. It still is. Not only from Arab or Islamic countries, but from our partners as well. Particularly from Western Europe. This War on Terror requires partner nations to help build capacity in the countries where these extremist groups are operating, and when we alienate them because of the demonstrated values of our own soldiers, it has significant consequences.

Further, in a war like this, we are not only fighting a ruthless enemy, but also supporting moderate Islam in what is known as the "war of ideas" within Islam. Most Islamic anthropologists will talk about how Islam is struggling with how to deal with globalization and the incursion of western values into their societies. Some say they need to put up barriers and return Islam to its orthodox ways, which include lack of women's rights, human rights, and the return to Sharia law (like Taliban-run Afghanistan). They also advocate using violence as a means of accomplishing these ends. The other side encourages tolerance and pluralism, and inclusion, and advocates dialogue as a means to resolve differences. Caught in the middle are the majority of Islamists who believe in a fundamental orthodox of Islamic values but are swayed between the arguments of the extremists and the encouragement of using dialogue from the moderates. But when they see their own culture abused by westerners, like they did at Abu Ghraib, we do more to encourage this great majority to join the ways of the extremists, than to remain off the battlefield. We are essentially losing the "hearts and minds" of greater Islam.

So that is the effect of the actions of a few of our soldiers. What is important at West Point is that we are developing junior leaders. Each of these soldiers at Abu Ghraib had a junior leader and that leader had a set of values which we would assume would help provide the leader with a sense of what is right or not. This value set helps provide the parameters of what behavior is acceptable or what is not. In the war we're fighting, where each corner holds a complex set of variables, and where the most junior leaders are making decisions of what is right or not on a daily basis, we must do our best to inculcate in each of these leaders a set of values to help define acceptable behavior or not. And then to develop in them the moral courage and candor when they find themselves in compromising situations, to chose to do the harder right. That is why the teaching of our values at West Point—duty, honor, and country—and the teaching of the values of our Army (loyalty, duty, respect, selfless service, honor, integrity, and personal courage) is so critical to the development of our future leaders.

"The harder right." The phrase struck me. My usual M.O. is to cut and run—when a situation gets too emotionally hot to handle, I withdraw. For me, the harder right was to stick it out. If I had gotten divorced, I would have left not just my husband, but the Army world as well—its misdeeds, its challenges, and its imperfections. Once gone, I might be offended, but in no way could I be implicated in guilt by association.

There's simply no way I can make peace with everything that occurs in the military. Instead, I have to learn to make peace with imperfection, and how best to use whatever power I'm afforded, a commitment that involves balancing the patriot's twin responsibilities of discretion and dissent—a struggle as old as war itself. That the Academy would view the tragedy of Abu Ghraib as a teachable moment gave me the hope I needed to hang in.

I realized that I didn't have to ignore or dismiss the ugliness of Abu Ghraib. It was a lesson for me, too, in locating my own limits within a larger institution. I didn't have to deny my outrage over Abu Ghraib any more than I had to tamp down my disapproval over the fact that some lower-rank enlisted soldiers are paid so little, they have to resort to WIC to get groceries for their family. Nor did I have to hide my alarm over a study conducted by Veterans Affairs researchers that states, "One in seven female soldiers who were deployed to Iraq or Afghanistan and later sought healthcare for any reason reported being sexually harassed or assaulted during their military service. The women who reported harassment or assault were 2.3 times as likely to suffer post-traumatic stress disorder as those who did not, and were also more likely to suffer from depression or engage in substance abuse." Sometimes, disgust is an entirely appropriate response.

I knew that if I were to ever reconcile the horrors of war and military corruption with the goodness of my marriage—and the military itself—I would have to go beyond Rumsfeld's smarmy advice to overlook the "few bad apples" and work the grid in reverse: For every crooked soldier, there are hundreds of thousands more who are honorable; for every hurtful military tactic and policy, there are scores more that help. For every politician who would exploit the troops, there are plenty who only care to see our military might used for good. And the Army isn't some great green unified mass that throbs to Rumsfeld's pulse. I recalled that after the West Point Class of 2004 graduation ceremony, where the Secretary of Defense was the featured speaker, Mike came home and told me that Rumsfeld actually got booed. Not loudly. Not unanimously. But still. The dissenters, the watchers. They're out there.

With that in mind, I resolved, Let me embrace this Army life. Let me enjoy what there is to enjoy, and appreciate all that is good. When Mike went on temporary duty to Washington, D.C., I traveled with him. Like any traditional military officer couple, he went to the Pentagon and I went to the mall. I prowled the racks at the Crystal City Galleria and found a deeply discounted off-the-shoulder Calvin Klein gown to wear to the Yale Club, where Mike had been asked to deliver remarks at a charity ball. At the end of the afternoon, Mike returned from One of Those Secret Meetings I'm Not Allowed to Hear About. I said, "How was your day?" He replied "It went okay," and I didn't think twice about it.

I had also bought black satin opera-length gloves for the ball—a receiving line second nature to me by now, the theatrics of being an officer's wife soothing in their familiarity. I sat in the glittering ballroom, its walls lined with formal portraiture of all the Yale-educated Presidents, and watched the audience as Mike stood at the podium. Their faces turned toward him, rapt and attentive, he told them about West Point's ongoing commitment to creating leaders of character, women and men of courage and candor, even in this difficult military and political climate. When he finished, the attendees rose and gave him a standing ovation. More than anything, they wanted assurance, a place to direct their good faith. I knew a little bit about that myself. Throughout the rest of the evening, I smiled, greeted, conversed, "Hey, do you think when no one's here late at night, the Clinton portrait and the Bush portrait have a cage match?" I presented the image of poise and trust, and for the first time, it wasn't an act.

Back in our new house, I relaxed like a woman who had finally taken off a too-tight girdle. I felt like I hadn't really exhaled since 2003, when we moved to West Point. But now we were moving on, together, to something new, in a town poised at the brink of renewal, where the sound of church bells on the main street mingled with the Islamic teaching center's call to prayer. We drew up radical plans to raise ceilings and move walls and doorways to make a bigger space and to create a better flow. We spent weekend hours at the paint store (whatever colors we wanted!) and on Mondays hauled dumpsters full of garbage symbolically away. We began remodeling, needing the tangibility of rebuilding this place that was half-historic, half-insane. Half-gorgeous, half-broken. It was imperfect, but it was our home. A house of hope.

For now, the renovations have stopped and it's back to basics. Back to Boggle. Alena shakes up the lettered dice with a noisy rattle while Mike flips the timer for the three-minute run. Nate lifts the lid and we pick up our pencils. Game on.

My eyes scan the little board. I spot, then scratch on my notepad a three-letter palindrome: R-A-W. W-A-R. Good for a point apiece, these three-letter words, back to front, say it all about the ongoing challenge in being an Army wife. How at times it is a visceral, gut-felt battle between the culture into which I married and the ideals that I hold dear. How it's a skirmish between needing to be my own person yet wanting to belong to something larger than myself. How sometimes, no matter how much I love my soldier, I hate the military. Maybe that makes no sense if you haven't been there. Maybe someone can't see how I can bounce between the polar extremes, yet manage to find a center that holds. Maybe someone might wonder why I even bother with the battle at all. If that's the case, and it seems too contradictory to understand, then come to my house. I'll spell it out for you.

16

You and What Army?

Am I terrible person because I fired my house-painter for setting our American flag on fire? I know it was an accident, but still, not cool. He was stripping the cracked, knobbed-up hundred-year-old paint from our front porch with a torch and a spackle knife, and the next thing I knew, I looked out the front window to see him frantically waving Old Glory around. Flames lapped the edges of the red and white stripes. Then he dropped the flag in the grass and started stomping on it.

I ran out the front door, yelling, "Dude!" First of all, I told him, who in their right mind uses a torch to strip paint from dried-out, nineteenth-century woodwork? A house this old is like a tinderbox. Secondly, we're a military household. I can't have you pulling an Abbie Hoffman out on the front lawn.

I'm protective of the American flag. The symbol of democracy is important to me. I know that the flag on the upper sleeve of an Army uniform looks backward because it is always worn on the right side, i.e., the side of honor. I also know that the canton field—the white stars on blue—must always be positioned to face forward, toward the soldier's heart, to suggest the direction of movement. When it's being stored, the flag should be folded thirteen times, with the canton field on top, and it should never touch the ground. I hate the idea that one political party claims to have greater respect for the flag. The flag is not a partisan prop. It belongs to every American. Trust.

With Mike now an Academy directorate head, I was, in the eyes of the twenty people in his shop, the Boss's Wife. I had kind of flown beneath the radar before, but now I had increased visibility. It's what happens when your husband gets promoted—people are more likely to notice what you do, how you act, and what you contribute. Since I'd married Mike, I hadn't really done much by way of volunteering or social niceties, and I wanted to change that. Not just to show the people in Mike's shop that we cared about them or to apple-polish his professional image, but because so many people had stepped up to help me, and I wanted to pay it forward.

I started by sending holiday care packages. I found a Web site that posted specific items that units wanted. One Airborne unit in Iraq requested, of all things, scrapbooking materials so they could document their deployment. I immediately went through my stash of papers, ribbons, stickers, and adhesives and put together a box for my fellow scrappers overseas. I hauled it to the post office, where the clerk told me it weighed fourteen pounds. For a scrapaholic, restraint is always a challenge.

About three weeks later, an envelope came in the mail. It was a letter from the unit's commanding officer, a lieutenant colonel. She thanked me profusely for the care package, and as a token of her esteem, she sent me a unit coin and a tree ornament—a blue enameled bell with the image of a camel on one side and a silhouette of Iraq on the other, with "Merry Christmas from Iraq" stamped under it. You know a war is long when it has its own specially fabricated holiday ornaments. I hung it on our tree next to the frosted glass snowman wearing a tiny black West Point sweater.

I sent holiday cards and called women I knew at other posts whose husbands were deployed. I dropped off blankets and clothes for families in need. If I saw a soldier from Mike's shop out and about on post, I made sure to tell him to pass along my regards to his wife.

But after every card, call or package, I was left wondering: What else can I do?

My husband's least favorite sentence is: "This week, on *Army Wives* . . ."

He cannot stand the Lifetime Network series *Army Wives*. He will flee the room when it comes on. At first, I thought the show was ridiculous, too. A brigadier general's wife being all buddy-buddy with a private's wife? Not likely. And what's up with that female lieutenant colonel wearing her hair below her collar? Don't they have a military consultant on this show? Please. But the soapy plot-lines drew me in, and I'd find myself sneaking into the den on Sunday nights to watch the show, just to find out if Trevor was going to beat his addiction to the painkillers he was prescribed when he was injured in Iraq, or if Pamela had figured out who was stalking her. As implausible as the plotlines could be (and they were *very* implausible), I got a good cry out of almost every episode, and there's nothing I love more than running the ol' waterworks.

Periodically, Mike would give the show another chance, but then he'd see an extra dressed in ACUs barbecuing on his front lawn like a dweeb, or that the general didn't have a lieutenant aide glued to his side and he'd give up. The only way I could keep him from changing the channel was to sit on the remote.

My friend Iggy was also obsessed with *Army Wives*. She's a heavily tattooed lesbian tomboy, living in East L.A. Not exactly the target demographic for the show, but she was as hooked as I was. When I lamented that I didn't have super-close friendships like the women on the show, Iggy said, "Man, you've *got* to meet Bean."

Bean, a retired active duty major turned reservist had gone to high school with Iggy in the San Fernando Valley in the '80s. They never dated, but they went to a Go-Gos show together once. Bean had just taken a job at West Point. I invited her out to lunch in Highland Falls. She was tall and rangy. It wasn't too hard to figure out why people called her "Bean."

"So," I asked, "how have you dealt with 'Don't ask, don't tell' all these years? Weren't you afraid you'd end up at Fort Homophobe, somewhere in the boonies?"

Bean grinned. She's a big grinner. "I always just told my assignments officers, 'Don't send me anywhere where they'll give me crap for being Jewish.'"

That meant being stationed for two years at Fort Lewis, outside of Seattle. Through subtle hints and innuendo, she'd found other gay soldiers on post. Some nights, they'd go to the gay bars in Seattle, but soon they realized that someone at Lewis was sending in other soldiers to spy on them. There was nothing the Lewis brass could do to them, officially—don't ask, don't tell, right? But they manipulated the situation by letting the soldiers know that they were being watched—which was enough intimidation for some gay soldiers to leave the Army.

If sexuality is a continuum between 100 percent heterosexual and 100 percent not, I wondered, what point on the scale is "too gay" for the military? A long-ago experimentation with someone from basic training? Identifying as bisexual while partnered in a heterosexual marriage? Getting drunk at a party and making out with another girl? Having Katy Perry's "I Kissed a Girl" on your iPod? The criteria seemed frighteningly mushy. Especially if just being in a gay bar—in civilian clothes, and on your own free time—could get you noticed.

Bean knew she was in hostile territory at Lewis and acted accordingly. She deployed for a year, and when she came home, she told her civilian girlfriend not to be at the airport for the homecoming. The thought of it made my heart ache.

We started hanging out together a lot. Bean-n-Lily, Lily-n-Bean. Bean liked West Point fine, but she found some of the soldiers to be a little full of themselves. Respectable and storied as it is, West Point does have a bit of a rep for being a country club assignment. Bean, on the other hand, had not only deployed, she had volunteered to deploy. Twice. She liked to needle the soldiers who'd been at West Point for years. "You've been at West Point for how long now? Oh, since 1998, you say? So, basically you're telling me you've been here for the entire length of the war. That's nice." *Sarcasm* fit neatly between *sacrifice* and *service* in the Bean lexicon.

Bean and I went to a cadet parade review together. We sat in the front row, and while we waited for the review to start, Bean elbowed me as a major walked by. "Check out the name tag." I looked. "It's Major Wood," she whispered. "Pardon me," I whispered back, "but I do believe I just saw Major Wood over there!" Bean snickered. "The Plebes have Major Wood first thing in the morning!" We think we're hilarious.

I finally had a friend with whom I could talk about Army regulations and vintage New Wave, Santa Cruz vegans and

MREs, General Petraeus and Susie Bright. With Bean, I didn't have to partition. As friends, we could be everything we were at once, uncensored and undivided.

Shortly after I met Bean, an old acquaintance from San Francisco, Stephanie, e-mailed after fifteen years of radio silence to say hello and to let me know she was now living in New York. The last time I'd seen Stephanie was in San Francisco. She and I were working on a pinup photo shoot on the tracks of the J Church streetcar line, and we had to run into the bushes to avoid getting creamed by the oncoming train. "I heard you're with a soldier now," she wrote. "Me, too!" Last I knew of Stephanie, she only dated women. Either she'd undergone a change in her sexual orientation, or her girlfriend was a soldier. It turned out to be the latter.

We met for Cuban sandwiches at a bustling café in Nolita and talked for hours. She told me that she had met her girlfriend Dana at a publishing convention and was immediately smitten with her buzz cut and her steely blue eyes. And once she'd seen Dana in uniform—forget about it.

"I know how that goes," I said. "So how does your relationship work? Are you the Invisible Woman all the time?"

"It actually works pretty well!" she said. "I couldn't live with her on post when she was at Fort Drum, obviously, so we lived in Watertown, but I still went to all her company functions with her as her 'friend.' It was pretty obvious who I was, but since we didn't talk about the nature of our relationship or touch each other, there was no room for anybody to bitch."

(As she spoke, I thought, Man, Stephanie has *got* to meet Bean.)

Because Stephanie's relationship wasn't recognized as legitimate, she wasn't afforded the same benefits and privileges as I; she wasn't officially an Army spouse. I don't live on post with my mate because I don't want to; Stephanie didn't live on post with her mate because she couldn't. Even though she was a fine soldier's girl—loyal, supportive, and domestic—she was seen as a deviation from the American concept of wifedom, her relationship not real. She was marginalized by military shortsightedness. In my odd-duck moments, I check myself: There is feeling like you don't fit in, then there's being told explicitly that you aren't welcome.

Stephanie was deeply moved that one night, the company commander, a macho guy, deep in his cups, pulled her aside. "I just want you to know, you're always welcome here. You and Dana are family to us." He was not-asking, not-telling her that she was accepted, just as she not-was.

Nonetheless, Stephanie's girlfriend decided to retire her commission, join the reserves, move to Brooklyn, and take a civilian job. She couldn't tell her assignment officer exactly why she had chosen to retire, couldn't call it out by name, so she simply said it was too hard to live two different lives, to have an identity cleaved apart by circumstance. She wanted to continue serving her country, but the moral and practical challenges had become insurmountable. She could handle the physical demands of being a soldier, but toggling between the two disparate worlds was too hard on her heart. To keep serving full-time, she had to keep lying, and she just couldn't do it anymore.

A few months after seeing Stephanie, I attended a benefit for a volunteer organization in the city with a major and two cadets. During the drive home in the major's minivan, the cadets started talking about the event. "You know, sir," one of them said, "some of the people there were pretty flamboyant."

The major asked what he meant by that, and the cadets started down a more than slightly homophobic path.

I held my breath. I had only recently met this major, and I knew that he and his wife had four kids and went to church every Sunday. I braced myself, thinking he was about to give the cadets a free pass on their judgmental attitude.

The major cleared this throat. "You know, tolerance is an important element of character . . ." He went on at length about the foolishness of "Don't Ask, Don't Tell," and about how the value of an institution lay in its diversity. By the time he finished, the cadets were totally schooled.

I told Bean about my night out. She was less interested in the discussion of tolerance than she was in what happened when we had gone to the parking garage after the event. As we waited for the minivan to be brought around, a woman came up to one of the cadets, who was wearing his white-over-gray uniform of gray trousers and a white short-sleeve button-down belted with a maroon sash, and a white service cap. Mistaking him for a parking attendant, she handed him the ticket for her car.

In 2004, the *Washington Post* reported that within the prior two years, thirty-seven Arabic interpreters had been discharged from the military's Defense Language Institute for admitting to homosexual behavior. (Way to keep America safe, Department of Defense!) The conventional argument against admitting homosexuals into the military is that they would disrupt morale. Is the belief that straight soldiers are so unsophisticated, they'll ignore their own watch to be on alert against the dread homos?

John M. Shalikashvili, chairman of the Joint Chiefs of Staff from 1993 to 1997, was an early advocate of the military's "Don't Ask, Don't Tell" policy. He had a change of heart, however, and wrote, in a *New York Times* Op-Ed in early 2007, "I now believe that if gay men and lesbians served openly in the United States military, they would not undermine the efficacy of the armed forces. Our military has been stretched thin by our deployments in the Middle East, and we must welcome the service of any American who is willing and able to do the job." He quoted a Zogby poll of more than five hundred plus troops returning from Iraq and Afghanistan, 75 percent of whom said they were comfortable interacting with non-heterosexual people. He also pointed out that twenty-four countries, including Britain, Israel, and other GWOT allies, allow gays to serve openly, with no ill effects on morale or recruitment.

His opinion was an important bellwether, but it was by no means universally held. Later that year, then-head of the Joint Chiefs of Staff Peter Pace told *The Chicago Tribune*, "I believe homosexual acts between two individuals are immoral and that we should not condone immoral acts . . . I do not believe the United States is well served by a policy that says it is okay to be immoral in any way."

The question isn't whether or not gays should be allowed to serve in the military. They already are serving in the military—admirably and honorably. What remains to be seen is how long will it take for them to be granted the dignity of serving without fear of negative repercussions. Until that day, it's just more suck to be embraced.

"Dude, why is there lettuce on the floor of your car?" Bean had just climbed into the passenger seat. We were on our way to the monthly meeting of our book club.

"Oh, I signed up to drop off a meal for those families whose housing burned down in Gray Ghost. I braked fast and the salad tipped over. So did the stuffed shells. Notice it smells like marinara in here?"

The book club was small—only a dozen or so women. Lorna was essentially the heart of the club. The wife of a West Point academic department head, she had been an

Army wife for twenty years. There was Bean, Sondra, an attorney who worked in the JAG office, and Kelly, who was married to a major on faculty with Lorna's husband. The rest of the group members were civilian employees who worked at the Academy, including a couple of mental health professionals (none of whom I'd seen during my crisis). It was only my third meeting since I'd been invited in, but I liked the group tremendously.

My hospitality panic had become something of a joke to Bean. She made light of my insecurity every time I brought something to the book club potluck. Tonight was no exception. She took a bite of my stuffed shells and announced to the room, "Lily! These shells are *really* good! Wow!"

Our friend Sondra was more polite in her support; she took a helping and hid it behind everything else on her plate. Sondra is hardcore. An active duty major married to a physician, and a mother of a young son and daughter, she not only knows how to fire off a .50-caliber machine gun, she also knows that the proper purse to carry with camouflage is a Kate Spade tote.

Why, oh why didn't I seek out female soldiers as friends the first second I got here? Their outgoing nature and expressiveness is so appealing. Timidity won't cut it in the testosterone-heavy Army world, so they know how to bring it, personality-wise.

At my first meeting, the monthly selection was a book by a civilian professor who taught literature at the Academy. We debated every point of the book, from her depiction of the wives on post to the influence of Christianity in the military, the exception, of course, being our opinions on the war. At some point in the discussion, Sondra said, "Just because you don't support the war doesn't mean you don't support the troops." The comment hung in midair, everyone backing away as if it were a ticking bomb.

This month, after we discussed the month's selection, *The Secret Garden*, the conversation turned to a book the group had been writing together, exquisite-corpse style. Each member wrote a chapter then passed it on to the next.

Bean piped up. "Hey, you know, Lily's a writer."

I shot her a look: *I am totally going to throttle you, Bean.*

"Yeah," she told the group. "She wrote a memoir."

I mumbled a few words about *Strip City*, how I used to be a stripper and that the book was about my farewell-to-stripping adventure, *mumble mumble mumble*, and I was *so* going to kill Bean for outing me to our entire book club.

Lorna listened intently. "Not for nothing," she said, her smile turning cryptic, "but there are a lot more Army wives who used to be strippers than you might think." She paused for a moment then said, "Lily, will you teach *me* how to strip?"

That was it? Seriously? All those hours of angst and paranoia about being judged and ridiculed by other Army wives, and the minute I'm outed as a former stripper, one of the most respected women on post wants me as her tutor?

With that question, the wall that divided the two worlds I moved between came crashing down.

I'm sympathetic to the public's war burnout. I'd love a break from this war business myself. When I thought about what more I could do for military folks as a volunteer, I thought long and hard about what I like to do for someone if I could.

I finally figured it out because of the semi-annual sale at Victoria's Secret. I'd made the mistake of tossing my lingerie into the same load of wash as Mike's ACUs and the Velcro on his uniforms cannibalized my good bras, rendering about three hundred dollars' worth of laundry carnage. Off to the mall I went. I noticed that the young salesgirl wore a set of dog tags around her neck.

"Is someone you know deployed?" Asking may have been nosy on my part, but whenever I see anything that indicates a connection with the service, I want to reach out.

She wrapped my purchases in hot pink tissue. "My husband."

"He deployed from around here?"

"We were at Fort Campbell, but I decided to come home to stay with my family while he's gone." This girl was a stranger to me, but I thought I recognized the effects of a prolonged deployment bummer in the weariness of her face.

My DEERS card is always tucked into the first slot in the billfold section of my wallet so I can easily pull it out to hand to the gate guards whenever I go on post. When I took out my credit card to pay, I showed the ID to her. "I've been there. I know it's hard when he's gone."

She smiled.

"Thank you both for your service," I said, taking my bag from her. "Good luck." I wanted to say, "I'm sure he'll be fine," but there was no way for me to know that.

What I did know, at long last, was how I wanted to help. It came to me on the drive home.

I wanted to help the wives. The military already provides spouses with financial advice, family support, deployment survival tips, and crisis assistance. What it doesn't offer is what I wanted to give women the most: a break. Some time when they didn't have to worry about their husband or their kids or the Army or the war. When they could do something creative and out of the ordinary.

I wanted them to feel confident that when they faced their husbands again, they'd be strong and sexy. But mostly, I wanted them to be there for themselves. I couldn't bring home the husbands who were deployed. I couldn't heal the husbands who were injured. But I could offer these women one hour out of their everyday lives to learn something new, to get in touch with their inner glamour girls, and to leave the stress of the military wife life behind, if only for a little while.

I stood on the shiny wood surface of the roller skating rink at Fort Hood, Texas, and smiled at the dozen women gathered before me."Welcome to the inaugural class of Operation Bombshell, the only burlesque class exclusively for military wives."

Once I got the flash of inspiration to start Operation Bombshell, I mobilized right away. I got back in touch with Robyn, whom I hadn't seen since she married Joe after his graduation from West Point in 2004. I knew that she and Joe were at Fort Hood, where Joe was now a captain. Given that Fort Hood was home to several units, many of which were deployed, I knew there were probably lots of wives there who were missing their husbands, and eager for something fun to do. "Oh, yeah," Robyn said. "It's unheard of for someone here to not deploy within a year." I figured Robyn would make a good accomplice, so I asked for her help. She'd invited me to her wedding, sight unseen, so she was nothing if not plucky, right? She scouted places on post where I could teach the class, and I bought a couple plane tickets for Mike and me. I told Robyn to spread the word among the wives at Fort Hood. She sent out the notice I typed up and Operation Bombshell was a go.

Things are bigger in Texas, and Fort Hood is no exception. Fort Hood is the largest military installation in the world, covering 340 square miles of Texas hill country, and it is the Army's only two-division installation. During the week, the post roads are busy enough to have morning and evening rush hours. There are two commissaries and several mini malls. Mike and I looked around the PX, which is the size of a football field. We examined the book section, brimming with popular non-fiction, novels, and military history. On display at the end of an aisle was a chilling array of books on bereavement: *How to Go On Living When Someone You Love Dies; Military Widow: A Survival Guide; Life and Loss: A Guide to Help Grieving Children.*

We left the PX and drove toward the post gate. At the corner of Tank Destroyer Boulevard, a big sign was staked into the dirt. "What's wrong? You OK? Depression is serious."

The night before class, Mike and I met Robyn and Joe for dinner at the Olive Garden in Killeen. Robyn looked much the way I remembered her—slender and pretty, with an irrepressible energy that mixes determination with Gidget-like cheer. Joe and Mike shook hands when they were introduced, Mike telling Joe not to bother calling him "sir."

Sitting at a table across from us at the restaurant was a young couple, the man in ACUs. The woman had a handbag made of the new Army camo, with a name tape on it, plus the First Cavalry patch and sergeant's rockers—all of which matched the patches on her husband's uniform. Robyn told me these bags were a big trend on post. So I guess now a wife can wear her husband's rank, literally.

While we enjoyed our Endless Pasta Bowls, Robyn and I talked about the class tomorrow, and how when we married our husbands, neither of us was prepared to become an officer's wife. We both had to learn the unspoken rules as we went. Mike and Joe were embroiled in a parallel conversation. When Joe was deployed to Iraq the first time, a suicide bomber blew himself up at the recruiting station where Joe worked, killing thirty people, so he and Mike bonded over what it's like to clean up after a bombing, "bagging and tagging" exploded bodies. Until that moment, I hadn't known that during Desert Storm, Mike and his unit had been tasked with helping the Red Cross collect and identify remains on the Basra Highway.

So much had transpired since I first met Robyn—she and Joe had moved twice, Joe had been deployed, they'd bought a home in Killeen, and they'd had their first child, Dylan, who was now eighteen months old. Robyn was active in the Family Readiness Group and had recently gotten certified as a financial planner. She knew she wanted a career of her own, and was planning to use her skills to help military families.

Though I wouldn't have told her so because it seemed corny, when I thought of how beautifully she'd matured into the role of military wife, I was impressed. I was proud of her.

In true military wife style, all the Op Bombshell girls showed up for class right on time, Sunday at 2 p.m. Robyn and I had decided that the Fort Hood roller rink was the best site for the class because there was a good sound system, and we'd be able to accommodate a large class. The rink was a relic from the early 1970s, but I didn't mind. Burlesque wasn't exactly modern, either, and the rink manager didn't care when we dragged the chairs for the routine across the rink's wood surface.

One by one, the Op Bombshell girls introduced themselves. They came from every region of the country—some had Texas drawls, others spoke with a Midwestern twang. One had been in the Army herself. One was pregnant. Two had husbands who had been sent home from combat with injuries, and of the other ten students, each had a husband who was deployed, and Robyn's husband, Joe, was leaving for his second deployment the following week.

With the women lined up in three rows before me, I stood at the head of the class. I nodded to the DJ to start the music. "Let's get started." It was about to get a lot steamier in the roller rink that time forgot.

The song "Hey, Big Spender" comes from the musical *Sweet Charity,* the movie version of which was choreographed and directed by Bob Fosse. Fosse got his start as a performer in burlesque houses when he was barely a teenager, and the bawdy influence shines through in his work. But my friend Jo, a bump-n-grind Einstein, tweaked the routine to give it a decidedly New Burlesque twist, simplifying the moves while retaining the sizzle. It's two minutes of pure attitude, and the Op Bombshell girls loved every second of it.

Like jazz, Coca-Cola, hip-hop, and the hula hoop, burlesque is a uniquely American invention. The appeal of New Burlesque lies in its modern, big-tent approach to flirty sexuality and performance. Girls of all shapes, sizes, and ages pay homage to the dancing girls of days past by reinventing classic routines and exalting old-school glam-ourpuss style and the art of the tease. It's sexual theater, retro-style, with a peppery kick of kitsch. Despite its pop-ularity, New Burlesque is not a big-money enterprise—even Dita Von Teese, the one true star to emerge from the scene, is no billionaire. The women are purely in it for love and glamour—two things that are very important to me, too. New burlesque is different from modern stripping, with the poles and the Lucite heels and the "do you want company" table dance grind. The outsize persona of the performer takes precedence. The whole vibe is fun, ex-pressive, creative, and democratic in its embrace of diver-sity. I think it's safe to say that stripping is all about giving the customer what he wants, while New Burlesque is all about leaving your audience wanting more.

They were dedicated students, paying rapt attention and asking to repeat the more intricate combinations. The rou-tine starts with the woman seated in a chair, looking away, like a bored cabaret girl. *Oh, do you want something from me, mister?* They snapped up the intro sequence in a jiffy, and soon these dutiful Army wives were working their way through shoulder pops. Cleavage spills. Working the props. *Work the chair*, I yelled over the music. *Pop your hip. Own it.*

So let me get right to the point . . .
I don't pop my cork for every guy I see. . .

We did about ten seconds' worth of material at a time, piecing the moves together like a choreography quilt. After ninety minutes, the girls were ready to do the song straight through with no coaching. A minute and thirty seconds into the song, the trumpets started blazing, and the girls were grinding the routine into a fine powder, each move crisp and defined.

Hey Big Spender!
Spend . . . a little time with me.

Then a final flourish of crazy-hot trumpets, and the song drew to its dramatic close. When the last note fell, I spontaneously burst into applause. I looked around the room and saw exactly what I'd hoped to see: Everyone was smiling. They did it!

At the conclusion of the class, we put our chairs away. Robyn set up her camera, and the class clustered together for a group photo, all of us making kissy-faces as the flash popped. In that moment, our politics didn't matter. Rank or operational specialty didn't matter. We were united in our purpose and focused on our mission. We came together for one reason—because when the going gets tough, the tough get shakin'.

That day, none of us had to perform to survive; we did it purely for the joy of movement and the escapist thrill. We got lost in the moment and got a little bit naughty. For years,

I'd kept these two parts of my self completely separate—the wife and the wild girl—as if they might contaminate each other. How nice it was to finally accept that, instead, they complemented each other. I could knit these two halves together, then give them as a gift to other women: Have fun. Be glamorous. Be free. Be yourself. Enjoy.

It takes all kinds of people to make a military, and it takes all kinds to make a military marriage. If I am, in fact, a freak show of a wife, I embrace it. At last. I may never be held up as an example of spousal perfection, or see my face grinning out from a "Army Wife of the Year" poster, but I finally realized that even if I'm not perfect, I have something to contribute. Some of us are poster girls, some of us are pinup girls, and, apple pie or cheesecake, we've all got a spot at the table. However humble, I'd finally found my place—where the saucy side of self-expression meets the military spouse tradition of volunteerism.

I started planning to take Operation Bombshell nation-wide. I knew that Operation Bombshell: Cross Country was an audacious undertaking. A one-woman traveling burlesque school, roving from military installation to military installation? *What*? But I wanted to do it, for myself, and more importantly, for the other wives. I can't cure post-traumatic stress disorder or post-traumatic spouse disorder. I can't bring their husbands home or heal their wounds. But I can offer these women a little flash and dazzle. I believe that when properly applied, glamour heals.

When you really throw down and put all your weight behind something you want to do, periodically a naysayer
pops up to taunt you by saying: *Oh yeah? You and what
Army?* When it comes to Operation Bombshell, the answer is: Why, me and the United States Army, that's who.
Packing up my Peggy Lee CDs and my makeup case, I felt
very much a part of the whole. My heart drummed a
snazzy patriotic beat in my chest. As Mike and I drove out
of Killeen on Route 190, hundreds of American flags
waved us farewell—rippling on flagpoles, hanging in store
windows, and draped with great respect and care on the
facades of buildings. I wondered, Could Operation Bombshell even be possible in any other country? No, I decided,
looking out into the cloudless, open-jawed Texas sky. Only
here. Only in America. The land of the freaks and the
home of the brave.

17

Rendering Honors

Washington, D.C., in June is a hot, muggy mess. Anti-American upstarts make much of our nation's capital having been built on a swamp. Me, I'm just annoyed that the second I got into town, I had to jam napkins into my armpits to stay the outpouring of sweat. Mike and I had come down for the annual Army Birthday Ball—the branch's biggest gala—and we hadn't left our air-conditioned room at the Grand Hyatt since we'd gotten in the night before.

Heat index be damned, Mike got into his gym clothes and laced up his running shoes. He left to take a jog through the streets of Chinatown, and I threw back the sheets, rose from the bed, and quickly set to work.

I was in the bathroom washing my hair when he came back. Over the spray from the shower, I heard him say, "What's *this*?"

Wrapping a towel around me, I stepped into the room to find him staring at the bed. While he was out, I'd

pinned up a huge American flag and covered the head-
board on the bed in so much red, white, and blue bunting
it looked like a parade float. With the aid of some packing
tape, poster board, and a Sharpie, I had whipped up some
signs, I LOVE YOU, YOU ARE MY HERO, and most importantly—to me—was the one that read: WELCOME
BACK FROM OIF (a little late). It was the welcome
home from the war that he'd never had.

I hadn't forgiven myself for not properly heralding his arrival back from the war. Whenever anyone shook his hand
or expressed gratitude for his serving, I'd berate myself. *A
grateful nation thanks you for your service. Your wife, on the
other hand, didn't do squat.*

He sat on the bed and asked over and over, "Why did
you do this? You didn't have to do this. Why?" I knew that
if I explained at length, my throat would get tighter and
tighter until I could only squeak out my words. Then I'd
cry. Happy tears, and there's nothing wrong with that,
really, but hadn't I shed enough tears in this marriage already? He wrapped me in his arms—him in his sweaty
running gear, me in my damp towel—and we embraced in
silence. There was so much to say, and so little room to say
it. Thank you for your commitment to serving our country. Thank you for picking me to be your wife. Thank you
for being man enough to get help when you needed it.
Thank you for fighting for our marriage as valiantly as you
fought any war. Thank you for being both my husband and
my hero.

Thank you for everything.

We almost didn't make it to the ball because of Mike's medals. The cheap metal rack that keeps the medals straight on his mess dress blue uniform came apart and no amount of SuperGlue would hold it together. "I can't go with my uniform messed up," he said. "I'm sorry."

I was used to this by now—five years of beret scrunching and shoe polishing and sending various types of uniforms on trips through the dry cleaners and the washing machine. Still, I couldn't hide my disappointment. We'd come all this way, we'd paid a lot for the tickets, and I was already dressed in my black satin Rita Hayworth dress with red roses pinned in my hair.

In a stroke of military wife meets MacGyver ingenuity, I found a safety pin at the bottom of my cosmetic bag that Mike was able to use to fix the medals in place. A quick check in the hotel room mirror and we were on our way.

The convention center ballroom held fifteen hundred people, gathered together for no other reason than to celebrate the birthday of the United States Army. There were generals and privates, war heroes and West Point cadets. One of the hosts was a sergeant turned Miss Utah. During a lull in the ceremonies, her cohost, country singer Michael Peterson, challenged her to a push-up contest, "You do as many as you can, then I'll do one more." So she dropped to the stage in her skintight beaded evening gown and did thirty perfect military-style push-ups, which the crowd received with a standing ovation. Then her co-host then got down on the stage and did one more. *Hyuk hyuk.*

The secretary of the Army took the stage. At the prompt, we filled our glasses with wine and stood for the toast:

To the Commander in Chief
To the President
To Our Fallen Comrades
To Our Fallen Comrades
To the United States Army
To the Army
To Our Soldiers and Their Families
To Soldiers and Their Families
To Our Guests
To Our Guests

After we left the convention center, Mike and I went for a walk at the National Mall. When I was in high school, my sophomore history class had visited the great monuments of the Mall and I was unmoved. At the time, statues of founding fathers were boring. Veterans Day just meant no school. Things were very different now. Mike and I walked along the reflecting pool and down into the marble cleft of the Vietnam Memorial. We traced our fingers over the etched names. Father, son, brother, friend. And female nurses and medics, too. I knew then why I had taken Abu Ghraib so personally—it was not just a criminal act, it was an insult to these good soldiers and the ones who came before and after. What I expected in return for my faith was infallibility, and complete freedom from any disappointment, but that's not possible. Surrounded by all those monuments—to struggle, to honor, to country—I felt deeply that while my faith had been insulted, I hadn't abandoned it entirely. I still had it, and held it a little closer there in the dark and muggy Washington night.

Mike squeezed my hand. "Kind of chokes you up, doesn't it?"

I nodded. I stood by my husband's side, virtually atop these monuments yet feeling like I was observing them from a respectful distance, mindful that for me, the two defining emotions of being an Army wife are the pride of involvement and the loneliness of anxious detachment. I'm not a soldier, yet not a seamless fit with civilians. I'm entrenched in a subculture, yet for so long I despaired of ever fitting in. Isolation and pride are the warp and weft of it, with a baseline anxiety as the thread that runs throughout. The Army asks a lot of its families. You sacrifice your time with your loved one—if they're called away, you have to let them go, under whatever conditions and for whatever length of time. You sacrifice your autonomy— where you will live and for how long. And some make the ultimate sacrifice—a fact that is never far from my mind.

When I lived outside of Philadelphia as a little girl, the neighborhood kids would tease anyone in the gang who bragged by saying, "So what do you want, a monument or a medal?" There are now plans to build a monument to the military spouse. The very idea lights me up. I can't help it; it turns me into a sap. But in a way, I think, maybe we don't need one. Our very survival is a monument to our strength and value, and we build it a little more every day.

I suppose choosing to marry an Army officer tapped into some deeply buried vein of idealism within myself. Cynicism is a dependable, but wearying, default, and on some level, our marriage (any marriage, really) was an attempt to change that. They say in the Army, "Hope is not a planning factor," but when it comes to marriage, hope is the ultimate planning factor. Which is not to say that every day is a fabulous party full of rainbows, cupcakes, and unicorns. And I certainly would not say my husband is perfect, or, to put it in Army argot, a zero-defect water-walker. I have loved people besides Mike, but the difference between them and him is the faith that he inspires—in his character, his capabilities, his essential goodness as a person.

My beloved third-grade teacher, Miss Mailey, when trying to explain to the class the difference between optimists and pessimists, pointed to me. "You're a pessimist," she said. This newfound faith thing is huge for me, a complete systemic reversal. So if my marriage is some emblematic statement, of the What Does It Mean type, it means that I *believe*. In this country, in this military, in this man. Where fatalism had once been my talisman, now I'm learning a new way to exist in this world. Life is random and anything can happen. It's true. But you burn up a lot of precious daylight expecting the bad times to come. There are other ways for things to go besides south. What didn't kill me is making me stronger, for now.

My inner skeptic is not totally at rest, however. I'm constantly on guard against people who might view my husband as an instrument of their agenda. If you want to valorize him as some American all-star, that's fine. But no dice to racists and xenophobes who would exhort him to "get over there" and kick some brown, non-Christian ass. Turn foreign soil into a parking lot? Wow, thanks for the suggestion, but I don't think so. The same goes for those who are obsessed with bloody theatrics and body count, who want to attach their sense of helplessness and loss to someone real, thereby reducing my husband and his fallen comrades to little more than war meat. Yes, we have known terrible tragedy, but circle elsewhere for your stories of injury and despair, carrion birds. Not my husband. Not on my watch.

Each summer at West Point, a new class of cadets comes in, dependable as the tide. After being signed in at R-Day, the Plebes truck off to Camp Buckner for six grueling weeks of Cadet Basic Training, a.k.a. "Beast Barracks," learning rifle marksmanship, rappelling, hand grenade and bayonet training, and other skills critical to modern warfare. Beast concludes with a ritual known as March-back, during which the Plebes, some of them still a few growth spurts away from adulthood, march the full twelve miles from the camp to the Academy. They return sweaty and smudged, their usual eyewear and contact lenses swapped out for ugly regulation BCGs (birth-control glasses). With their faces almost obscured by the spectacles' heavy frames, they file through the Academy gate and tramp down Washington Road like a weary tribe of Elvis Costellos. At the very end, they march past the VIPs clustered on the porch of Quarters 100, the home of the superintendent, presenting, for the first time, the banner that bears their class motto. Of all the pageantry and ritual at West Point, Marchback is my favorite, for it marks the conclusion of the cadets' first trial by fire, in which they both test themselves as individuals and forge their group identity. They are learning, as I have, that the reward of association with the military lies in the paradox—the gamble and the security both, of defining your individuality through folding into something far greater. It twines together anxiety and hope, fatigue and elation, and ceremony and grit in a way that drills down to the ferment of your being. Even if I don't see eye-to-eye with the military on everything, being an Army wife has, in a complex and unexpected way, turned me around and handed me back my life.

I move through the world differently now. I know that all around me, everywhere I go, people are suffering in silence, faking it to make it and in many cases, barely hanging on. Even at West Point, within all that expert form and function, there may be chaos beyond any measure. I know that people are keeping secrets, from others and from themselves, just to get by. You can't tell what kind of hell someone's carrying between their ears. Best to proceed with care.

Among the negative emotions that soldiers may face post-deployment is profound isolation. A sociologist studying this phenomenon among Vietnam vets called this sense of stigmatization and loneliness feeling "out of tribe." Though I don't know my allies personally, I know my tribe—the stumpers in the PTSD Army, we who bear the psychic scars of being in the wrong place at the wrong time. PTSD is the infirmity of the unlucky, and alas, our numbers are legion. In our craptastic, wounded way, we are unified—battle buddies in a different kind of war.

The military, to its credit, is now acknowledging that PTSD is a real problem, as is the tough-guy posture that prevents suffering troops from getting help. "Stigma is a challenge," Army Secretary Pete Geren said at a Pentagon news conference on military health care. "It's a challenge in society in general. It's certainly a challenge in the culture of the Army, where we have a premium on strength, physically, mentally, and emotionally."

The stigma is being bucked by soldiers like Army Reserve General David Blackledge, who commanded a civil affairs unit on two tours in Iraq, and now works in the Pentagon as Army assistant deputy chief of staff for mobilization and reserve issues. During his first deployment in 2004, his convoy was ambushed. An Associated Press story reports, "In the event that he since has relived in flashbacks and recurring nightmares, Blackledge's interpreter was shot through the head, his vehicle rolled over several times and Blackledge crawled out of it with a crushed vertebrae and broken ribs. He found himself in the middle of a firefight, and he and other survivors took cover in a ditch." During his physical recovery at Walter Reed Hospital, he also had several sessions with a psychiatrist to deal with the psychological fallout. Said Blackledge, "He really helped me. I tell (troops) that I've learned to deal with it. It's become part of who I am."

The military is aiming to bring relief right where it's needed most. My own miracle worker, Victoria Britt, was excited to tell me that her colleagues are collaborating with the Veteran's Administration in Philadelphia to train medical personnel to do EMDR in the field.

As horrific as the trauma of combat may be, and as important as it is for the stigma within the military to lift, I understand that also every day women, men, and children are traumatized in settings no more foreign than their own home.

At West Point, all's quiet on the domestic front, and I don't take the peace of this place for granted. I know what's waiting for us just outside these gates, that another deployment looms at the next duty station. Mike will pack up his ACUs, with his blood type stamped inside each garment, and I'll have a whole new host of challenges to meet.

Recently, I was standing in Lorna's kitchen before a meeting of our book club. Her home, perched high on the steep bank of the river, had a perfect view of all the new-money mansions being built on the bank of the other side. When I saw the lovely spread she had laid out—service for thirteen people, gold-rimmed plates on chargers, blue ombré Austrian crystal stemware, cadet gray napkins tied with ribbons in West Point black and gold, and, as a centerpiece, a large nutcracker doll in the style of a West Point cadet in parade uniform—I complimented her on her table and lamented that hostessing was a dying art, even in the Army. She said she liked to host, enjoyed the ceremony of it, but admitted that it was alien to her at first.

"When I first got married," she said, "my husband and I were sent to Fort Hood. This was in the '80s and Hood was still a very formal post. At my first coffee group, the hostess had written out calligraphied name tags, and she served hand-dipped chocolate strawberries. I couldn't believe the fuss. But my husband was early in his career, so I did a lot of volunteer work for the unit. I can't even say how annoyed I was at assembling the newsletters and making the phone calls . . . but I will tell you something. A few months later, the men were called up for Desert Storm and we had maybe a week to prepare for all of us to be alone without our husbands for God only knows how long. But we already had our system in place." What she said made me realize that all the domestic marshaling and networking has significant purpose. It isn't a formality; it's a drill. One week it's a domestic field exercise, then, when the men are called away to dangerous duty, it transforms into a critical parallel mission.

I nodded knowingly as Lorna served dessert—Paula Deen brownies, freshly warmed, covered in fudge sauce and served in a stemmed, cut crystal glass. I had assimilated that marshaling spirit into my own life that fall, when my mom, a three-pack a day smoker, had a chest X-ray that showed a suspicious spot on her lung. I didn't think twice about helping. Household Six, reporting for duty. I split doctor-visit duties with my sister who lived near her in New Jersey, drove Mom to appointments and follow-up consultations, dispatched info to the rest of the family, and coordinated trips to the hospital.

On the rainy afternoon when my mother got her cancer diagnosis—stage 1B adenocarcinoma, which she felt was a mere slap on the wrist for someone who's smoked heavily for sixty years—I went out into my backyard as the storm cleared and saw an enormous double rainbow. I called my mom and told her about the time I'd seen the double rainbow when I was staying in the hotel after I'd first separated from Mike, terrified and alone. I said, "Mom, I think Dad's trying to let us know that he's watching you and that you'll be okay," and we wept together.

When the doctors recommended a lobectomy, I took

Mom to the hospital for surgery and still got a full Thanksgiving dinner on the table three weeks later, served on the
Noritake china my father had bought for her fifty-five
years earlier when he was in Korea. She sat at the table,
with her therapy pillow tucked under her arm (pink fleece,
shaped like a pair of lungs embroidered with a smiley
face), and said, tiredly, "This is so nice."

Before, I'd have called off the whole holiday. The Army,
specifically, Army wives, gave me the drive to keep going.
I could not have done it without the inspiration of the
women I know who moved their family twelve times in ten
years, or had babies while their husbands were out of the
country for months, or held their head high while they
walked friends through the agony of loss. Some people call
it self-sacrifice; I call it kicking ass. Army wives know that
no matter what, life truly does go on. Not easily, not pain-
lessly, but it goes on nonetheless. You may be fed up to your
back teeth with frustration and pain, but your mission,
should you choose to accept it, is to meet it with as much
feminine grit as you can.

There are women who are truly heroic in the lengths they
will go to for family and country. And there will always be
a woman who can put a fancier polish on the job. One day
Mike told me about his new boss's wife. "She's great," he
said. "Very salt of the earth. Whenever someone in the department has a birthday, she bakes them a cake."

When he said this, tires screeched in my head. Brakes

slammed on. Wait just a minute here: She bakes an individual, personalized birthday cake for *each* person in the department?

I had to ask. "Just how big is this department?"

"I dunno. About twenty people?"

Twenty birthday cakes? Per year? That's a cake every other week. Now come on, there's gotta be a medal for *that*. The golden cake pan, the meritorious frosting ribbon. Hell, just make that lady an honorary Pillsbury doughgirl.

Of course, I had to share this bit of Olympic-grade hospitality with anyone who would listen. The response from my civilian girlfriends was uniform:

"Psycho."

"Mental."

"Pathological."

(It bears noting that these are all career women with small children, so their cake-baking time is snatched up by work and kid detail.)

But my acquaintances married to other prominent men at West Point were like, "Carol's so thoughtful, isn't she?" In other words: "Well, *duh*."

There's a saying about being married to a soldier: "The Army is the wife, you're the mistress." I've worked so hard to get comfortable with the role of wife that I refuse to cede the title, even in jest. And let's face it: *I* wash his socks, therefore, *I* am the wife. I prefer to say, "I'm the wife, the Army is my husband's bossy mutant cojoined twin." He's attached to the grisly sucker for now, might as well learn to make friends.

Every evening on every United States military post, the flag is lowered. All Army personnel within viewing distance face the flag in salute as it gets rung down, even if it means stopping their cars and exiting the vehicles to pay homage. This daily retreat is part of a larger tradition of rendering honors, and when I see it taking place, I am always deeply moved.

Being married to the military is not always fun, and is not always safe. But when has hardship ever dampened conviction? Nothing steels your sense of purpose like a challenge or two. Or two dozen. In the dark times, I drag along like Beckett: "I can't go on. I'll go on." In my proudest moments, it feels less like a sacrifice than an honor, and maybe, just maybe, a cool-ass cosmic duty.

As long as there have been soldiers, there have been women (and men) who love them. We may soon have our monument, but we don't get any medals. Our accomplishments aren't worn on our chests, but rather, inside of them. The heart of every dedicated spouse pumps out lifeblood that binds all of us together as both a family of sorts and heirs to a unique national legacy. The gratitude for that singular designation keeps you moving forward, for better or for worse, steady as cadence and strong as your own heartbeat.

Acknowledgments

Thank you to Mike, the heart, soul, and centerpiece of this story.

Thanks, on the "garrison side," to my Weinstein Power Trio, Judy Hottensen, Kristin Powers, and Catherine Finch, my agent Tina Bennett of Janklow and Nesbit, Svetlana Katz, and Carin Besser for her thoughtful read and remarks.

Thanks also to my beloved friends, Deb, Molly, Jeanette, Mary Beth, Vanessa, Bill, Eleni, Susan, and everyone else who rallied 'round to help pull me out of the ditch.

I owe my life to Victoria Britt, and I owe Linda Lavin a debt of gratitude for making my life worth living again. Bless you both for your good works.

Thanks to the inaugural class of Operation Bombshell. I'm so privileged to get to know and teach wonderful women like you. You are the future of the Army family and I couldn't be more proud.

Thanks to my dear friend Major Bean McBean, the World's Most Organized book group, Major Sara Holland,

Ann Campbell, Dynamite doctor-lady Terry B-to-the-L and Captain Brian B-to-the-L, Major General Robert Caslen, and "of corps," the West Point Corps of Cadets for letting me trip alongside the Long Gray Line.

Thanks to General David Petraeus for his enthusiasm for my writing, and to Major Everett Spain for bringing the good news to my attention.

Finally, thanks to my family for their continued patience with my writing habit, and to the United States military family for doing what you do. Godspeed.